The Confident Student

Fourth Edition

The Confident Student

Carol C. Kanar
Valencia Community College

Houghton Mifflin Company
Boston   New York

To Steve, again

Director of Student Success Programs and College Survival: Barbara A. Heinssen
Assistant Editor: Shani B. Fisher
Editorial Assistant: Jonathan Wolf
Senior Project Editor: Nancy Blodget
Editorial Assistant: Elisabeth Kehrer
Senior Production/Design Coordinator: Sarah Ambrose
Senior Manufacturing Coordinator: Sally Culler
Marketing Manager: Stephanie Jones

As part of Houghton Mifflin's ongoing commitment to the environment, this text has been printed on recycled paper.

Library of Congress Catalog Card No.: 00-105153

Student Edition ISBN: 0-618-04662-3

Instructor's Manual ISBN: 0-618-04663-1

123456789-WEB 04 03 02 01 00

Contents

Preface

The Confident Student, Fourth Edition is informed by my desire to help students gain the confidence that comes from self-knowledge and achievement to meet the challenges of college, life, and work. The vital study skills, critical thinking strategies, self-discovery techniques, and self-management tools that made previous editions of *The Confident Student* successful have been retained in the Fourth Edition. New to this edition are its attractive, full-color format; new exercises and features in every chapter; an expanded emphasis on technology with computer applications and web site activities in every chapter; and an improved organizational framework. As others who have used previous editions have learned, students who use *The Confident Student,* Fourth Edition will find in this book all the strategies they need to become confident, successful, life-long learners.

New to the Fourth Edition

A new full-color format enhances the book's strong visual appeal and supports the pedagogy incorporated in *The Confident Student.* For example, the pre-reading questions highlighted on each chapter-opening page help students apply the all-important skill of accessing prior knowledge before reading. The new formats for the end-of-chapter activities—Chapter Review and Your Reflections—engage students' attention, encouraging them to review and reflect on what they have learned.

New icons designate exercises and activities by theme: computer/Internet, collaborative, learning styles, and critical thinking.

New computer applications include computer/Internet exercises in each chapter and several new Computer Confidence topics. Additional exercises and copies of fill-in charts and forms can be accessed through the Houghton Mifflin web site at http://college.hmco.com.

Thinking Ahead, a new chapter feature, takes students from the classroom to the workplace, showing them how chapter concepts and skills can be applied in real-world situations requiring decision making and problem solving.

Chapter Review, a new summary feature, frames the interactive concept review section with lists of attitudes to develop and skills to practice.

New Chapter Organization and Content

The Fourth Edition's fourteen chapters are organized into two parts to more clearly reflect this book's dual emphasis on self-management skills and academic skills. **Part 1, Becoming a Confident Student,** helps students develop the affective strategies and practical skills they need to immediately see a positive difference in both their academic performance and the life choices they make. **Part 2, Studying with Power and Confidence,** shows students how to create and use study systems, think critically, concentrate, read with understanding, and manage their learning to achieve the outcomes they want. Instructors can present the chapters in the order that best suits their course content and organization.

A New and Exciting Way to Teach!

The materials in *The Confident Student,* Fourth Edition, are now available in a new modular format. By selecting only the chapters you want from a database of 19 possible chapters of *The Confident Student,* you can create a customized version of the text geared specifically towards the individual needs of your students. You can even select the sequence in which you wish the chapters to be presented. The 14 chapters in the Fourth Edition are available for modularization, along with 5 additional chapters, including *Becoming a Confident Writer, Gaining Math Confidence, Developing Science Strategies, Developing Your Vocabulary,* and *Using Your Library, Doing Research.* To find out more about the modules, contact your Houghton Mifflin Sales Representative or visit the Student Success Programs web site.

PART 1   BECOMING A CONFIDENT STUDENT

CHAPTER 1   CHOOSING SUCCESS IN COLLEGE

Form an Academic Support Group, Embrace Diversity, Know Where to Find Help, Stay Informed. Get Involved

■ **NEW:** A section on forming an academic support group has been added. The section on diversity has been expanded and retitled "Embrace Diversity." A Computer Confidence box on using Email has been added. A section on Greek organizations and Success Strategies for Immediate Use (Figure 1.1) are also new.

CHAPTER 2   MOTIVATING YOURSELF TO LEARN

Assess Your Strengths and Weaknesses, Discover and Use Your Learning Style, Adapt to Others' Styles, Develop Critical Thinking and Study Skills

■ **NEW:** A new Confidence Builder on Howard Gardner's multiple intelligences and a new Critical Thinking exercise on Clair Weinstein and colleagues' concept of skill, will, and self-regulation expand the information on learning styles.

CHAPTER 3   SETTING GOALS AND SOLVING PROBLEMS

Set Goals for Success in College, Set Reachable Long-Term and Short-Term Goals, Use the COPE Method to Solve Problems

■ **NEW:** Exercise 3.1 for the Internet expands this chapter's thorough coverage of goal-setting and problem-solving techniques.

CHAPTER 4   SHARPENING YOUR CLASSROOM SKILLS

Prepare for Class, Become an Active Listener, Develop a Personal Note-Taking System, Learn to Make Effective Presentations, Participate in Class and Group Activities

■ **NEW:** A new collaborative focus is achieved through group exercises featuring an activity on listening behavior and another on practicing note taking with a classmate to match note-taking styles with learning styles. Using the Internet to find resources for making speeches and giving reports will aid students in their research skills.

CHAPTER 5   MAKING THE MOST OF YOUR TIME

How to GRAB Some Time, Scheduling Your Time, Procrastination

■ **NEW:** A new Confidence Builder with time-management tips for student athletes has been added. Several exercises have been revised to incorporate computer/Internet activities.

CHAPTER 6   MAINTAINING YOUR HEALTH AND WELL-BEING

Health, Well-Being, and Success in College, Staying Healthy, Your Emotions, Your Interpersonal Skills, Making Friends, Your Sexuality

■ **NEW:** The section on sexuality has been expanded. New material on binge drinking and an alcohol use and abuse survey round out this chapter's coverage of avoiding harmful substances. Also new: a Computer Confidence box on how to avoid Internet addiction.

PART 2   STUDYING WITH POWER AND CONFIDENCE

CHAPTER 7   CREATING YOUR STUDY SYSTEM

SQ3R: The Basic System, Devising Your Study System

■ **NEW:** A new Computer Confidence box on surveying web sites to save time on the Net has been added. A new Confidence Builder relates being proactive—one of Stephen R. Covey's seven habits of highly effective people—to studying. The section on SQ3R has been trimmed and tightened, and the figures have been reformatted.

CHAPTER 8   ORGANIZING INFORMATION FOR STUDY

Concept or Information Maps, Comparison Charts, Time Lines, Process Diagrams, Informal Outlines, Branching Diagrams

■ **NEW:** A new Confidence Builder helps students build the right attitudes toward study. A new Computer Confidence box explains how to use a computer to make study guides.

CHAPTER 9   CONTROLLING YOUR CONCENTRATION

Eliminate Distractions, Eliminate Other Causes of Poor Concentration

CHAPTER 10   IMPROVING LEARNING AND MEMORY

How Memory Works, Why You Forget, Increase Your Memory Power

CHAPTER 11   PREPARING FOR TESTS

How to Prepare for Tests: Three Steps, Develop a Test-Taking Routine, Master Objective Tests, Know How to Answer Essay Questions

■ **NEW:** New Exercises and some organizational changes enhance Chapters 9–11.

CHAPTER 12   REDUCING TEST ANXIETY

Eliminate the Causes of Test Anxiety, Learn to Relax, Face Your Fears, Fight Distractions, Talk Positively to Yourself, Find Your Best Solution

■ **NEW:** The coverage of test anxiety, its causes, and ways to eliminate them is now more focused as a result of new features and some revisions in content and exercises.

CHAPTER 13   BECOMING AN ACTIVE READER

Reading Actively; Find Main Idea, Details, and Implications; Use a Textbook Marking System

■ **NEW:** The section on active reading has been expanded and now includes a new Figure 13.1 listing traits of active and passive readers. New material and an exercise on evaluating printed sources and Internet sites has been added.

CHAPTER 14   USING CRITICAL THINKING STRATEGIES

Examine Your Assumptions, Make Predictions, Sharpen Your Interpretations, Evaluate What You Learn

■ **NEW:** Chapter content has been extensively revised to make this material more accessible to students.

Features Retained from the Third Edition

The Confident Student, Fourth Edition, continues to be a highly visual, highly personal text with a strong academic base. The features that help students acquire knowledge and make it their own have been retained.

Awareness Checks in every chapter are brief checklists or assessment questionnaires that orient students to a chapter concept or discussion topic. Followed by a brief explanation, the Awareness Checks help students assess their attitudes, skills, and prior knowledge.

Confidence Builders in every chapter address study skills, attitudes, and job or career skills. Their purpose is to broaden students' understanding and build confidence by extending the discussion of chapter topics into related areas of interest or research. Several new Confidence Builders have been added to the Fourth Edition.

Computer Confidence is a feature that adds a technological dimension to the text. Several new Computer Confidence topics have been added to the Fourth Edition.

Critical Thinking exercises enhance the text's pedagogical foundation. Through this feature, students learn to integrate critical thinking naturally into their approach to studying and interacting in the classroom as they are asked to question, more fully process, and consider different viewpoints surrounding the issues and concepts presented in the chapter. Most of the exercises have been revised or updated, and several are new to the Fourth Edition.

Your Reflections at the end of each chapter poses several questions for students to think about and respond to in writing. The Reflections provide an excellent opportunity for students to assess their progress, reflect on what they are learning, and plan ways to apply their new skills. The Reflections can be used as a journaling activity, a personal log, or a springboard to discussion between student and instructor.

Themed Exercises in every chapter, designated by icons, address learning styles and collaborative activities. Many of these have been revised and some are new. Computer/Internet exercises in every chapter are new.

Skill Finder is a pre-assessment test students can take to assess their strengths and weaknesses and identify areas of knowledge covered in the text and where to find them. The post-assessment Skill Finder in the Instructor's Resource Manual has also been retained.

Ancillaries

The Instructor's Resource Manual that accompanies *The Confident Student* contains an answer key for the exercises and chapter-by-chapter suggestions for using the text. Also included are sample course syllabi, a brief bibliography, and a set of reproducible masters for overhead transparencies and handouts to use as supplementary materials. Collaborative activities by Candy Ready of Piedmont Technical College have been retained from the Third Edition. The sections on integrating SCANS workplace competencies with course objectives and on portfolio assessment in student success courses have been retained from the Third Edition.

New! The Myers-Briggs Type Indicator® (MBTI®) instrument*—the most widely used personality inventory in history—is now available to be shrink-wrapped with this text for a discounted price at qualified schools. The standard Form M self-scorable instrument contains 93 items that determine preferences on four scales: Extraversion–Introversion, Sensing–Intuition, Thinking–Feeling, and Judging–Perceiving. For information on obtaining a shrink-wrap package, contact your local sales representative or Faculty Services at 1-800-733-1717.

Houghton Mifflin's Student Success Roundtable Discussion Videotapes can be used to supplement the text. Reproducible exercises for use with these videotapes are in the Instructor's Resource Manual.

Additional activities and worksheets for *The Confident Student* can be found on Houghton Mifflin's web site by selecting "Student Success" at http://college.hmco.com.

Acknowledgments

I want to thank everyone who helped me in writing this text: my husband, Stephen P. Kanar, for providing the encouragement and support I needed to complete this book; my friend Lyn Gray, for her moral support and secretarial help; and all the other family members, friends, and colleagues who encouraged me.

I am grateful to Barbara A. Heinssen for her continuing support of *The Confident Student* and its message. My special thanks go to her for conceiving the Fourth Edition's new design and to Carol Dirga, designer, for carrying it out. Once again, I thank Melissa Plumb for her wise counsel and excellent suggestions that have guided me through three editions of this book. Nancy Blodget deserves special

*MBTI and Myers-Briggs Type Indicator are registered trademarks of Consulting Psychologists Press, Inc.

credit for her tireless work on the production of *The Confident Student*. I thank also Vici Casana for her expert editorial help, Ann Schroeder for securing permissions and helping to select the wonderful photographs that grace this book's pages, Maria Sas for the lovely art program, and Shani Fisher for the many, many things she does for me and *The Confident Student*. My acknowledgments go to Tim Krause for his assistance with adding computer applications. I am indebted to the whole family of Houghton Mifflin editors and others who played a role in the publication of the Fourth Edition. Thank you, everyone.

The following reviewers who read my manuscript and provided me with many fine suggestions for developing the Fourth Edition into its present form have my thanks:

Linda Bagshaw, *Briar Cliff College*
Glenda A. Belote, *Florida International University*
John C. Bennett, Jr., *University of Connecticut*
Ronald Burdette, *Montgomery College*
Susann B. Deason, *Aiken Technical College*
Kevin M. Dohrenwend, *Middlesex County College*
Barbara S. Doyle, *Arkansas State University*
Lynn Ingraham, *Erie Community College*
Paula S. Krist, Ph.D., *Florida Institute of Technology*
James V. Muniz, *University of Scranton*
Sherry Reid, *Bowling Green Community College*
L. Harold Stevenson, *McNeese State University*
David A. Strong, *Dyersburg State Community College*
Dr. Peggy Walton, *Howard Community College*
Esther J. Winter, *Northwest Missouri State University*

Finally, I am deeply grateful to my students, for without them I wouldn't have been inspired to write this book.

CCK

To the Student

This book is designed to help you discover the ways in which you learn most easily and most enjoyably, and to help you define your own goals and preferences as you embark on your college career and look ahead to life and work in the future. It includes thorough discussions, illustrations, and easy-to-understand suggestions on ways to develop all the skills you will need to perform well in your courses and achieve the success that will make you a confident student.

How to Use This Book

Begin with the Skill Finder on pages xix–xxii. Use it to get an idea of what the book covers, to discover which of your study skills need improvement, and to find out which chapters may be most useful to you. In addition, try these suggestions to get the most you can out of *The Confident Student.*

1. Use the chapter-opening questions to assess your prior knowledge about the chapter topic. This prereading activity will put you in the frame of mind for maximum learning.

2. Read each chapter one section at a time. If you have questions, write them in the margin or in a notebook so you can bring them up in class discussion.

3. Pay special attention to the photographs, figures, and other visual elements that may clarify and expand your understanding of chapter concepts.

4. Complete the Awareness Checks. Do the chapter exercises and try out the suggestions in the Confidence Builders, Computer Confidence boxes, and Critical Thinking boxes to reinforce your grasp of each new strategy or skill.

5. To relate what you are learning to real-world situations in life and work, complete Thinking Ahead.

6. To round out your understanding of a chapter, complete the Chapter Review.

7. For a personal assessment of what you have learned and how it may affect your life, complete Your Reflections at the end of each chapter.

8. Finally, talk over the chapter with a friend or with members of a study group. Discussing a chapter is an excellent way to review it and fill any gaps in your understanding.

Make *The Confident Student* a Better Book

When you've completed your course, I'd really like to know your opinion of *The Confident Student,* Fourth Edition. Tell me what works and what doesn't work for you. I would be grateful for any suggestions you have that will help me improve the text.

Carol Kanar
c/o Houghton Mifflin Student Success Programs
215 Park Avenue South
New York, NY 10003

Skill Finder

This questionnaire will help you determine which of your skills you need to develop or improve. Read each statement. If the statement applies to you, check YES. If the statement does not apply to you, check NO. To interpret your results, see the end of the questionnaire. To take the questionnaire online and get a printout of your results, visit the Student Success Programs web site by selecting "Student Success" at http://college.hmco.com.

Yes	No	**Adapting to College, Using Resources**
☐	☐	1. I know what courses are required at my college.
☐	☐	2. I have a college catalog, and I check it often to keep up with important dates and deadlines.
☐	☐	3. I know what kind of help is available to me on campus and where to find it.
☐	☐	4. I get along well with people from diverse races, ethnic groups, and cultures.

Yes	No	**Motivating Yourself**
☐	☐	5. I know what my basic skill strengths and weaknesses are.
☐	☐	6. I know what my learning style is and how to use it.
☐	☐	7. I am able to adapt to others' teaching styles.
☐	☐	8. I am able to keep myself motivated.

Yes	No	**Goal Setting and Problem Solving**
☐	☐	9. I set goals for myself and work to achieve them.
☐	☐	10. I have no trouble making decisions.
☐	☐	11. I am not a person who gives up when things get difficult.
☐	☐	12. I have learned how to use problem-solving techniques.

Yes	No	**Listening and Taking Notes**
☐	☐	13. When I am listening to a lecture, I do not become distracted.
☐	☐	14. I know the signal words to listen for in a lecture that will tell me what's important.
☐	☐	15. When I take notes, I am able to keep up with the speaker.
☐	☐	16. The notes I take are readable and useful.

Yes	No	**Time Management and Class Preparation**
☐	☐	17. I have no trouble finding time for studying.
☐	☐	18. I almost always arrive on time for classes.
☐	☐	19. I hand in assignments on time.
☐	☐	20. I am absent only in case of sickness or emergency.
☐	☐	21. I ask questions and participate in discussion.

Yes	No	**Health and Well-Being**
☐	☐	22. I know how to maintain a balanced diet.
☐	☐	23. I know what exercises will keep me fit.
☐	☐	24. I have learned ways to control my emotions.
☐	☐	25. I know how to have fun without engaging in harmful activities or abusing substances.

Yes	No	**Using Textbooks Effectively**
☐	☐	26. Before reading, I look over the material briefly to familiarize myself with the author's topic.
☐	☐	27. I am able to tell what is important in a chapter.
☐	☐	28. I have no trouble maintaining interest in what I read.
☐	☐	29. I always take time to read tables, charts, and other graphics.
☐	☐	30. I use mapping techniques to organize information.
☐	☐	31. I take notes on my reading to help me study.
☐	☐	32. I know what to underline or mark in a chapter.
☐	☐	33. I know and use strategies for learning special terms and definitions.

Yes	No	**Memory and Concentration**
☐	☐	34. I can usually remember what I've studied well enough to get good grades on tests.
☐	☐	35. I know how my brain processes information, and I control the process.
☐	☐	36. I have learned various memory-enhancing techniques.
☐	☐	37. I am not easily distracted when I am reading or studying.
☐	☐	38. I have no trouble concentrating in class.

Yes	No	**Preparing for and Taking Tests**
☐	☐	39. I have no trouble determining what to study for tests.
☐	☐	40. I am usually well prepared for tests.
☐	☐	41. I have learned special strategies for taking objective tests and essay exams.
☐	☐	42. I use guessing strategies only if I don't know an answer.
☐	☐	43. Taking a test does not make me nervous if I know that I am well prepared.
☐	☐	44. I never have test anxiety.

Yes	No	**Reading and Critical Thinking**
☐	☐	45. I am an active rather than a passive reader.
☐	☐	46. I know what strategies to use to help me remember what I read.
☐	☐	47. Before learning anything new, I examine my assumptions and assess my prior knowledge.
☐	☐	48. I know the difference between what an author says and what an author means.
☐	☐	49. I evaluate what I read for reliability, objectivity, and usefulness.

Yes	No	**Using Computers to Enhance Studying**
☐	☐	50. I am able to use email to keep in touch with instructors, classmates, study partners, and others who can help my learning.
☐	☐	51. I know how to use a computer to organize my notes.
☐	☐	52. I know how to use a computer to improve my time management.
☐	☐	53. I know what Internet addiction is and how to avoid it.
☐	☐	54. I know how to survey web sites to find what I want.
☐	☐	55. I know how to use a computer to make several types of study guides.
☐	☐	56. I know how to evaluate Internet sources.

How to Calculate Your Score

Count the number of NO answers for each section. If you have more than one NO answer in a section, then you may need to improve or develop the skill identified by the section heading. Use the list on the following page to help you find the chapter in *The Confident Student,* Fourth Edition that covers these skills. See the Contents or the Index to find specific page numbers where a topic is covered. Your instructor may ask you to answer these questions again at the end of your course to assess your mastery of the skills.

Skill Finder	Corresponding Chapter in *The Confident Student,* Fourth Edition
Questions 1–4, 50	Chapter 1
Questions 5–8	Chapter 2
Questions 9–12	Chapter 3
Questions 13–16, 51	Chapter 4
Questions 17–21, 52	Chapters 4 and 5
Questions 22–25, 56	Chapter 6
Questions 26–33, 54–55	Chapters 7 and 8
Questions 34–38	Chapters 9 and 10
Questions 39–44	Chapters 11 and 12
Questions 45–49, 56	Chapters 13 and 14

The Confident Student

CHAPTER

1

Choosing Success in College

ARE YOU TAKING advantage of

everything your college has to offer?

Do you know what resources are available to help you?

What are your hopes, your dreams, for your college

experience?

GETTING ALONG IN college and being able to take advantage of everything it has to offer depend on how well you can adapt to change. If this is your first semester or quarter in college, you may need time to find your way around campus, make new friends, and begin to feel comfortable in your new setting. Even if you are a returning student, you still may need a period of adjustment as you orient yourself to a new schedule of classes, new instructors, and a different set of requirements and expectations.

College is as much an experience as it is a place, and it is *your* experience. The choices you make will control the outcome. By adopting confidence-building attitudes and by engaging in productive learning behaviors, you will be choosing *success* as your outcome.

Your first step is to look around you. Discover everything you can about your college campus and the resources it offers to help you become a successful, confident student and a participating member of your learning community. This chapter explains how you can choose success.

Awareness Check 1

HOW WELL DO YOU KNOW YOUR CAMPUS AND ITS RESOURCES?

Check the following statements that describe you or your behavior.

- [ ] 1. I know what courses are required for graduation from my college.
- [ ] 2. I know what my instructor's attendance and grading policies are.
- [ ] 3. I believe that my attitudes and values reflect those of many of the students who attend my college.
- [ ] 4. I respect the values of students whose race, ethnicity, or sexual orientation differs from mine.
- [ ] 5. I know what services are available to all students at my college.
- [ ] 6. If I should happen to be in academic difficulty, I know what services are available to help me and where to go to obtain them.
- [ ] 7. I know where to go to apply for campus employment.
- [ ] 8. I know where to go on campus to apply for a grant or scholarship.
- [ ] 9. I have a college catalog or know where to get one.
- [ ] 10. I know what other college publications are available to students and how they can help me.

If you have checked yes to eight or more of the previous statements, you may already be making a successful adjustment to college life. If you checked no to three or more of the items, you may need to develop or improve your adaptive strategies.

- Form a support group.
- Embrace diversity.
- Know where to find help.
- Stay informed.
- Get involved.

Form an Academic Support Group

IN A COMMUNITY of learners the primary function of each faculty member, administrator, employee, and department is *to help you reach your goals.* Everyone in your college community hopes that you will succeed. Therefore, your college is rich in resources that can guide your progress. For example, people are an important resource. If you have not already done so, you need to form a *support group:* a network of people to whom you can turn for advice, answers to questions, or a boost in confidence.

Faculty

Your instructors are in the best position to advise you concerning all matters related to their classes. Instructors welcome questions because students' questions help them determine the effectiveness of their teaching. In fact, your questions are often your primary means of interaction with your instructors. Do not hesitate to ask questions or seek information. If you are having difficulty in a course, for example, don't postpone getting help or hope that your problem will go away. Make an appointment with your instructor as soon as possible

Find an instructor with whom you are especially comfortable and turn to this person when you need advice. If your instructor is unable to answer one of your questions or to suggest ways to solve a problem, he or she can direct you to another person or office where help will be available.

Advisors and Counselors

Academic advisors and career counselors are among the most helpful people on campus. These professionals handle academic and personal problems of every kind all day long, so they know what you are going through. If you need help preparing a schedule, an academic advisor will show you how to select the courses you need. If you want help deciding on a major or choosing a career, a career counselor can provide valuable assistance, both in determining where your interests lie and in assessing employment opportunities. If you have a problem that you don't know how to handle, such as test anxiety, an advisor may talk the matter over with you or refer you to someone else.

Counselors and advisors know your college's rules and requirements. They may offer such services as keeping you informed of important dates and deadlines, explaining your assessment-test scores, and informing you of any skill-development courses or programs you may need. Some advisors may work only with students having unique needs, such as learning or physically disabled students, international students, adult learners, or minority students.

Your instructors want you to succeed in their courses. They can answer questions about material that they cover in class and assignments and tests, and they can give you sound advice about where to seek extra help if you need it.

At some colleges you may be assigned to an advisor during your first semester or quarter. The advisor will track your progress throughout your academic career. If you plan to transfer from a two-year college to a university, an advisor can help you select courses that will meet the university's requirements so that you won't lose credits. Therefore, it is important to meet with an advisor as soon as you decide that you want to transfer. If you need academic advice or career or personal counseling, find the office or department on your campus that provides these services. Since department names may differ from campus to campus, check the college catalog or inquire at your admissions office—or ask your instructor.

Mentors

A *mentor* is an ally, a friend, someone who takes a personal and professional interest in you. On many college campuses today, instructors may serve as mentors to students in special programs funded by federal grants or other sources. Students are assigned to mentors during their first term. They meet regularly with their mentors, usually four or more times during the term, to set goals, assess progress, and work through problems. Mentors may offer tips on how to study, take tests, and reduce stress. They may also help students plan their schedules for the following term.

The relationship between student and mentor serves several purposes. It gives the student a contact person on campus to turn to for advice, help in solving a problem, or specific suggestions on how to meet course requirements. If you begin to experience academic difficulty, for example, the mentor may help you find a tutor. Mentors stay in contact with their students' instructors throughout the term, and mentors and instructors often work together to help students be successful.

In adjusting to college, many students complain that the close relationships that they enjoyed with faculty in high school are not available in college. Mentoring programs may be one way to fill the gap. Such programs may operate differently from campus to campus, but the goal of any mentoring program is the same: to help students choose success. To find out whether there is a mentoring program on your campus, call the admissions office.

Extend Your Support Group

Each subject area department, such as English or math, may have special requirements and services that pertain only to that department and the courses it offers. On some campuses, the heads of departments deal with students seeking permission to enroll in courses that are already filled. If you have a question or a problem related to enrolling in a course, see the department head. He or she will either answer your questions and help you solve the problem or refer you to someone who can.

COMPUTER CONFIDENCE

Use Email to Keep in Touch

Email is a widely used communication tool or information-sharing medium available to colleges, businesses, and individuals through the Internet. Email is a quick and easy way to keep in touch with classmates, instructors, and family members. You may not have time to write, address, and mail a letter, but you can always work in a few minutes to email a message to someone with whom you want to stay in touch. Email has several other advantages as well.

- You can email classmates to share notes and materials, update group members with whom you are working on projects, and keep each other informed about meeting dates and times.

- You can email students at other colleges and universities to share ideas or collaborate on research projects and other activities.

- You can email your instructors. Many instructors encourage email and distribute class notes, handouts, and the course syllabus through this medium.

- You can use email to communicate with researchers in your field of interest, seek information from employers concerning jobs and careers, or submit a résumé or job application.

(Continued)

- Email is more convenient to use than the telephone and may be more economical, saving you money on long-distance calls. Also, you can send and receive messages at times that are convenient for you. By encouraging friends and family members to keep in touch through email, you may be able to avoid the telephone call that interrupts you when you are studying. Thus, email can have a positive effect on your time management.

- Composing email messages may also provide you with some needed practice in writing skills as you plan what to say and experiment with ways to put sentences and paragraphs together to get your ideas across.

To send and receive email, you need not have a computer of your own. Most college campuses allow students to set up email accounts through the campus computer system. Some require students to enroll in a computer class or pay a fee. Check with your campus computer center, the library, or the media center to find out how you can gain access to the Internet and send email. Then, all you need is your email address, a password, and the recipient's address.

The best way to get the addresses of classmates and instructor is to ask for them. To find addresses of people you may not know but to whom you want to write, check your campus email directory if one is available. Many campuses have a web page or a campuswide information system (CWIS). For off-campus addresses, you can use an Internet "search engine" such as Netfind. Once you have your address and the other person's address, you will be ready to send mail.

Keep in mind that computer systems, mailing programs, and specific commands differ, so if you are new at using email, your campus computer center can help you get started.

Tips for Effective Communication Through Email

1. The main advantage of email is that it's fast. Messages that are too long or wordy waste time—both yours and the reader's. Therefore, keep your messages brief and to the point.

2. Be aware of your reader and adjust your tone accordingly. For example, is your message business or personal? Your tone for a personal message will be more casual than the tone for a business message and will be more formal when you are writing to an instructor than when you are writing to a friend.

3. Stick to simple typing. Avoid using features like bold type, italics, and different fonts. These may not translate well when you send your message and could cause confusion.

4. Observe rules of *online etiquette* (polite communication). Because email is spontaneous—messages and responses can be transmitted instantly—you may have a tendency to dash a response off the top of your head. Avoid this tendency. Think before you write and choose words carefully. Do not type in all caps; your reader will think that you are shouting. Avoid profanity; in fact, do not put anything in writing that you wouldn't say in person. When in doubt, wait a while before sending your message, giving yourself time to review it and to make changes as needed

5. Perhaps most important, check your mail regularly and answer your messages as soon as you can. You know how you feel when your messages go unreturned. Remember that the other person feels the same way.

© Ron Sherman

Other students might be the most helpful people in your college life. Exchange phone numbers with a friend in each of your courses who can help you catch up on classes you may have to miss.

EXERCISE **1.1**

FIND OUT IF EMAIL IS available on your campus. If it is, find out how to open an account and get an email address. Then practice sending and receiving messages with one of your instructors, a classmate, and a student at another college. Complete the following items.

1. What is your email address?

_____

2. List the names and the email addresses of the instructor and the students with whom you exchanged messages for this exercise.

_____

_____

3. Explain where you had to go and what you had to do to set up an email account on campus.

_____

_____

SELECT A COURSE IN WHICH you really want to put your best effort this term. Ask the course instructor if you can conduct an interview with him or her by email. Explain to the instructor that this interview will help you to determine what you can do to succeed in the course. Ask the instructor the following questions:

1. **What is the best way to prepare for your class?**

   _____

2. **What special study or reading techniques do you think I should use to get the most out of my textbook?**

   _____

3. **Do your test questions come mainly from lectures, reading assignments, or both?**

   _____

4. **What is the best way to study for one of your tests?**

   _____

5. **How would you describe your teaching style?**

   _____

6. **Is there anything else you can recommend that I should do to succeed in your class?**

   _____

Departmental secretaries can be very helpful, too. They can answer questions about departmental requirements and course offerings. They can tell you who is teaching each section of a course. They can also tell you where an instructor's office is and give you the instructor's campus telephone number, or they can leave a message for an instructor whom you have been unable to reach.

If you live in a residence hall on campus, your resident advisor, or RA, can advise you about campus services or student affairs. RAs are easy to talk to because they are usually students like you. They have lived through some of the same problems you have, and they have asked and found answers to some of the same questions. An RA can usually point you in the direction of a helpful person, department, or office. On some campuses, a graduate assistant or fellow, house master, or faculty master may be someone to whom you can turn for advice.

If you are involved in athletics, your coach can be an ally. Your coach wants you to remain eligible to participate in sports. Coaches are well aware of grade requirements, and they keep track of your progress in your courses. Your coach wants you to do your best in class and on the team. He or she is someone you should find easy to talk to if you need advice.

Club and organization sponsors are people who tend to take an active part in campus life. Like coaches, they share some of your interests, and they may know you as a person in a way that your instructors or advisors may not. Although a club sponsor may not be able to answer some of your questions, he or she will probably know someone on campus who can.

Don't underestimate the value of making friends with other students. Exchanging phone numbers with a student in each class gives you someone to call when you are absent so that you can find out what you missed. Having friends in each class may allow you to form a study group or to find a ride to campus if you need one.

Thus, your academic support group might include an advisor, an instructor, a departmental head or secretary, a coach or club sponsor, and a friend in each class. Their roles are not to provide answers to questions or solutions to problems that you can find on your own, but to *support* you in your effort to be successful. In a community of learners, you need never be alone.

EXERCISE **1.3**

HAVING A SUPPORT GROUP TO turn to when you need information, the answer to a question, help with a problem, or a boost in confidence makes adjusting to college easier. Write the names, addresses, and phone numbers of several people in your support group on the following chart. Include email addresses if you know them. Then, post the chart in a handy place. If you need space for more support group members, see http://college.hmco.com/success to download additional copes of the chart.

My Support Group

	Phone number	Address/office	Email address
Family members 1. 2.			
Instructors 1. 2.			
Classmates 1. 2.			
Advisor, coach, or other person 1. 2.			

Embrace Diversity

BEFORE THE 1960s, college students in the United States typically were white males who had similar social and economic backgrounds. However, the percentage of women attending college has steadily increased since the 1960s, and they now outnumber men on many college campuses. The student body has also become increasingly diverse. Students come from a variety of backgrounds. They differ in age, race, gender, socio-economic level, sexual orientation, and learning ability. Many are international students, and some are disabled. Some grew up in urban neighborhoods; others are from rural communities. Today there is no typical college student.

The composition of the U.S. population is also changing. By 2020, according to U.S. government projections, African Americans, Asian Americans, Cubans, Puerto Ricans, Mexican Americans, Native Americans, and others will account for one-third of the population. By the last quarter of the twenty-first century, these groups collectively will constitute a majority of the population.

Your Diverse Campus

What does *diversity* mean to you? For one thing, you are likely to have classmates and instructors who come from many different cultural and ethnic backgrounds. Second, colleges have responded to student diversity by offering services and opportunities to meet a variety of needs. Moreover, diversity has many benefits. Exposure to different customs and ways of thinking challenges your ideas and broadens your world-view. Because your campus is a small slice of the larger society, it provides you with an opportunity to hone your interpersonal skills and to develop intercultural communication skills before you begin your career in an increasingly diverse workplace.

A campus that embraces diversity welcomes all students in a spirit of friendship and community.

© Gary Conner/PhotoEdit

Creating a learning environment where all are treated with respect and where all are free to pursue their educational goals is everyone's responsibility. Do your part by being open to ideas and customs that may differ from your own. If you harbor any stereotypical thinking that prevents cross-cultural communication, now is the time to let it go. Look around you at your classmates and instructors. They are people—first.

Embrace diversity by reaching out to others in a spirit of friendship and community. Make all students feel welcome, just as you want to be welcomed. Accept others' differences, listen without being critical, and establish friendships based on shared interests and values. As you form your support group, think of others' differences not as barriers to communication but as bridges to understanding. Let your support group ring with the harmony of different voices.

Diverse Students, Needs, and Services

Your college probably offers a number of programs, services, and interest groups that serve the needs of a diverse student population. The Black History Association, a group found on many campuses, plans programs and events that raise everyone's awareness of African Americans' achievements. On some campuses, women's groups, international student organizations, lesbians' and gay men's coalitions, and religion-based student associations provide a place to socialize and conduct special-interest activities.

Although socializing with others like yourself is important, it is equally important to reach out to those who differ. Getting involved in extracurricular activities can help you find new friends who share your interests. Joining a group that appeals to students interested in an art such as dance, drama, or music; a career such as engineering or teaching; or an issue such as SADD (Students Against Driving Drunk) can serve as a starting point for getting involved in campus life. By becoming active in student government or another campus service organization, you can have a voice in the issues that affect all students. All of the previously mentioned groups can provide many opportunities for you to meet people from diverse cultures and backgrounds with whom you may have much in common.

Adult Learners

A woman, now retired after many years of successful teaching, remembers her first attempts to enroll in college:

> *I was 35 years old and a divorced mother. My dream was to continue my education, which I had postponed because of marriage, and become an elementary school teacher. I made an appointment with the head of the education department at the college of my choice to discuss application procedures. He told me I was too old. He said it was not their policy to accept students my age. Also, I was divorced and would not be a good role model for their young women. But I did not give up. Eventually, I was accepted at a state university that admitted a few older students each year. Even so, I had to endure discouraging words from professors and students alike who did not think I should be there. That was 1962. Fortunately, attitudes about older students have changed.*

Attitudes *have* changed. Adult learners are welcomed on campuses today for several important reasons. First of all, adult learners bring with them knowledge and skills that enrich the college experience for everyone. Second, most people change jobs or careers two or more times during their lives and seek additional skills or training. Moreover, learning does not end at graduation—it is a lifelong process. Despite such current positive views about adult learners, these students often enter college feeling out of place, wondering whether they will be able to catch up and keep up. Adult learners have jobs and families and may feel pressured as they add course requirements to their already full calendars. Embracing diversity means learning from each other's unique experiences and remembering that all students, no matter what their ages, face similar problems of adjustment in college.

Students with Disabilities

Most colleges provide special services for disabled students, such as note takers for blind students or extra testing and writing time for the learning disabled (students who have dyslexia, for example). Physical or learning disabilities need not prevent students from being successful in college. Many disabled students have developed coping strategies that would benefit all students. The key to successful communication and interaction with disabled students is to treat them as you would any other students. When goals and interests are shared, there are no barriers.

Non-Native Speakers of English

Even on a campus that embraces diversity, the temptation may be great for non-native speakers of English to restrict their interaction with others to those who speak their own language. Many of these students go home to families that also do not speak English. The time that they spend in class may be the only opportunity that non-native speakers of English have to use English. It is crucial for these students to make friends with and to interact with native speakers. Therefore, if you are a non-native speaker of English, seek opportunities to practice your English skills. Participate in class discussions. Join clubs or organizations in which you will meet native speakers who share your interests.

If you are a native speaker of English, reach out to the non-native speakers in your classes. Invite them to join a study group after class or take the initiative to collaborate with them in group activities within class.

Students with Diverse Sexual Orientations

Many heterosexuals react negatively toward gays and lesbians because of learned stereotypes that act as barriers to communication and obscure the truth. For one thing, you cannot determine a person's sexual orientation based on his or her outward appearance. Within the lesbian and gay community, as in any community, a variety of values, behaviors, and personality traits are represented. Finally, gay and lesbian students, like most students, just want to make friends, pursue their educational goals, find meaningful work after college, and build lasting relationships.

Any student can choose success. No matter what your age or background is, and no matter what your academic performance has been, college offers a new beginning. Every chapter in this book contains strategies that will help you build the confidence and skills needed to achieve your goals. For a list of strategies you can begin using now, see Figure 1.1.

EXERCISE 1.4

WRITE A MEANINGFUL ESSAY ABOUT yourself. Describe your background: your age, your racial or ethnic group, your native language, the place where you grew up, and one or two values that are important to you and your family. Then explain how your background makes you similar to or different from others. Finally, focus on your skills, talents, and abilities. What unique contribution can you make to your learning community? When you are finished, exchange papers with a class member. Read and discuss each other's papers. What do you have in common? What differs? Share your conclusions with the rest of the class.

CRITICAL THINKING

What is your college doing to embrace diversity? You can find out by answering the following questions. To answer these questions, you will have to do some research, either by finding relevant printed materials or by interviewing the appropriate people. Your instructor or a librarian may be able to tell you how to begin. You may find answers to some of the questions by going to your college's web site.

1. Assess the diversity on your campus. What ethnic, racial, international, or other kinds of groups are represented? What percentage of the students, faculty, administration, and staff does each group comprise?

2. What courses that address diversity issues are offered?

3. Is diversity mentioned in your college's mission statement? If so, how?

4. What college policies or procedures are designed to meet the needs of a diverse student population?

5. To what extent does your college promote interaction among students from diverse backgrounds?

6. Do you find any discrepancies between your college's policy on diversity and actual practice? If so, explain the discrepancies.

7. Based on the facts you have found, what conclusions can you draw about your college's commitment to diversity? For example, how does diversity benefit your campus? Do all students feel welcome? What, if anything, should be done to improve relations among the diverse groups on your campus?

Present your answers orally or in writing as your instructor directs.

CONFIDENCE Builder

How Flexible Are You?

Learning to be flexible in your daily activities prepares you to meet life's greater challenges and makes adapting to change seem easier and less overwhelming.

Do you hold on to cherished opinions, even in the face of conflicting evidence? Do your first impressions of people remain largely unchanged, even after you get to know them? How do you handle broken relationships, changes in plans, or personal and financial setbacks? If you have difficulty adapting to change, then much of your life—whether at college, at work, or at home—is probably filled with stress. Change, according to many experts, is one of life's greatest sources of stress. People who are inflexible in their beliefs, attitudes, and plans set themselves up for disappointment, discomfort, and distress.

The way to adapt to change is to be flexible. Flexibility is a trait employers often cite as being a valuable personal skill, and it is one you can develop. What are some of the situations at college that call for flexibility? You painstakingly make out a schedule—only to find out that one of your courses is closed. Your roommate is a day person; you are a night person. You spend hours studying for a test, you are motivated and ready to perform, and then your instructor postpones the exam until next week. How can you adapt to day-to-day changes such as these that can make your life miserable if you let them? How can you become more flexible? The following three tips may help.

Watch your attitude. Remember that you are not perfect, and neither is anyone else. Life does not always proceed according to schedule. It isn't the end of the world if things don't go as planned. Learn to shrug instead of vent.

Have a contingency plan. You can't plan for all emergencies or temporary setbacks, but you *can* anticipate some changes. For example, have alternatives in mind when you select courses. Expect that in any situation in which two people live together, conflicts will arise. Remind yourself to stay calm, talk things over, and be willing to compromise. Whenever you make a schedule, set a goal, or plan for a future event, try to build into your plans some alternatives in case things don't work out.

Keep an open mind. Change has its good points. Change keeps you from getting in a rut. Change also opens up possibilities you may not have previously had a reason to consider. Above all, adapting to change successfully makes you grow and makes it easier for you to accept the next change that comes along.

College is a great place to loosen up rigid ways of thinking and behaving in order to become a more flexible person. The challenges that a college education offers, the diverse learning community, and the opportunity to expand your mind will enable you to meet the even greater challenges in your life that lie ahead. For more help in accepting the need for change and in coping with the stress that results from life's major changes, see Chapter 6.

To pursue this topic further, do an online search using these key words as a starting point: *flexibility, adapting to change, stress* and *change*.

Figure 1.1	**Success Strategies for Immediate Use**
1. **Believe in yourself.**	Choose success and believe that you will succeed. Your belief will motivate you to study and to be persistent.
2. **Expect a welcome.**	Your instructors are glad to see you. Your knowledge and experience are valuable contributions to the learning community.
3. **Head off stress.**	College can be stressful. Know this in advance and be prepared. Create a schedule you can live with. Adjust working hours accordingly.
4. **Seek support of family.**	Spouses or partners and other family members can help or hinder your success. Let them know how much you need their support.
5. **Look to your peers.**	Make friends right away. Find an ally with whom you can study, share notes, or have a snack and conversation between classes.
6. **Brush up on skills.**	Your reading, writing, and math skills are prerequisites for many courses. If your skills in these areas are rusty, find out what help is available and take advantage of it.
7. **Become computer literate.**	Learn how to use a word processor, access online library and research materials, send and receive email, and use the Internet. Find out where on campus you can get the instruction you need.

Know Where to Find Help

SUPPOSE YOU HAVE a question or a problem that you do not think anyone in your support group can help you resolve. Where are you most likely to find assistance? The following is a list of typical campus offices and centers and the services they provide. Your college catalog, campus directory, telephone book, or your college's web site can direct you to the office you seek.

Registrar's Office. This office keeps records of students' grades and issues transcripts. If you have a question about graduation requirements, applying credits toward a degree, dropping or adding a course, transferring credits, or changing majors, see someone in this office.

Career Center. If you are having trouble setting career goals or deciding on a major, someone in this office can help. Here you may find printed career materials or a computerized guidance program. Either for no charge or for a small fee, you can take one or more tests that will assess your interests, personality, and skills. By taking these tests you might discover the job or career that is right for you. Some career centers also provide a job placement service for graduates. If you want this service, all you have to do is file a résumé. In addition, your career center may invite prospective employers to recruit on campus. Meeting these visitors is a good way to decide whether the businesses or professions that they represent would interest you.

Academic Advising and Counseling Office. The name of this office varies from campus to campus, but it may offer two kinds of services: academic advising to help you with course selection and planning, and counseling to help you with personal or other problems that affect your adjustment to college. Some campuses may have separate offices for academic advisement and for personal counseling. Since you may need these services at some point in your college career, find the name and location of the office or offices that provide them.

Financial Aid Office. Go to this office to apply for scholarships, loans, and work-study grants. People in this office are best qualified to answer your questions about financial matters, including special financial aid options such as scholarships and loans for which you may be eligible. If you want a campus job, your application process begins here. For some jobs, you may have to meet special requirements or demonstrate financial need.

If you have a fee or a fine to pay, or if you need to pick up a paycheck for work done on campus, the financial aid office may also handle those transactions. On the other hand, your campus may have a separate office—the *bursar's office*, for example—that collects fees and fines and issues checks.

Student Health Services. What happens if you get sick or have an accident on campus? If your college provides health services to students, you can get medical assistance from a campus nurse or physician. Some may provide mental health services as well. If you have a chronic health problem such as diabetes or epilepsy, you should make sure that your instructors know about it. If you become ill in class, they will be able to get help for you.

Learning Labs and Centers. Do you need to develop your reading, writing, math, or study skills? If your college has a learning lab or center, you can find help there. In the lab you will probably work independently on programs or materials that you select yourself or that are selected for you. These will be based on your needs and level of ability. Some labs are voluntary, but at some colleges spending time in a learning lab may be one of a student's course requirements. If you are required to attend a reading, writing, or math lab, think of it as a great opportunity to strengthen your skills so that you will be successful in courses that are going to become increasingly more difficult.

Library. Your campus library contains all the resources that you will need for research and recreational reading such as books, magazines, newspapers, journals, reference books, documents, and microfilms or microfiche. It may also have audiovisual holdings such as audiotapes and videocassettes. Most libraries have computerized information retrieval systems that are networked with other libraries and document centers. If you have never done any research, a librarian or library assistant can show you how to do it. Most libraries provide an orientation to explain their holdings and the services that they offer.

Tutorial Center. If you are having trouble in a course, your instructor may suggest tutoring. A *tutor* is often a student who has taken your course and earned an A in it. The tutor probably has completed a training program and knows how to explain the course material. Working with a tutor can sometimes be easier than working with an instructor because the tutor is your peer, and you can talk to him or her as you would to a friend. You may or may not have to pay a fee for the tutor's services. To find out whether tutorial services are available on your campus, ask your instructor or academic advisor.

EXERCISE **1.5**

TAKE A WALKING TOUR OF your campus. Your college may not have all of the places listed here, but find as many of them as you can and write down their building and office or room numbers. If an office on the following list is not on your campus, write *none* in the space provided. Post this list in a handy place.

Important Campus Locations _____

Registrar's office _____

Student health service _____

Career center _____

Advisors' offices _____

Athletic director's office _____

Learning labs and centers _____

Financial aid office _____

English department office _____

Library _____

Tutorial center _____

Computer center _____

Veterans office _____

Office of Diversity _____

Housing office _____

Campus security _____

EXERCISE **1.6**

APPLY WHAT YOU HAVE LEARNED about the places to find help on campus. Discuss and answer the following questions, doing any research that may be needed. Resources to consider include your college catalog and your college's web site.

Do this exercise by collaborating with a group or partner. Before beginning the exercise, follow the guidelines for successful collaboration explained in Figure 1.2.

1. **Adult Learners**

   a. **What special services or programs exist on your campus for adult learners?**

     _____

   b. **Where is the service or program offered (office or other location)?**

     _____

   c. **Give the name of a contact person to ask for information.**

     _____

2. **Women**

   a. **What special services or programs exist on your campus for women?**

     _____

   b. **Where is the service or program offered (office or other location)?**

     _____

   c. **Give the name of a contact person to ask for information.**

     _____

3. **Students with Disabilities**

   a. **What special services or programs exist on your campus for the learning disabled and physically disabled?**

     _____

     _____

   b. **Where is the service or program offered (office or other location)?**

     _____

     _____

   c. **Give the name of a contact person to ask for information.**

     _____

4. **Does your campus provide help for students who need to reduce stress? Where is the service offered, and who is a person to contact for information?**

     _____

     _____

5. **Does your campus provide help for students who need a tutor? Where is the service offered, and who is a person to contact for information?**

_____

_____

Group Evaluation:

Evaluate your discussion. Did everyone contribute? Did you accomplish your task successfully? What additional questions do you have about places on campus to go for help? How will you find answers to your questions?

_____

_____

Figure 1.2	**Collaborating with Group Members**

Every chapter of _The Confident Student_ contains a _collaborative_ exercise—an activity that is intended for partners or a small group. Exercise 1.6 in this chapter is a collaborative exercise. Successful collaboration requires teamwork. When collaborating in a small group, each member has a role to perform, and each member's full participation is required. The following is a list of typical group roles and responsibilities.

Before beginning a collaborative exercise, form a group and decide which members will perform the following roles and responsibilities. If you are collaborating with a partner, you can divide the responsibilities equally.

Roles	**Responsibilities**
Leader	The leader is responsible for interpreting the exercise directions, keeping the discussion on target, and making sure that everyone participates.
Recorder	The recorder acts as the secretary by taking notes and summarizing the group's findings or recording answers after the group achieves consensus (agreement).
Researcher	The researcher consults the textbook, the instructor, or other resources as needed to settle matters of confusion or controversy.
Reciter	The reciter reports back to the class, using the recorder's notes for reference.

Some collaborative activities may require different roles and responsibilities other than those described here. For example, if you are given a time limit for completing a task, someone must act as timekeeper. This could be a separate role, or it may be another responsibility added to the leader's or recorder's tasks. For groups that are larger or smaller than four members, new roles or new divisions of responsibilities can be created.

© Ron Sherman

Your library or media center may offer a tour that you can take to learn about all of its resources. It's a good idea to get an overview before you begin your first research project.

Stay Informed

WHENEVER YOU HAVE a question about some aspect of college life—whether there is a chess club on campus, for example, or what the number of credit hours required to graduate is—you can probably find the answer in one of your college's publications. One way to become a more confident and self-sufficient student is by familiarizing yourself with the kind of information contained in these sources:

The college catalog

The college newspaper

The student bulletin

The student handbook

Informational flyers and posters

Note that many of these resources may also be available on your college's web site. Frequently referring to these materials will make you a well-informed member of your college community.

The College Catalog

Your *college catalog* contains a wealth of information about your college's programs, policies, requirements, and services. The calendar in your catalog is one of the items you will use most frequently. The college calendar lists dates, deadlines, and a fee payment schedule for which you are responsible. The calendar is usually among the first few pages of your catalog. It shows when classes begin and end, when holidays occur, when the drop-and-add period is over, when final exams are scheduled, and when you should make an application for a degree. The catalog will also tell you whether a fee is involved in applying for a degree and under what conditions you can get your money back if you withdraw from a course.

To save time, many students like to prepare a schedule in advance. To do this, you will need to know what courses are available, how many credits each course is worth, and the names and numbers of courses. You will find courses listed in the catalog under department or subject area names, followed by course descriptions and any fees or prerequisites that may apply.

At the end of each semester, you will get a computer printout of your grades. The printout will show a grade for each course, your average for the semester, and a *cumulative GPA,* which is the average of all grades you have earned from the time of your enrollment. The GPA is usually stated as a number from 1.00 to 4.00. Your catalog explains, using examples, how to calculate your GPA.

Most campuses have numerous kiosks and bulletin boards for posting important academic and social events. You can easily check for new listings on your way to and from classes.

© Bob Daemmrich/Stock Boston

Have you ever wondered what an instructor's full name is, what degrees he or she holds, or what college he or she attended? Look in your catalog. Toward the end, you may find an alphabetical list of instructors and their degrees and colleges attended.

Your library or media center will have copies of the catalog available for use as a reference. Furthermore, you may find a shelf or more devoted to the catalogs of many other colleges. If you are attending a two-year college and plan to continue your education after graduation, one good way to learn more about a college in which you are interested is to look through its catalog.

EXERCISE 1.7

USE YOUR COLLEGE CATALOG (online or hard copy) to find the answers to the following questions, noting the page number where you found each answer. *Hint:* Use the contents and index to help you find the topics each question covers.

1. **How many credits are required for graduation?**

_____

2. **What degrees are offered?**

_____

3. **What GPA must you maintain in order to avoid being placed on probation?**

_____

4. **Does your college offer a grade of I (incomplete)?**

_____

5. **What happens if you don't make up an incomplete grade?**

_____

6. **Is class attendance required? Is there an attendance policy stated in the catalog? On what page?**

_____

7. **What are the degrees held and colleges attended by one of your instructors?**

_____

8. **Where do you go to get a campus parking permit?**

_____

9. **What courses are all students required to take?**

_____

10. **On what dates are final exams given?**

_____

11. **When does the next registration period begin?**

_____

12. What are the number and title of a reading course offered?

_____

13. How many math courses are all students required to take?

_____

14. What are two clubs or organizations you can join?

_____

15. What is the college president's name?

_____

More Publications

Your *college newspaper* is a mirror of campus culture. It contains information of interest to the college community along with articles that report on local and world events from a student's point of view. The newspaper is probably published at least several times a semester or quarter. Reading it is an excellent way for you to stay informed about campus affairs.

Your college may also provide a *student bulletin* or other weekly publication that keeps you informed of campus activities and events and contains additional items of general interest. The bulletin is usually sponsored by the student government association, which may also publish a *student handbook.* The handbook condenses and summarizes information contained in the catalog concerning the college's policies and regulations, but it is usually written in a style that is more appealing to students.

Throughout your campus—on bulletin boards and kiosks; in the cafeteria, bookstore, and student union; in the library and learning labs; and in some classrooms—you will find various informational flyers about services and events that are printed by the people or departments sponsoring the events. These flyers will only contain the essentials about the service or event: the time, the place, and whether it costs anything. All of these publications and materials are additional means by which people at your college express their interest in you, your needs, and your continued success as a student.

Get Involved

ONE OF YOUR reasons for coming to college is to gain the knowledge and develop the skills needed to find a job or career that is both financially satisfying and personally rewarding. But as you pursue these goals, do not overlook two other important reasons for coming to college: to learn how to work and interact socially with a diverse group of people and to develop personal interests that can enrich your life and leisure. One more advantage of getting involved is that through interaction with others you will develop the skills, interests, and relationships that may help you build an impressive résumé. Interacting with others through clubs, activities, sports events, fraternities and sororities, and study groups can provide a few ways to get involved in campus life.

Greek Organizations

For many students, fraternities and sororities can be strong support groups. These *Greek organizations* provide a place for members to live, eat, study, and play together. The benefits of membership may include the development of social skills, involvement in campus and community affairs, lasting friendships, and a link to a network of former members who can ease the transition from college to career. However, fraternities and sororities are both exclusive and expensive. Not everyone who wants to join a Greek organization will be chosen. Also, Greek organizations have a reputation on some campuses for excessive drinking and socializing. Members who lack self-discipline may find themselves on academic probation if they participate in these activities. In the end, Greek organizations, like all other organizations, have advantages and disadvantages. Whether you join one or choose to remain independent, you will still be able to make friends and build a support group if you make the effort.

Special Challenges for Commuters

If you commute to college, you may be at a disadvantage in one respect. It may be less convenient for you to become involved in activities and events than it would be if you lived on or near campus. But there are ways for you to take a more active part in campus life. Consider your interests. What are your career aspirations? Is there an activity that you would like to try but have not had an opportunity to pursue? Many clubs and organizations on your campus would be happy to have you as a member. If you join one of these groups, you will meet people who share your interests, and you may learn even more about an activity you already enjoy. You may also meet people with whom you can share transportation to and from campus activities and events. Your catalog and student handbook contain a list of campus organizations. You could also drop by your student government office and introduce yourself. Someone there can tell you about the many activities and upcoming events in which you can take part. Forming a study group that meets on campus or scheduling some on-campus study time is another way to remain on campus and stay involved.

thinking *ahead*   - - - - ▶

What practical knowledge have you gained from this chapter that you can use to solve real-world problems? To find out, read the following scenario and complete the items that follow it.

You have completed your degree program and have been hired for the career of your dreams. The company you work for is in a town far away from your family, friends, and the campus that has been your home for the past several years. You are eager to make a good impression, you have several innovative ideas that you hope to put into practice, and you have confidence in your skills. Although you have made a few new friends at work, you are still feeling the stress of finding yourself alone in a new town at a new job. You know it is just a matter of time until you feel at home in your new environment, but you wish there were something you could do in the meantime.

1. **Define the problem as you see it.**

   _____

   _____

   _____

2. **Consider the strategies you have learned in this chapter:** *form a support group, embrace diversity, know where to find help, stay informed,* **and** *get involved.* **Think of these strategies as possible options or solutions to your problem. Which one do you think would be most helpful? Why?**

   _____

   _____

   _____

   _____

   _____

3. **Explain how you would use one of the strategies to solve the problem. For example, if you choose** *form a support group,* **how would you do it? Who would be the members?**

   _____

   _____

   _____

   _____

4. **What else have you learned from this chapter that could be helpful in the situation that this scenario describes?**

   _____

   _____

   _____

   _____

   _____

chapter **re**view

To review the chapter, reflect on the following confidence-building attitudes, complete Concepts to Understand, and practice your new skills at every opportunity.

ATTITUDES TO DEVELOP

- openness to new ideas and willingness to seek help
- flexibility in your activities, plans, and opinions
- respect for others' differences
- belief in yourself

CONCEPTS TO UNDERSTAND

Choosing success in college means adopting confidence-building _____, building skills, and engaging in productive _____ _____ that will help you reach your goals. To choose success, you can begin by forming a _____ group. Your group may include your in-structors, an academic advisor or counselor, department heads and secretaries, your resident advisor, your coach, club sponsors, and classmates—people to whom you can turn for help or advice.

Choose success by embracing _____. Reach out to students whose age, race, ethnicity, sexual orientation, and abilities differ from yours. Expect to learn something from everyone you meet. Do your part to make every student feel as comfortable in the college learning community as you want to feel.

Choose success by knowing where to find _____. Whether you need a loan, a part-time job, as-sistance in selecting a major, or a tutor for one of your courses, familiarize yourself with the people or places on campus that provide these services.

Choose success by staying _____. Use your college catalog as a reference to keep up with dates, deadlines, degree and program requirements, and course offerings. Read the college newspaper, stu-dent bulletin, college web site, and the various flyers and posters displayed around campus.

Choose success by getting involved. Whether you live on campus or commute, participate as much as you can in campus activities, events, and organizations.

To access additional review exercises, see http://college.hmco.com/success.

SKILLS TO PRACTICE

- using email and the Internet
- interacting with diverse people
- choosing and using resources at your campus
- finding information
- collaborating in group activities

Your Reflections

Your Reflections

Reflect on what you have learned about choosing success in college and how you can best apply that information. Use the following list of questions to stimulate your thinking; then write your reflections. Your responses may include answers to one or more of the questions. Incorporate in your writing specific information from this chapter.

- Would you describe yourself as a flexible person? Why or why not?

- What campus resources to you think will be most helpful to you?

- If you were assigned the task of helping a student get adjusted to campus life, what advice would you give?

- What are you doing to increase your chances of success in college?

- Of all the attitudes and skills listed in the chapter review, which do you think will be the most useful to you at work or in your career?

Motivating Yourself to Learn

WHAT ARE YOUR strengths and

weaknesses as a student? Do you know

that you have a learning style? What is the connection

between motivation and learning?

MOTIVATION IS THE incentive or desire that moves you to take an action. What motivates you to ask someone out? The desire for companionship could be a motivating factor. What motivates you to take a job? The need to support yourself or your family, the desire to serve or help others, or some other incentive may be the reason. What motivated you to come to college, and what will motivate you to study, learn, and be successful in your courses? This chapter will help you find answers.

The motivation to learn lies within you—it is your responsibility, not anyone else's. In fact, a quality that is extremely valuable to develop, if you do not already possess it, is *personal responsibility*. This quality is essential not only in college but also in the workplace, where you will be challenged with tasks that will require you to continually upgrade your skills.

To help you get motivated and stay motivated, this chapter explains four keys to success in college. They will help you unlock your learning process and free the confident student within you. Moreover, they may open doors for you in the workplace as well.

- Assess your strengths and weaknesses.

- Discover and use your learning style.

- Adapt to others' styles.

- Develop critical thinking and study skills.

Assess Your Strengths and Weaknesses

THE FIRST OF this chapter's keys to success in college is a realistic assessment of your strengths and weaknesses in the basic skills of reading, writing, math, and

Your academic advisors can help you select courses that take your academic strengths and weaknesses into account and enable you to build new skills.

© Bob Mahoney/The Image Works

using computers. If you do not know what your strengths and weaknesses are in those areas, you may overestimate your skills and take courses for which you are unprepared. Or you may underestimate the value of your experiences outside of college, which can make up for some skill deficiencies. For example, you may have gained knowledge and abilities from reading, working, traveling, or serving in the military that you can apply to your college courses. Knowing what you can and cannot do, and making decisions based on that knowledge, will help you make responsible course selections.

Your self-assessment should take into consideration the advice you have received from helpful people at your college. Your academic advisors and instructors are eager for you to be successful. That is why they have invested so much time in testing you, advising you, and perhaps requiring you to take a skill-development course in reading, writing, math, or computer literacy. They also know that a strong foundation in these skills is a career asset.

Self-assessment is a key to success in the workplace as well as in college. When confronted with any new learning situation, ask yourself questions such as "What do I already know?" "What skills do I have that I can use?" "What personal qualities apply?" "What additional knowledge, skills, or qualities do I need?" Your answers will provide the self-knowledge you need to make good choices.

For an informal assessment of your strengths and weaknesses in the basic skills, complete the following Awareness Check.

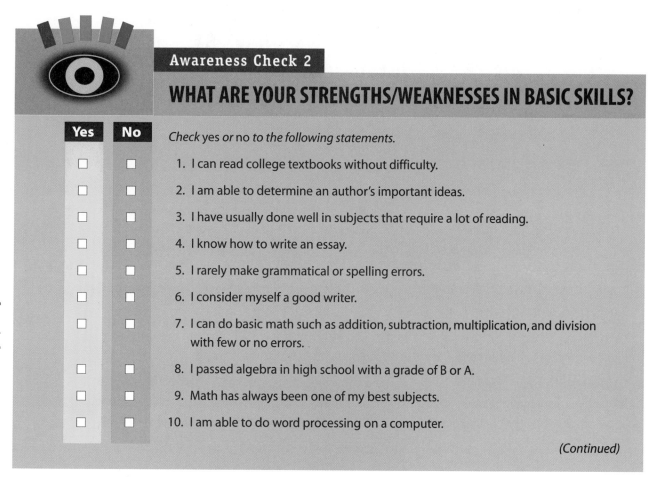

Awareness Check 2

WHAT ARE YOUR STRENGTHS/WEAKNESSES IN BASIC SKILLS?

Yes	No	
☐	☐	*Check* yes *or* no *to the following statements.*
☐	☐	1. I can read college textbooks without difficulty.
☐	☐	2. I am able to determine an author's important ideas.
☐	☐	3. I have usually done well in subjects that require a lot of reading.
☐	☐	4. I know how to write an essay.
☐	☐	5. I rarely make grammatical or spelling errors.
☐	☐	6. I consider myself a good writer.
☐	☐	7. I can do basic math such as addition, subtraction, multiplication, and division with few or no errors.
☐	☐	8. I passed algebra in high school with a grade of B or A.
☐	☐	9. Math has always been one of my best subjects.
☐	☐	10. I am able to do word processing on a computer.

(Continued)

Yes	No	
☐	☐	11. I can use email, do Internet searches, and perform other basic computer tasks.
☐	☐	12. According to an assessment-test score or an advisor, my reading skills need improvement.
☐	☐	13. According to an assessment-test score or an advisor, my writing skills need improvement.
☐	☐	14. According to an assessment-test score or an advisor, my math skills need improvement.

If you checked no to statements 1–3 and yes to statement 12, you may need to improve your reading skills. If you checked no to statements 4–6 and yes to statement 13, you may need to develop your writing skills. If you checked no to statements 7–9 and yes to statement 14, you may need to strengthen your math skills. If you checked no to statements 10 or 11, you need to develop computer skills. Since strong reading, writing, math, and computer skills are essential to success in college, you need to build on your strengths and overcome your weaknesses in these areas. However, academic skills alone are not what make you intelligent. You may be smart in other ways.

CONFIDENCE
Builder

Howard Gardner's Seven Intelligences

Book learning is only one kind of intelligence. Researchers have found other categories of intelligence that are changing our definition of what it means to be smart.

Those who study intelligence are divided between two camps: Some believe intelligence is a single ability measured by IQ tests, and others think intelligence is multifaceted. Howard Gardner, a professor at Harvard University's Graduate School of Education, belongs to the second camp. Author of *Frames of Mind* (1983) and *Multiple Intelligences: The Theory in Practice* (1993), Gardner argues that we have seven intelligences. Everyone possesses these intelligences to some degree, but some people may show greater strength in one or more areas. Gardner also believes that we can encourage the development of our intelligences and that we can learn to use them to our advantage.

Linguistic. This intelligence is characterized by skill with words and a sensitivity to their meanings, sounds, and functions. If your linguistic intelligence is high, you probably learn best by reading.

Logical-Mathematical. This intelligence is characterized by skill with numbers, scientific ability, and formal reasoning. If your logical-mathematical intelligence is high, you probably learn best by taking a problem-solving approach to learning. Outlining or making charts and graphs may be good study techniques for you.

Bodily-Kinesthetic. This intelligence enables people to use their bodies skillfully and in goal-oriented ways such as playing a sport or dancing. If your bodily intelligence is high, you may be able to learn more effectively by combining studying with some physical activity.

Musical. This intelligence is characterized by the ability to find meaning in music and other rhythmical sounds and to reproduce them either vocally or with an instrument. If your musical intelligence is high, you may want to choose a career in music or engage in leisure activities that allow you to pursue your musical interests. Although studying to music is a distraction for some, you may find that it aids your concentration.

Spatial. This intelligence is characterized by the ability to perceive the world accurately and to mentally reorganize or reinterpret those perceptions. For example, an artist perceives accurately what a bowl of fruit looks like—the colors and sizes of the fruit and how the fruit is arranged. However, the artist's painting of the bowl of fruit is a new interpretation—the artist's mental image of the bowl of fruit—and this image may distort the sizes or change the colors of the fruit. If your spatial intelligence is high, you may learn best by finding ways to visualize or restructure the material that you want to learn.

Interpersonal. This intelligence is characterized by the ability to read people's moods and intentions and to understand their motives. Empathy is another characteristic of interpersonal intelligence. *Empathy* is the ability to identify with another person's feelings. People who have a high degree of interpersonal intelligence may be said to have "good people skills." If your interpersonal intelligence is high, you may learn best by collaborating with others on projects or by participating in a study group.

Intrapersonal. This intelligence is characterized by self-knowledge: the ability to read your own emotions, to understand what motivates you, and to use that understanding to shape your behavior. If your intrapersonal intelligence is high, you should be able to make use of all of your other intelligences to find the best study methods that will work for you.

Gardner's theory of multiple intelligences (MI) is widely accepted among educators. However, opinions about the theory's usefulness differ. Some psychologists and educators praise Gardner for raising public awareness about the many facets of intellectual ability. But others are concerned because the theory has never been formally tested. It is well to remember that most employers place great value on verbal and math skills, believing that they are stronger predictors of success at work. The practical value of Gardner's theory may be that it encourages students to discover and use all of their talents and intellectual capacities to create success in college and in life.

To pursue this topic further, do an online search using these key words: *learning styles, multiple intelligences, Howard Gardner.*

Discover and Use Your Learning Style

DISCOVERING AND USING your learning style is the second key to success in college. Like everything else about you, your learning style is uniquely your own, different from anyone else's. *Your learning style is your characteristic and preferred way of learning.* Another way to look at learning style is to think of it as the conditions under which you find it easiest and most pleasant to learn and to work. For example, suppose you buy a new piece of software. What would be the easiest, quickest, and most pleasant way for you to learn how to use it? Would you read the manual, follow the instructions on a tutorial disk, ask a friend who knows how to use it, or sign up for a course? None of these ways is the *best* way to learn how to use new software, but one of these ways, or a combination of them, may be the best way for *you* to learn.

Your Five Senses

Is your learning style primarily visual, auditory, or tactile? *Visual learners* prefer to learn by reading or watching. *Auditory learners* like to learn by listening. *Tactile learners* learn by doing, by touching or manipulating objects, or by using their hands. Figure 2.1 provides a chart with examples of each learning style and shows how learning style preferences affect how you go about completing a task such as learning how to use a computer or assembling a child's toy. As you read the chart,

EXERCISE 2.1

TRY THIS EXPERIMENT FOR A vivid example of the way your learning style affects you.

1. **Fold your hands.**

2. **Look at which thumb is on top. Is it your left or right?**

3. **Now fold your hands again so that the other thumb is on top. Does this position feel comfortable to you?**

4. **Fold your hands your preferred way and notice any difference in feeling.**

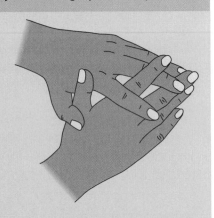

Folding your hands is something you do automatically, and because you always do it your preferred way, you feel comfortable. But when you fold your hands differently, you feel uncomfortable because that position is not natural for you. Your learning style is automatic in a similar way. When you are in a classroom environment that matches your learning style, everything feels right. But if the environment does not match your style, you may feel out of place, uncomfortable, and unable to do your best. To combat feelings of discomfort in a classroom environment, understand your learning style. Find ways to adapt your style to fit the environment, and you will be successful. Adapting your style is like learning to live with the wrong thumb on top. At first, it may feel a little strange, but with practice the difference will not be noticeable.

Your learning style has many components. We will discuss four of them:

1. **Your five senses**

2. **Your body's reactions**

3. **Your preferred learning environment**

4. **Your level of motivation**

Figure 2.1	Learning Style Preferences		
LEARNING PREFERENCE	**EXAMPLE**	**LEARNING TO USE COMPUTER**	**ASSEMBLING A CHILD'S TOY**
Visual	Prefers visual sense. Must *see* to understand Learns best by reading and watching.	Looks at diagrams. Reads a manual. Watches someone demonstrate the process.	Tries to duplicate picture on the box. Reads instructions silently while assembling toy.
Auditory	Prefers auditory sense. Must *hear* to understand. Learns best by listening to an explanation.	Attends a class or workshop to hear explanation. Listens to someone read the instructions.	Reads instructions aloud while working. Asks someone to read each step.
Tactile	Prefers tactile sense. Must *touch* or *feel* to understand. Learns best by engaging in hands-on activity.	Uses trial-and-error approach. Attends a hands-on workshop.	May ignore the instructions or resort to them only when trial-and-error method fails.

remember that it illustrates *preferences:* what each type of learner feels most comfortable doing. The most successful learners are those who take control of the learning situation by adapting to different modes of instruction and by using a combination of learning methods.

Though everyone can learn to adapt to different learning styles, most people have difficulty at first when asked to do something that seems unnatural to them. Imagine the frustration of a secretary, an auditory learner, whose boss says, "Now watch how I fix this copy machine because the next time it breaks down, "I'll expect you to fix it"—or the child, a visual learner, whose teacher says, "I am going to explain how to turn on your computer and start the program. Listen to the steps, and do exactly as I say." You may have felt a similar frustration in classrooms when the instructor presented material in a sensory mode other than your preferred one. For example, if you are a student who dislikes lecture courses, loses concentration, or has trouble following ideas, maybe you're not an auditory learner. To be successful in a lecture class, you may need to develop strategies that will help you adapt to auditory modes of instruction. For one thing, you could concentrate on developing good note-taking skills and listening techniques as explained in Chapter 4. To fill in gaps in your notes, compare them with those of someone in the class who does have a strong auditory preference and who is good at taking notes.

Because instructors' teaching styles and methods differ, you must be flexible enough to adapt to whatever instructional mode is being used. Figure 2.2 illustrates some common teaching methods, the learning style preferences they appeal to, and some adaptive strategies for you to try.

Figure 2.2	Adapting Learning Style to Teaching Method	
TEACHING METHODS	**LEARNING STYLE/ SENSORY PREFERENCE**	**ADAPTIVE STRATEGIES TO TRY**
Lecture/class discussion	Auditory	Take notes. (tactile and visual) Watch for visual cues such as gestures and facial expressions that emphasize important points. (visual) Pay attention to visual aids or information written on chalkboard. (visual)
Videotaped presentations Use of visual aids	Visual	Listen to instructor's explanations or comments and copy them into your notes. (auditory and tactile) Summarize presentation in your notes and read it aloud to review. (auditory)
Hands-on activity	Tactile	Summarize the activity in your notes to read later. (auditory and visual) Listen to any explanation that accompanies the activity. (auditory)

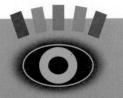

Awareness Check 3

WHAT ARE YOUR SENSORY PREFERENCES?

Check all of the statements that seem true of you. An explanation of your responses follows the Awareness Check.

☐ 1. I learn best by reading on my own.

☐ 2. I get the best results from listening to lectures.

☐ 3. I enjoy courses where there is some physical activity involved.

☐ 4. I can learn how to do something by watching a demonstration of how it's done.

☐ 5. Class discussions are helpful to me.

☐ 6. I like to type and to use computers.

☐ 7. Illustrations, charts, and diagrams improve my understanding.

☐ 8. I'd rather listen to the instructor's explanation than do the assigned reading.

☐ 9. I get more out of labs than lectures because of the hands-on approach.

☐   10.   How-to manuals and printed directions are helpful to me.

☐   11.   I like to use audiocassette tapes of lessons and exercises.

☐   12.   I'd rather work with machines and equipment than listen to or read explanations.

☐   13.   I can learn to do something if someone shows me how.

☐   14.   I can follow directions best when someone reads them to me.

☐   15.   It's not enough to show me; I have to do it myself.

Statements 1, 4, 7, 10, and 13 are characteristic of visual learners. Statements 2, 5, 8, 11, and 14 are characteristic of auditory learners. Statements 3, 6, 9, 12, and 15 are characteristic of tactile learners. If your checks are spread evenly among two or more categories, you may be equally comfortable using one or more of your sensory modes. But remember that this Awareness Check is only an informal survey. For a formal assessment of your learning style, see an academic or career development counselor, who may be able to give you one of several well-known tests.

Your Body's Reactions

When you are in a classroom or study area, lighting, temperature, and the comfort of the furniture may or may not affect your ability to pay attention or to get your work done. If your body does react strongly to these and other influences such as hunger, tiredness, or mild illness, then you may lose concentration. You should take care of these physiological needs before attempting to do anything that demands your full attention. Determining your physiological preferences and building your schedule accordingly is one way to use your learning style to create the conditions under which you will stay most alert.

Like most people, you probably have a peak time of day during which you are most alert and energetic. Throughout the day your concentration, attention, and energy levels fluctuate. In the morning you might be alert and ready for anything, but by afternoon you might feel sapped of energy. If you are a morning person, for example, then it would make sense to schedule your classes in the morning if you can. But if you are alert and can concentrate better in the late afternoon or at night, then schedule as many of your courses as possible in the evening hours. If you anticipate that a certain course will be difficult, make every effort to schedule it at your peak time of day. You should also plan to do as much of your studying as possible at this time of day.

If you learn to accept what you cannot change, then you can adapt to situations that don't meet your preferences, knowing that you will have to try harder to pay attention and remain on task. Moreover, although you have limited control over your classroom environment, you can set up your own study environment to reflect all of your important preferences. See Chapter 9 for a detailed discussion and suggestions.

The next Awareness Check will help you understand how your body's reactions might affect your ability to learn.

Awareness Check 4

HOW DOES YOUR BODY REACT?

Check the statements that best describe you.

- ☐ 1. I feel most alert in the morning hours.
- ☐ 2. I don't "come alive" until afternoon or early evening.
- ☐ 3. I am definitely a night person.
- ☐ 4. I concentrate and work best in a brightly lighted room.
- ☐ 5. Bright light distracts me; I prefer natural or nonglare lighting.
- ☐ 6. Overhead lighting is never right; I need an adjustable lamp.
- ☐ 7. The temperature in a classroom does not usually affect my concentration.
- ☐ 8. I can't work or concentrate in a room that is too hot or too cold.
- ☐ 9. I usually get chills when sitting next to a fan, air conditioner, or open window.
- ☐ 10. If my chair or desk in class is uncomfortable, I am usually able to ignore it and concentrate.
- ☐ 11. If my chair is not the right height, my back or neck aches.
- ☐ 12. If I feel a little ill or headachy, I can't think about anything else.
- ☐ 13. I can ignore feelings of hunger or tiredness long enough to keep my attention on my work.
- ☐ 14. Mild feelings of illness usually don't distract me from my work.

Your answers to the Awareness Check indicate the following about your body's reactions: the time of day when you are most alert (items 1–3), your lighting preferences (items 4–6), your temperature preferences (items 7–9), your comfort in relation to furnishings in your classroom (items 10–11), the extent to which hunger, tiredness, and illness affect your ability to concentrate in class (items 12–14).

EXERCISE **2.2**

ANSWER THE FOLLOWING QUESTIONS ABOUT your best class and your worst class. Compare your body's reactions to each classroom environment (questions 1–6). Then determine to what extent your body's reactions affect your learning in each class and what you can do to adapt more effectively (questions 7–8).

1. **What time does the class meet, and are you most alert at this time?**

   best class _____

   worst class _____

2. **Is the temperature in the classroom generally comfortable for you?**

   best class _____

   worst class _____

3. **What type of lighting is available in the classroom, and do you find the lighting acceptable?**

   best class _____

   worst class _____

4. **Are you generally rested or tired when you go to class?**

   best class _____

   worst class _____

5. **Have you eaten recently before class, or do you become hungry during class?**

   best class _____

   worst class _____

6. **Would you describe the seating arrangement and the furniture in the classroom as comfortable or uncomfortable?**

   best class _____

   worst class _____

7. **What relationship do you see between your body's reactions and your performances in your best and worst class?**

   _____

   _____

8. **What can you do to improve your performance in your worst class? What can you do to make your worst class seem more like your best class?**

   _____

   _____

Your Preferred Learning Environment

A learning environment is much more than the place where your class meets. The way the class is structured is also an important part of the learning environment. In what kind of learning environment are you most comfortable? Do you like a traditional classroom, where desks are arranged in rows and the instructor directs activities? Or are you more comfortable in a looser arrangement, where instructor and students sit together in a circle, for example, or where small groups of students sit together at tables?

Perhaps you are a self-directed student who prefers to work alone in a self-paced class or lab. Or you may need a lot of direction and supervision while you learn. You may be a student who learns more from the instructor's lectures and comments than from class discussions. Or you may be a student who doesn't get much out of class unless you have opportunities to share ideas with others in group activities. The following comments illustrate three learning environment preferences. Can you hear yourself in one of these comments, or do you have yet another preference?

1. **Carol:** The instructors are the ones I've paid my money to hear; they're the experts. I resent it when class time is taken up answering questions that are covered in the reading assignments.
2. **Andy:** I hate this class. All the instructor does is lecture. I learn more from class discussions and listening to different people's opinions.
3. **Grant:** I don't like it when I have to adjust my pace to the rest of the class. I'd rather work independently so I can progress at my own rate, taking as much time as I need.

Carol likes a traditional, teacher-centered classroom. Andy prefers a student-centered environment. Grant, who likes to work alone, prefers individualized instruction.

The learning environment for your course may affect your feelings about the subject matter as well as your performance.

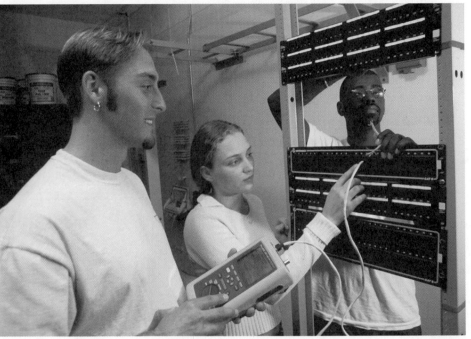

© Ron Sherman

Most of the time you will have to adapt to whatever learning environment is available. However, understanding your preferences will enable you to select the kind of classes in which you are most comfortable, if you have a choice. Advisors and other students are good sources of information about the type of learning environment a specific course or instructor provides.

EXERCISE **2.3**

TO FIND OUT MORE ABOUT your learning preferences, you can take informal inventories like the ones in Awareness Checks 3 and 4.

For this exercise, take another informal learning styles inventory. Your instructor may suggest one or may direct you to a person on campus who will provide one. Or you can check the Internet. Try the search phrases *Learning styles, learning styles inventories,* and *learning styles and testing.* See also http://college.hmco.com/success for suggested sites.

Compare your results on whatever inventory you take with your results from Awareness Checks 3 and 4. What is your preferred learning style? What do your results suggest that you do to improve your learning and studying?

EXERCISE **2.4**

IN ADDITION TO INFORMAL INVENTORIES, formal tests like the ones listed next may provide a more complete picture of your learning style.

- **Myers-Briggs Type Indicator® (MBTI®)**
- **Kolb Learning Style Inventory**
- **Hogan/Champagne Personal Style Inventory**
- **Keirsey Temperament Sorter**

These tests identify personality traits or preferences that may influence your life interests and career choices and the ways in which you learn, interact with others, and handle problems.

Find out which formal tests are offered on your campus and where they are administered. Then make an appointment to take a test and have it scored. Compare your results on the formal test with your results on the informal inventories. What additional information have you learned about your personality and learning style? How can you use this information to enhance your learning and studying?

Your Level of Motivation

Your motivation and your attitude—positive or negative—toward college, work, instructors, and your abilities may depend on your *locus of control*. J. B. Rotter, a psychologist, first explained the concept in 1954 as part of his social learning theory. *Locus* means place. Your locus of control is where you place responsibility for control over your life. Do you believe that you are in charge? If so, then you may have an *internal* locus of control. Do you believe that others more powerful than you are in control of what happens to you? If so, then you may have an *external* locus of control.

What does locus of control mean to you as a student, and how can it affect your motivation? To find out, complete the next Awareness Check; then read the explanation that follows.

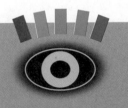

Awareness Check 5

WHAT IS YOUR LOCUS OF CONTROL?

Yes	No	
		Check yes *if you agree with a statement; check* no *if you do not agree.*
☐	☐	1. If I can do the work, I can get a good grade in any course, no matter how good or bad the instructor is.
☐	☐	2. If the teacher isn't a good speaker or doesn't keep me interested, I probably won't do well in the class.
☐	☐	3. I believe that i have the power to control what happens to me.
☐	☐	4. I believe that I have very little control over what happens to me.
☐	☐	5. When I make a mistake, it's usually my fault.
☐	☐	6. When I make a mistake, it's usually because someone didn't make clear to me what I was supposed to do.
☐	☐	7. My grades are the result of how much studying I do.
☐	☐	8. My grades don't seem to be affected by the amount of studying that I do.
☐	☐	9. I can adapt easily to a change of plans or events.
☐	☐	10. Adapting to change has always been difficult for me. I like things to be as predictable and orderly as possible.
☐	☐	11. When I fail a test, it's either because I didn't study or because I didn't understand the material.

Yes	No	
☐	☐	12. When I fail a test, it's either because the test was unfair or because the instructor didn't cover the material.
☐	☐	13. I usually don't need anyone to push me or make me study.
☐	☐	14. I can't seem to make myself study.
☐	☐	15. I am a self-motivated person.
☐	☐	16. I need someone to motivate me.

If you checked yes to mostly odd-numbered statements, then you may have an internal locus of control. If you checked yes to mostly even-numbered statements, then you may have an external locus of control. Now, read the following descriptions of students who have an internal or external locus of control and decide which most accurately describes you.

The Internal Locus of Control. Students who have an internal locus of control can see a direct connection between their efforts and their grades. These students tend to be self-motivated, positive thinkers. They believe they can do whatever they set out to accomplish. They are not afraid of change. They welcome challenges. When they make a mistake, they can usually trace it to something they did wrong or something they did not understand. These students don't believe in luck or fate. They are in control of their lives. When things go wrong, they try to figure out what they can do to make things right again.

The External Locus of Control. Students who have an external locus of control see no connection between their efforts and their grades. They may believe teachers award grades on the basis of personal feelings or that their grades result from good or bad luck. These students tend to be negative thinkers who need someone to motivate them and give them a push to succeed. They believe that many of the things they want in life are out of reach or that other people are holding them back. They may be afraid of change and may prefer to follow familiar routines. When they make mistakes, they blame others for being unfair or for not giving them the right information. They believe that they have little control over their lives. When something goes wrong, they may believe that they can do nothing about it.

Research shows that locus of control affects achievement. The more internal your locus of control, the greater your chances for success in college. Thinking positively about yourself and your abilities, accepting responsibility for motivating yourself, and doing what is necessary to succeed will produce results not only in college but also in your job or career and in your personal life. If you already have an internal locus of control, recognize it for the asset that it is. Use your ability to motivate yourself to stay in control and on track. If your locus of control is

To be successful in a course, be willing to adapt to the learning environment.

external, it is well worth your time to begin developing a more internal one. Here are some ways to do it:

1. **Become a positive thinker.** Earlier in this chapter, you assessed your strengths and weaknesses. Focus on your strengths. Remind yourself of all the things you do well and take action to overcome your weaknesses.

2. **Take responsibility for motivating yourself.** Realize that only you can make yourself study. When you study as you should, congratulate yourself and enjoy your good grades. When you don't study, accept the consequences and don't blame others.

3. **Accept the fact that success results from effort.** If you are not getting where you want to go, then apply yourself with more determination and be persistent. The greater your effort and persistence, the more likely you are to get what you want.

4. **Start listening to yourself talk.** Eliminate the nameless "they" from your vocabulary. "*They* made me do it," "*They* keep me from succeeding," and "If only *they* had told me" are comments externally motivated students make when things go wrong. By replacing *they* with *I* in your vocabulary, you are taking control of your life.

In conclusion, the internal and external loci of control represent extremes of behavior. The more internal you are, the more you believe that you are in control of your life. The more external you are, the more you believe that someone or something outside yourself is controlling the circumstances that affect your life. In other words, the degree to which you *believe* you can control what happens to you largely determines the amount of control you *actually* have.

EXERCISE **2.5**

DISCUSS THE FOLLOWING SITUATIONS WITH your group members. Follow the guidelines for successful collaboration that appear on the inside back cover. Determine whether each of the following situations is one that you can control and be able to explain why or why not. Share your answers with the rest of the class. Then evaluate your work.

1. **You arrive late for class because:**
   Your alarm didn't go off.
   Your ride didn't come.
   You had to work late the night before.
   You had car trouble.

2. **Studying is difficult for you because:**
   There are too many distractions at home.
   You have a family to take care of.
   The textbooks are difficult or boring.
   You don't know what to study.

3. **You never seem to have enough time because:**
   People are always interrupting you.
   Your instructors assign too much outside work.
   You have too many things to do.
   You often procrastinate.

4. **You are often too hungry to concentrate in class because:**
   You usually don't have time for breakfast.
   You can't eat a snack in class to tide you over.
   You have no breaks between classes.
   Class and work make scheduling lunches and snacks difficult.

5. **You often leave homework undone because:**
   You are too tried to do it.
   You can't seem to turn down your friends' offers to socialize.
   You get stuck or don't understand how to do the assignment.
   You put work or family obligations first.

Group Evaluation:

Evaluate your discussion. Did everyone contribute? Did you accomplish your task successfully? What additional questions do you have about locus of control? How will you find answers to your questions?

_____

_____

_____

_____

Claire Weinstein and her colleagues at the University of Texas have developed a method for teaching students how to learn. They call the method *strategic learning* because it involves choosing appropriate learning strategies. For example, if you are taking a course in which the instructor's main teaching method is lecturing, then appropriate strategies for learning in that course would include *using effective listening habits* and *taking good notes.*

According to Weinstein and her colleagues, strategic learning has three components: *skill, will,* and *self-regulation. Skill* means knowing your strengths and weaknesses, understanding what a learning situation or task requires, and choosing the right strategy to complete a given task. *Will* is the desire to learn and the self-motivation to do what is required. If you have *will,* you are committed to learn, you adopt a positive attitude, and you avoid self-sabotaging thoughts and behaviors. *Self-regulation* is personal responsibility. If you are self-regulated, then you accept responsibility for your learning and its outcomes. You know that you—and no one else—is in control of your time, motivation, concentration, and stress. If your grades are not what they should be, then you, as a self-regulated student, must analyze the situation, determine what went wrong, and choose alternative learning strategies. (*Source:* Claire Ellen Weinstein, Gary Hanson, Lorrie Powdril, Linda Roska, Doug Dierking, Jenefer Jusman, and Erin McCann, "The Design and Evaluation of a Course in Strategic Learning," National Association for Developmental Education, Selected Conference Papers, *Vol. 3,* Denver, Colo.: 1997.) The strategic learning method is a way of helping students take control of their learning. To think critically about *skill, will,* and *self-regulation,* first be sure that you understand the concepts as briefly explained above. Then, see what connections you can make among these concepts and this chapter's four keys to success in college. The following questions will help.

1. When you assess your strengths and weaknesses, are you employing skill, will, or self-regulation?

2. How does will affect motivation?

3. How is self-regulation involved in learning style?

4. What roles do skill, will, and self-regulation play in developing good study skills or habits?

5. What do you need to be successful in an algebra course? (*Hint:* as a prerequisite for taking algebra, you need basic math skills. What other skills do you need? How do will and self-regulation fit in?)

Adapt to Others' Styles

EVERYONE HAS A learning style. In your college's diverse learning community, you must acknowledge and accept the different ways in which instructors teach and students learn. Being able to adapt to others' styles is the fourth key to your success.

When working collaboratively with classmates or when speaking in front of a class, be aware of others' styles. For example, a person who prefers to work alone may have to be encouraged to participate with group members. Similarly, if you are planning to give an oral presentation, you may need to supplement it with visual aids to appeal to the visual learners in class.

You probably won't find it difficult to adapt to your classmates' styles. Many of them are your friends, but you should try to get along with all of your classmates since you will be working with them throughout the term.

The greatest challenge lies in adapting to your instructors' teaching styles. Just as you have a learning style, your instructors have teaching styles. An instructor's teaching style determines, to some extent, the instructional methods he or she prefers to use. Although educational researchers define a number of teaching styles, we will consider only two basic types: *independent* and *interactive.* Each of these styles represents an extreme of behavior. However, many instructors' styles fall somewhere between these extremes. For example, an instructor may use *mixed modes:* a combination of teaching methods such as lecturing, collaborative activities, and group discussion.

The instructor whose style is *independent* is usually formal and businesslike with students and places more importance on individual effort than on group effort. This instructor expects students to assume responsibility for learning, to work independently, and to seek help when needed. Lecturing is the preferred teaching method of this instructor. He or she will often call on students rather than ask for volunteers. Students often feel competitive in this instructor's class. If you feel most comfortable in lecture courses and like working independently, then you may be able to do your best work with an instructor whose style is independent.

On the other hand, the instructor whose style is *interactive* is usually informal with students and places more importance on group effort than on individual effort. The interactive instructor guides students step by step through tasks and anticipates their needs. Small group activities and large group discussions are this instructor's preferred teaching methods. Rather than call on students, he or she will usually ask for volunteers. Students often feel cooperative in this instructor's class. If you feel most comfortable in classes where students do most of the talking, and if you would rather work with others than by yourself, then you may be able to do your best work with an instructor whose teaching style is interactive.

If you do not like or do not get along with one of your instructors, you may be reacting negatively to a teaching style that conflicts with your learning style. However, don't let personal feelings keep you from being successful in the course. Instead, focus on what you *can* do to meet the instructor's requirements and make an extra effort to adapt to his or her teaching style. If you make this effort, you may find that your relationship with your instructor will improve dramatically.

In an ideal situation, advisors would match students with instructors who have similar styles. But in the real world, you may not always get the courses and instructors that you want. Also, you may not know in advance what an instructor's teaching style is. A good rule of thumb to remember when dealing with instructors is that it is *your* responsibility to adapt to their styles, not the other way around. By learning to adapt to your instructors' styles now, you are preparing for the future. Throughout your career, you will encounter bosses, coworkers, and others whose styles differ from yours, and you will be expected to work effectively with all of them.

EXERCISE **2.6**

GET TOGETHER WITH A CLASSMATE who is taking one or more of your courses. Analyze the instructor's teaching style by completing the checklist that follows. Fill in the name of the course; then check each phrase that describes the instructor. If you analyze more than one instructor's style, complete a checklist for each one. To download an additional checklist, go to http://college.hmco.com/success. Then compare your checklist with your partner's. Do your results agree?

Course: _____

- ☐ **1. Formal, businesslike attitude**
- ☐ **2. Informal, casual attitude**
- ☐ **3. Encourages competition among students**
- ☐ **4. Encourages cooperation among students**
- ☐ **5. Lectures most of the time**
- ☐ **6. Holds class discussions most of the time**
- ☐ **7. Stresses importance of individual effort**
- ☐ **8. Stresses importance of group effort**
- ☐ **9. Often uses visual aids**
- ☐ **10. Rarely uses visual aids**
- ☐ **11. Calls on students**
- ☐ **12. Asks for volunteers**
- ☐ **13. Expects students to ask for help**
- ☐ **14. Guides students step by step**
- ☐ **15. Mainly sticks to facts**
- ☐ **16. Often shares personal experiences**
- ☐ **17. "Tells" what to do, gives directions**
- ☐ **18. "Shows" what to do, gives directions**

If you checked mostly odd-numbered items, your instructor's teaching style is independent. If you checked mostly even-numbered items, your instructor's teaching style is interactive. If you checked some even- and some odd-numbered items, your instructor's style may combine modes from both the independent and interactive styles.

Develop Critical Thinking and Study Skills

READ THE FOLLOWING student comments about studying and learning. Do any of them sound like statements you have made? Can you think of another one? Add it to the list in the space provided.

Student A: "My academic skills are OK, but I still don't make the grades I want."

Student B: "I study a lot, but I often study the wrong things."

Student C: "I usually get the main idea but forget the details."

Student D: "I never seem to have enough time for studying."

Student E: "I've found several Internet sources on my research topic, but I don't know how good they are."

Your Comment: _____

_____

_____

These statements illustrate common problems that students encounter as they attend classes and study. You can solve these problems by learning to think critically and study efficiently. However, you may have to work hard to overcome your difficulties and may need to devote some time to skills development.

Developing critical thinking and study skills is your third key to success in college. Knowing how to study helps you apply your knowledge and use your skills so that you can be successful in your courses. For example, if you learn how to listen effectively and take good notes, then you will be able to follow lectures and to record essential information for study and review. If you learn how to manage your time, then you will be able to keep up with assignments and meet deadlines. If you learn how to prepare for and take tests, then you will be able to make the grades you want. If you learn how to evaluate what you read, on the Internet and elsewhere, then you will be able to select appropriate sources when researching a topic.

Learning styles, critical thinking, and study skills overlap. Thinking critically is the means by which you make sense of the world around you. The learning activities that college students must do require critical thinking. For example, you must be able to make decisions, solve problems, reason logically, use your creativity, and know how to use appropriate learning strategies. Developing critical thinking skills will also make you more employable in the future. Those who can think critically and who know how to gather and use information will get the best jobs and will advance more rapidly in their careers than those who don't.

Studying is a kind of concentrated thinking that, at its best, involves more than one of your senses. For example, when you read and underline a textbook chapter, you are using your visual and tactile senses. Studying is easier and more efficient when you use what you know about your learning style to create the conditions in which your concentration will be greatest. Figure 2.3 shows how critical thinking and study skills work together to help you complete typical tasks that your instructors might ask you to do. Chapters 4 and 5 and Chapters 8–14 focus on the specific study strategies that can help you become a more confident, skilled student.

Figure 2.3　Using Critical Thinking and Study Skills

CRITICAL THINKING	TASKS TO DO	STUDY SKILLS NEEDED/USED
Making decisions	Decide when to study.	Set up a schedule.
	Decide what's important.	Read for main idea, details, key terms.
	Select courses.	Know requirements; use resources.
	Decide what to study.	Review notes, old tests, assignments.
Solving problems	Solve math problems.	Record problems and solutions on note cards.
	Avoid procrastination.	Make and follow a schedule.
	Reduce test anxiety.	Practice relaxation techniques.
Reasoning	Write a speech.	Make an outline.
	Follow an author's ideas.	Look for patterns of organization.
	Compare theories.	Make a chart or information map.
Knowing how to learn	Learn from reading.	Locate, understand, interpret information.
	Learn from listening.	Use listening and note-taking skills.
Thinking creatively	Compose an original piece of work.	Keep an "idea" journal.
	Develop a project.	Combine ideas in new ways.

Chapter 14 provides a more detailed explanation of critical thinking and how to develop and use your critical thinking skills. The fact is that you already have been using critical thinking for many everyday tasks. For example, choosing courses and making this semester's or quarter's schedule required you to *make decisions*—What courses should I take? At what times should I schedule them? If a course you had wanted to take was filled or if your work hours conflicted with the class hours, those situations required you to use your *problem-solving* skills. Moreover, two exercises in each chapter, Critical Thinking and Thinking Ahead, ask you to apply skills or knowledge that you have gained from the chapter to practical situations that you might encounter either in college, at work, or in your personal life. In other words, when you use what you already know to find out what you don't know, you are thinking critically.

thinking *ahead* ----→

What practical knowledge have you gained from this chapter that you can use to solve real-world problems? To find out, read the following scenario, and complete the items that follow it.

Jan graduated from college five years ago. She is an insurance agent for a large company, and she thinks by now she should have been promoted. She has applied for a management position whenever one has become available, but she is always passed over. Jan doesn't understand why. She has sold as many policies as her coworkers have, more than some, and she is good at what she does.

Now and then, of course, she does get angry with customers, but it's always their fault. Either they don't read their policies, or they don't listen to her explanations. She can't help it if they don't understand what their coverage is. Jan also argues with her supervisor. She can't understand why the supervisor expects her to be on time every day. Some mornings she's just tired, and sometimes she is "unavoidably detained." She thinks that the supervisor's demands are unrealistic.

As far as her coworkers are concerned, Jan can't be bothered. She's too busy to take part in office social activities, and she's too financially strapped to participate in the various charity drives that her coworkers organize. At her last evaluation, Jan's supervisor told her that her people skills needed improving. "You're not being fair," Jan said.

When a management position recently became vacant, and Jan's application was again denied, she blamed it on bad luck.

1. What does Jan want?

_____

_____

_____

2. Define the problem that keeps Jan from reaching her goal.

_____

_____

_____

3. What is Jan's locus of control, and how is it affecting her behavior?

_____

_____

_____

4. What can Jan do to change her behavior and to reach her goal?

_____

_____

_____

chapter **re**view

To review the chapter, reflect on the following confidence-building attitudes, complete **Concepts to Understand,** and practice your new skills at every opportunity.

ATTITUDES TO DEVELOP

- self-motivation
- personal responsibility
- willingness to adapt

CONCEPTS TO UNDERSTAND

Strategies for becoming a confident, successful student include making use of the four keys to success in college discussed in this chapter.

Assessing your _____ strengths and weaknesses is the most important key. Being realistic about what you are able to do will help you select the right courses.

Discovering and using your _____ style is another important key to your success. Use your five _____ to help you take in information accurately and remember what you learn. Let your body's _____ tell you when you are most alert; then try to plan your schedule accordingly. Know which learning environment you prefer but be willing to adapt to others. Increase your level of motivation by developing an _____ locus of control.

The third key is your willingness to _____ to others' styles. No matter how much an instructor's style or your classmates' styles differ from your own, it is still *your* responsibility to meet course requirements. Make whatever adjustments are needed for you to achieve success and to establish good relations with classmates and instructors.

A fourth key to success in college is to develop _____ thinking and study skills. Making decisions and solving problems are just two of the critical thinking skills involved in studying. All the important _____ skills you will need to develop or to improve—such as how to take notes, listen effectively, and prepare for and take tests—are covered in this book. To access additional review exercises, go to http://college.hmco.com/success.

SKILLS TO PRACTICE

- assessing strengths and weaknesses
- using and adapting to learning styles
- thinking critically

Your Reflections

Reflect on the knowledge that you have gained by completing the activities in this chapter. Then write a profile of yourself as a learner. Using the following questions as a guide, include in your profile specific information from this chapter.

- Based on your answers to Awareness Checks 2 through 5 and Exercises 2.3 through 2.5, how would you describe your basic skills, learning style, and locus of control?

- What do Gardner's seven intelligences and the strategic learning method developed by Weinstein and her colleagues tell you about yourself as a learner?

- Review the critical thinking and study skills listed in Figure 2.3. Which ones are your strong points? Which need developing?

- What is your greatest strength as a learner? What weaknesses do you need to overcome?

- Of the attitudes and skills listed in the chapter review, which do you think will be most useful at work or in your career?

Setting Goals and Solving Problems

 **WHAT ARE YOUR** goals, and how do you plan to reach them? Can you be flexible when things go wrong? Do your problem-solving skills need improvement?

GETTING WHAT YOU want from college, a career, or even a relationship takes planning. You can't just wait for something to happen. You must set a goal, make a plan to achieve it, and follow through. If your plan isn't working, you must be flexible enough to make the changes that will lead to success. How do you react when your plans don't work or your goals seem out of reach? How do you react to problems? Do you take steps to solve them, or do you figure they'll eventually work out without your help? You probably know some students who can't seem to cope with grades, work, relationships, or finances while others seem to lead problem-free lives. Is it luck? No. The students who cope have learned problem-solving skills.

Your third key to success in college, critical thinking and study skills, unlocks two more valuable life skills explained in this chapter: *goal setting* and *problem solving*. These skills can help you plan effectively and solve the problems that are bound to arise as you continue your education. They will also make your life at work easier and more productive.

This chapter will help you accomplish the following objectives:

- Set goals for success in college.

- Set reachable long-term and short-term goals.

- Use the COPE method to solve problems.

Set Goals for Success in College

YOU CAN BE successful if you set goals based on what you want to accomplish. If success in college is your goal, determine what you want out of your education. Do you have a career goal, or are you undecided? What other rewards does a college education offer? Ask yourself, "Why am I here?" To help you clarify your reasons for coming to college, complete Awareness Check 6.

Awareness Check 6

WHAT ARE YOUR REASONS FOR ATTENDING COLLEGE?

Check the reasons for attending college that match your own or add a different reason in the space provided.

1. I want to earn a degree, but I haven't yet chosen a major.

2. My friends are in college, and they want me to be with them.

3. My parents want me to get a college education.

4. I want to prepare myself for a career of some kind.

5. I have an athletic scholarship, veteran's benefits, or some other source of funding.

☐   6. I want to make a lot of money.

☐   7. I want to improve my skills so that I can get a better job than the one I have now.

☐   8. I want to broaden my knowledge.

☐   9. I wasn't able to go to college when I was younger; now I want that experience.

☐   10. Improving my education will help me advance to a higher-level position at work.

☐   11. I am a non-native speaker of English, and one of my goals is to improve my language skills.

☐   12. Your reason: _____

A goal should be something that you desire and that you will be motivated enough to reach. Your answers to the Awareness Check provide the key for understanding how your reasons for attending college can motivate you to reach your goals. If you checked only item 2 or item 3, for example, then you may have difficulty motivating yourself to do well because your reasons for attending college are based more on others' expectations than on your own. You need to decide what you want out of college. If you checked only item 7 or item 10, then you have a more specific goal in mind and are probably already working to accomplish it. You may need to find additional motivation only if you encounter a setback. If you checked only item 1 or item 4, then you have a practical reason for being in college, but you have not chosen a career or major. As soon as you do that, course selection will be easier because you will be motivated by a clearer sense of direction. If you checked only item 6, then you may have set an unrealistic goal. A college education, though it does prepare you for a career, does not guarantee that you make lots of money. Motivation is easier to find when your goals are realistic, and you believe you can achieve them. If you checked item 11, your college may have a special program for non-native speakers of English. You may have already recognized this program's value to your success in college and career.

Perhaps you checked several items. Checks beside items 7, 8, 9, and 10, for example, could mean that you are seeking a college education to broaden your understanding and to provide access to a better job. If you checked items 1, 4, and 5, then you may be a student who wants a degree and has the funding to get it, but you are still exploring the possibilities of what you might do with your education. A visit to your college's career center might help you decide on a major or set a career goal that will keep you motivated.

Here are some other reasons for attending college that you may or may not have considered. In the courses you take, you will be exposed to new ideas, beliefs, and ways of looking at the world. At times, you will be excited by what you are learning; at other times, you will be frustrated by opinions and values that challenge your own. A college education can help you develop a flexible and open mind, sharpen your ability to think, and enrich your life. Best of all, you may discover in yourself talents, skills, and interests that you did not know you possessed.

Set Reachable Long-term and Short-term Goals

A LONG-TERM GOAL takes a while to accomplish. A *short-term goal* is one of several steps you might take to reach a long-term goal. Suppose one of your long-term goals is to get a degree. Completing a course required to earn that degree would be one of many short-term goals you would accomplish in the process. Figure 3.1 contrasts long-term goals with some short-term goals you might set to reach them.

As you can see from Figure 3.1, long-term and short-term are relative terms. Though graduation from college may be a long-term goal since it takes several years to reach, it may also be a short-term goal when you view it as a step toward getting your dream job—a goal that may take many more years. Similarly, completing a required course may be a short-term goal needed to reach the longer-term goal of graduation. However, completing that course might also seem to be a long-term goal when compared with the short-term goals of completing the daily assignments or scoring well on the weekly quizzes needed to pass the course. The key to successful goal setting is to know what your long-term goals are and what short-term goals you need to set to reach them.

In general, we can think of goals as personal, academic, and career or work related. Figure 3.2 compares three types of goals.

Most students are in college because they seek the skills and knowledge that will make them employable. Although some enter college with a career in mind, many are undecided. Some students, like Ellen, change their minds. Ellen had always wanted to be a nurse, even though she knew little about what the job entailed. After completing her required courses, she was accepted into her college's nursing program. Ellen's math and science skills were strong, and she enjoyed tak-

Figure 3.1

LONG-TERM GOALS	SHORT-TERM GOALS
Complete a course successfully.	Attend regularly
	Arrive on time each day.
	Make a study schedule and follow it.
	Improve note-taking skills.
	Earn good grades.
	Keep up with assignments.
Graduate from college.	Complete required courses.
	Complete additional courses needed.
	Meet all degree requirements.
	Apply for graduation and pay fees.
Get a job in a chosen career field.	Get the degree or obtain the experience necessary to qualify.
	Prepare a résumé.
	Apply for the job.
	Have a successful interview.
	Repeat steps as needed until you are hired.

Figure 3.2	Three Types of Goals
Personal Goals	Losing weight
	Improving fitness
	Developing a positive attitude
	Increasing time spent with family
	Overcoming a bad habit
Academic Goals	Passing a difficult course
	Making a grade of A on a test
	Improving reading comprehension
	Developing good study skills
	Graduating from college
Career/Work Related	Getting the job you want
	Getting a raise or promotion
	Changing jobs or careers
	Improving relations with coworkers
	Upgrading job skills or learning new ones

ing her anatomy and physiology course as well as the other courses in her program. But when one of her courses required her to spend time in a local hospital tending to the needs of the sick, she realized immediately that nursing was not what she wanted to do for the rest of her life. She was suited neither to working in a hospital environment nor to the stress that accompanies a career in nursing. At first, Ellen was at a loss. She had invested her time and money in a career that she no longer wanted to pursue. To change her major could add a year or more to her graduation time; nevertheless, that is what she decided to do. Ellen is now the financial manager of an electronics corporation. She can't imagine having a more rewarding career, and she believes that changing her major from nursing to marketing was the right decision for her.

Ellen's story illustrates how personal, academic, and career goals can overlap. Ellen's career goal was to become a nurse. Her academic goal was to complete her degree in nursing. Ellen had hoped to find satisfaction in her work, so her personal goal was to have a career doing something she liked. At the time she thought she would enjoy being a nurse. As she learned more about her chosen career, however, Ellen's personal goal of job satisfaction was not being met. This led to her decision to change her career goal. She decided that she wanted a management-level position within a large business. As a result, her academic goals changed as well. Her new goals were to change her major to marketing and to complete the courses required for her degree.

What about values and ethics? Did they play a role in Ellen's goal setting? *Values* are your judgments about what is right and wrong. They are your standards of behavior, and they include such standards as reliability, respect, responsibility, fairness, caring, and citizenship. *Ethics,* on the other hand, are community standards of behavior. Cheating in college is unethical because the college community expects students to earn their grades. Making personal calls at work or taking office supplies to use at home are unethical practices because someone else has to pay for the calls and the supplies. Employers expect you not to steal from them.

EXERCISE **3.1**

CHOOSING SUCCESS MEANS SETTING GOALS. What do you want from college in terms of a career goal? What would be a satisfying job or career for you? Create a plan to achieve your dreams by following these steps:

1. **What is your major or career goal? If you are undecided, select a major or career that you think may interest you for the purposes of this exercise. Write your goal on the line provided.**

   _____

2. **Do an Internet search on your major or career goal. Some search words to try are *career planning, careers,* and *college majors.***

   a. **What job opportunities are available in your chosen field?**

   _____

   b. **What salary do you expect in the career or profession of your choice?**

   _____

3. **Check your college web site or catalog for information on majors and careers; then answer the following questions:**

   a. **What courses are required for your major/career?**

   _____

   b. **How long will it take for you to achieve your goal?**

   _____

4. **List three short-term goals that you must achieve in order to reach your long-term goal of completing your major or starting your career.**

   a. _____

   b. _____

   c. _____

5. **Briefly summarize your plan for achieving your long-term and short-term major or career goals.**

   _____

   _____

6. **Describe a personal value that is reflected in your choice of a major or career goal.**

   _____

Would it have been ethical for Ellen to pursue a nursing career, feeling as the did? No, because the medical community expects its workers to be dedicated. How dedicated could Ellen be to a job she didn't like? Ellen's values shaped her decision to change majors. She did not want to pursue a career in which she might not be able to live up to her employer's and patients' expectations.

Personal values and ethical choices not only are an important part of goal setting; they also influence every aspect of your life. They make up what is called "character." Character is an asset in college, at work, and in all your relations with others. Figure 3.3 lists values that build character. You can build your character by incorporating these values into your life and by considering them as you set goals.

A goal should be *reachable,* with an outcome you can expect to achieve given your skills, motivation, and values. As Figure 3.4 shows, reachable goals have six characteristics.

1. **A reachable goal is realistic.** It is based on your abilities, interests, needs, and desires. For example, when choosing a career goal, you should consider your skills and interests. If you dislike math and dread balancing your checkbook every month, then accounting may not be a realistic career goal for you. If you like to write, have always done well in English courses, and enjoy working with others to make reports and presentations, then a career as a technical writer might be a realistic goal for you. Your college may have a career center or provide career counseling that will help you evaluate your interests so that you can consider the jobs, professions,

Figure 3.3	Values That Build Character
Trustworthiness	Be honest and sincere. Don't deceive, mislead, or betray a trust. Stand up for your beliefs. Never ask a friend or colleague to do something that is wrong.
Respect	Be courteous and polite. Accept and appreciate differences. Respect others' rights to make their own decisions. Don't abuse, demean, or take advantage of others.
Responsibility	Be accountable for your actions. Think about the consequences of your behavior before you act. Don't make excuses or take credit for others' work.
Fairness	Treat all people fairly, be open-minded, and listen to opposing points of view. Don't take advantage of others' mistakes.
Caring	Show that you care about others through kindness, sharing, compassion, and empathy. Be considerate of others' feelings.
Citizenship	Play by the rules and obey the laws. Respect authority. Stay informed and vote.

Adapted from the Character Counts Coalition's "pillars of character." Appearing in Reece/Brandt, *Effective Human Relations in Organizations,* 7th edition, Houghton Mifflin Company © 1999, p. 122.

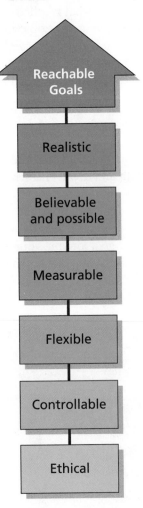

Figure 3.4

Six Characteristics of Reachable Goals

Reachable Goals

Realistic

Believable and possible

Measurable

Flexible

Controllable

Ethical

or public services best suited to your abilities and preferences. Career counseling can help you determine your chances for employment in specific fields. You might learn that jobs are scarce in a field you have been considering. Or you might discover a new field of interest that offers many employment opportunities.

2. **A reachable goal is believable and possible.** You must believe that you *can* reach your goal and that it is possible to reach it within a reasonable length of time. Suppose you want to buy a CD player. After doing some comparison shopping, you find that the price is more than you expected, and you decide to wait. You set a goal to save the money. Knowing how much money you need and how much you can afford to set aside each month, you determine that it will take five months to save the money. Each month you deposit the amount you have designated. Your goal is believable because you can afford the extra savings. Your goal is possible because you think five months is a reasonable amount of time. Your long-term goal is to save enough money to make your purchase. Each deposit you make represents the achievement of a short-term goal needed to reach the long-term goal.

3. **A reachable goal is measurable.** Establish a time frame and a foreseeable outcome. For example, if your goal is "to make a lot of money," decide how you are going to do it, when you are going to do it, and how much is "a lot." Have a foreseeable outcome at the end of which you can say, "I have reached my goal." If you set a goal to graduate from college four years from now, determine which courses to take and plan your schedule so that you can earn a sufficient number of credits each semester or quarter.

4. **A reachable goal is flexible.** Rarely do you set a goal and follow it through to completion without any problems. In working toward your college degree, for example, you may fail or withdraw from one or more courses, or you may change majors and lose credits that have to be made up. These are temporary setbacks that may interrupt your progress but need not keep you from reaching your goal. Reassess your plan for reaching the goal; then revise it, or make a new plan. Although it may take you longer to reach your goal, it is time well spent if you are doing what you want to do.

5. **A reachable goal is controllable.** You must be in charge. Set goals you can control and determine your own time limit for completing them. No one can, or should, set goals for you. Suppose you need to study for an important exam, and you know from past experience that you need at least three days to prepare yourself. Your study partner says, "We can ace this test with a four-hour study session the night before." That strategy may work for her, but will it work for you? If your goal is to make a good grade, set up your own study schedule and stick to it. You are the best person to determine how much time you will need to prepare for a test.

6. **A reachable goal is ethical.** It is fair to all concerned. The steps you take to reach your goal should not in any way cause you to violate rules, take advantage of others, or compromise your values. Suppose you are enrolled in a reading class that requires you to spend at least two hours a week in a learning lab practicing the skills you have learned in class. The reading class is required as a prerequisite for a composition course that is also required. You have set a short-term goal of completing the course with

a grade no lower than B. On your way to the lab, a friend says, "Let's cut today. We work on our own in there anyway. If we sign in and leave, no one will know." You know this is probably true because the lab is monitored by a technician who sends a copy of the sign-in sheet to the instructor.

What are the ethics involved in this situation? If you cut the class, you are engaging in unethical conduct for three reasons. First, you are breaking a rule. Second, you are taking advantage of your instructor by signing in and leading him or her to believe that you were present. Third, if honesty is one of your values, then you are compromising it. On the practical side, cutting lab doesn't help you reach

EXERCISE **3.2**

ANALYZE ONE OF YOUR PERSONAL, academic, or work-related goals in terms of the six characteristics of reachable goals.

1. What is your goal?

_____

_____

2. Which of your skills and interests make this a *realistic* goal for you?

_____

_____

3. What makes your goal *believable* and *possible*?

_____

_____

4. Is your goal *measurable*? For example, how long will it take you to reach your goal? When will you know if you have achieved it?

_____

_____

5. What makes your goal *flexible*? What will you do if you experience a setback?

_____

_____

6. Is your goal *controllable*? Is it something you can do on your own? Explain your answer.

_____

_____

7. Is your goal *ethical*? Explain how.

_____

_____

your goal. Avoiding practice time prevents your mastery of the skills and may lead to a poor grade. Is it possible to engage in unethical behavior and still reach your goals? In the short term, maybe. But in the long run, unethical conduct catches up with you. Since ethical behavior improves your chances of reaching these goals, it makes sense to say that a reachable goal is also an ethical one.

CONFIDENCE Builder

How to Develop a Positive Attitude

Changing your attitude is the first step toward solving many problems you will face in college. A negative attitude may be a habit you have developed, a characteristic response to problem solving that has prevented you from being successful in the past. Negative attitudes also affect self-esteem, destroying your confidence and creating an illusion of helplessness. But positive attitudes build confidence and self-esteem, enabling you to take control and find the motivation to do the work necessary to achieve your goals.

As Shakespeare said, "There is nothing good nor bad but thinking makes it so." Choosing to regard a problem as a challenge casts it in a positive light, focusing your attention on the actions you can take to find solutions. Here are four more things that you can do to develop a more positive attitude.

Visualize yourself being successful. Once you have set a goal, picture in your mind what you will have or will be able to do once you reach it. Keep that picture in your mind whenever you feel negative or are concerned about mastering a skill. For example, some golf instructors advocate using visualization during practice. Golfers picture themselves making a perfect swing, then repeat the process during a game.

Control your inner voice. You talk silently to yourself all the time. If your self-talk is mainly negative and derogatory, you are programming yourself for failure. Listen for those times during studying or test taking when you say to yourself, "I can't do this," or "I'm no good at this" and counteract those negative thoughts with positive ones: "I *can* do this; I just need to practice more," or "I am better at this than I used to be, and I will keep improving."

Reward yourself for doing well. When you know you have done your best or when you have accomplished a short-term goal that will help you reach a long-term goal, treat yourself to a movie, a new paperback novel, or lunch with a good friend. Be sparing with these rewards and save them for when you really deserve them. What you choose as a reward doesn't matter as long as it acts as a positive reinforcement for good behavior.

Be a positive listener and speaker. If you have trouble screening your own words for negative remarks that you need to change into positive ones, listen carefully to others. When a friend says, "I'm not going to pass algebra," explore this problem with him or her. Ask your friend to think of possible solutions. Make positive suggestions such as "Why don't you get a tutor to help you with the concepts you don't understand?" Being a positive listener and speaker may help you to think more positively about your own challenges as well.

To pursue this topic further, do an online search using these key words as a starting point: *work-related attitudes, positive attitudes, positive thinking.*

Use the COPE Method to Solve Problems

AS YOU STRIVE to reach your goals, you will encounter problems. Maintain a positive attitude about your problems by thinking of them as challenges that you can meet. To meet a challenge, you need a problem-solving method you can rely on and adapt to any situation.

One Student's Challenge

Kate, a mother of two children, thought the adjustment to college might be easier at a community college than at a university, where most of the students would probably be younger and unmarried. Kate wants a college education and the employment opportunities that will follow. She also wants to complete her education as quickly as she can, so she has enrolled in three morning classes and one night class.

When she first thought about attending college, Kate assumed that she would have plenty of time to manage the household and also do her assignments. By the end of the first week, however, Kate realized that she would have to do more studying than she had ever done before. By the end of the fifth week, she was behind, and her grades were not at all what she had expected. She couldn't find time to do all the reading that was required, so she relied on her notes and what she remembered from class discussions. Unfortunately, most of her instructors' test questions came directly from the textbooks. Although Kate understood what she read, she had trouble remembering information and deciding what to study. She could not always tell what was important in a chapter or what was likely to appear on a test. Although Kate was making an A in her algebra class—math had always been her best subject—and a solid C in her English course, she was barely pulling a C in her psychology course, and she was sure she would fail her computer course.

Kate has always thought of herself as a good student. Now, however, she is beginning to doubt whether she will make it through college. She knows that part of the problem is that she has too much to do. She never thought that juggling college and home responsibilities would be so difficult. Although her husband was supportive of Kate in the beginning, he is becoming concerned about the money her education is costing and the fact that it interferes with their family life. Kate is always tired, and her study time takes away from her time with him and the children. He feels that if Kate can't be successful, which to him means making an A in every course, she should give up. What do you think Kate should do? If you were in Kate's place, which of the following options would seem most reasonable?

1. Withdraw from college.

2. Withdraw from the two courses in which she seems most likely to fail.

3. See an academic advisor.

4. Ask her instructors for their advice.

5. Find out what additional help is available and take advantage of it.

6. Find a study partner or join a study group.

7. Take a study skills course.

8. Enlist the help of her husband and children.

Some of these options are better than others. Withdrawing from college would certainly get rid of the problem, but Kate would have wasted the time and money she has already spent, and she would have to make up the credits if she were to continue her education at a later time. Withdrawing from the two courses she is least likely to pass may or may not be a good idea. If there is no possibility that she can improve her grades, this strategy would leave her more time to devote to the remaining three courses. Since Kate is only five weeks into the term, she may still have time to raise her grades. Seeing her instructors before making a decision to withdraw would be a better option.

Kate could also see her advisor and explain the problem. The advisor may suggest ways to manage time more effectively. Although it would be too late for Kate to sign up for a study skills course, this is an option she should consider for the following term. Kate could also identify a person in her class with whom she could study or find a study group to join. Most colleges provide tutorial services at little or no cost for students who are having academic difficulty. Kate could consider getting a tutor.

Kate should not let a setback like this during her first term cause her to lose confidence. Adjusting to college is difficult for many students. The fact that Kate is making an A in the algebra course and is passing two other courses demonstrates that she *can* succeed in college. What she needs to do now is to find out how to improve her skills in the areas that are giving her trouble so that she can handle the workload more efficiently. Also, she needs to enlist more support from her family. Her husband needs to realize that success does not mean straight As. Both he and the children should relieve Kate of some of the household chores, and the family should work together to help Kate find the time to study so that she will also have more time for them. Finally, Kate should not set an unrealistic time limit for completing her education. Taking fewer courses a term might be the answer to many of her problems.

As you can see, students have much to consider when trying to solve a problem. More than one solution may be possible, and each may have advantages and disadvantages. You should always bear in mind that your first solution may not be the best one. Problem solving is a critical thinking skill that can be developed and improved. As you find effective solutions to more and more of your problems, you will gain confidence in your ability to meet difficult challenges.

A problem-solving approach, or method, is a consistent way of thinking through a problem until you find a solution. Some of these approaches are very specific, such as the method you use to conduct an experiment in a biology lab. Other approaches, such as the four-step COPE method explained in the next section, are more general and can be applied to problems you may have in your classes, at home, or at work.

The COPE Method

COPE stands for *Challenge, Option, Plan, Evaluation.* Figure 3.5 shows the COPE method's four steps.

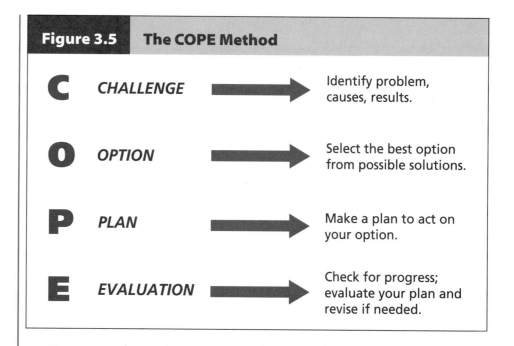

Figure 3.5   The COPE Method

C   *CHALLENGE* ➡ Identify problem, causes, results.

O   *OPTION* ➡ Select the best option from possible solutions.

P   *PLAN* ➡ Make a plan to act on your option.

E   *EVALUATION* ➡ Check for progress; evaluate your plan and revise if needed.

STEP 1   Clearly identify your **challenge**, *problem,* or its *causes,* and the *result* you want or *goal* you hope to reach.

This is the most important step. You must be able to identify your problem before you can solve it. Read the following two statements. The first is too general. The second is more specific because it clearly states a problem, its causes, and the desired result.

1. *My problem is that even though I study a lot, I still make poor grades on tests.*

2. *My problem is that even though I study a lot, I still make poor grades on tests because I get nervous, my mind goes blank, and I can't remember what I have studied until after the test is over. I want to overcome my nervousness so that I can take tests calmly and make better grades.*

To meet the challenge, ask yourself three questions. Then answer them. It may help to put your answers in writing.

- What is my problem?

- What causes my problem?

- What result do I want?

STEP 2   Choose the best **option** from the many possible solutions to your problem.

Rosalia says she cannot study at home because it is too noisy. The telephone rings frequently, her husband turns up the TV too loud, and her young children make noise playing and fighting with each other. After thinking about her problem and its causes, Rosalia came up with the following list of options.

1. Be assertive with family members about my need for some quiet time for studying. Enlist their cooperation and support so that they feel needed and involved.

2. Study in the bedroom with the door shut.

3. Find a study place away from home such as the library or an empty classroom.

4. Study during the day while my husband is at work, and my children are in school.

If you have trouble thinking of options for the solution to your problem, ask yourself this question: *What can I do to eliminate what is causing my problem?*

You might say, "If I knew how to solve my problem, I wouldn't have the problem!" Not necessarily. For example, smoking is a problem for many people. They may know of several options available that might help them quit smoking, yet they continue to have the problem because they do not act on their options. It may be that they don't really want to solve the problem, or they may want to but don't know how to get started. To act on your options, you need a plan.

STEP 3	Make a **plan** to solve your problem within a reasonable length of time and follow it.

To help create your plan, ask yourself this question: *What can I do to make my options work?* Then decide how you will act on one of your options. Set a time limit by which you expect to see some progress toward your goal or the elimination of the problem. For example, Rosalia, the student who had trouble studying at home because of the noise, had an algebra test coming up in two weeks. She decided to do all of her studying for algebra class in the library during the next two weeks. Her grade on the algebra test would tell her whether studying in a different place had paid off.

Suppose you want to quit smoking and know of several plans available such as the use of a patch that slowly releases small amounts of nicotine into the bloodstream to stop the craving. Or perhaps a nearby hospital offers a stop-smoking program that uses behavioral modification techniques without the use of drugs. You might want to try one of these methods. If you have tried to stop smoking in the past and failed, evaluate the plan that you followed. Why didn't it work? What detracted you from your goal? Make a new plan that allows you to try a different method so that you will be less likely to repeat your past unsuccessful behavior. Then set a reasonable time limit for breaking your habit, and try to stick to your plan.

STEP 4	Give your plan an honest **evaluation** to see what progress you are making.

To help evaluate your plan, ask these questions:

- Is my plan working?

- Have I given my plan sufficient time to work?

- Do I still have the problem?

- Is the problem situation improving?

- Should I make a new plan?

If you have solved your problem or if the situation is improving, continue what you are doing. If you still have the problem, and your situation has not improved, make a new plan.

Until the COPE method becomes second nature for you, try writing out the steps. Writing slows down the thinking process, enabling you to analyze your problem more carefully. Also, remember that when you put your plan into writing, you are making a commitment to yourself. Here is the commitment that Vernon, another student, made:

> *My problem is that I am a procrastinator. One cause of my problem is that I hate to study and will put it off until the last minute. I end up skimming over my notes and not absorbing anything. Another cause is that I'm easily distracted at home. I can think of a million other things to do. Also, I lack self-discipline. I want to overcome my procrastination and give myself plenty of time to study. I know this will make a difference in my grades. My plan is to do most of my homework and studying for tests in the library. I have two hours between classes on Mondays, Wednesdays, and Fridays. Also, I can study at home on Tuesday and Thursday mornings when no one is there to distract me. I am going to try to keep weekends free for fun unless I have work that I couldn't finish during the week or a big test on Monday. I'll try this plan for two weeks and see if I'm able to stick to it.*

Notice that Vernon clearly describes his problem, its causes, and the results he wants. He also devises a plan and sets a time limit of two weeks. At the end of two weeks, he can evaluate his plan to see how he is doing. He can then either keep following the plan or revise it if necessary. Vernon's plan is one that can work.

EXERCISE **3.3**

APPLY WHAT YOU HAVE LEARNED about problem solving by doing this exercise with group members. Follow the guidelines for successful collaboration that appear on the inside back cover. Read and discuss the following list of common problem situations. Choose any four of the problems and think of at least two options for solving them. Identify the advantages and disadvantages of each option. After reaching consensus, record your answers on the lines provided. Then evaluate your work.

(Continued)

1. Someone you live with distracts you from studying.

2. You need to lose ten pounds.

3. Your car was damaged in an accident, and it will cost more than the car is worth to fix it.

4. You forgot that you have an important test tomorrow, and you made a date for tonight.

5. A friend of yours wants to drop out of college.

6. Your friend owes you $20.

7. You're taking a required course, and you don't like the instructor.

8. You are not sure whether you will have enough money to pay for your tuition next semester or quarter.

1. Problem: _____

   Option A: _____

   Advantage: _____

   Disadvantage: _____

   Option B: _____

   Advantage: _____

   Disadvantage: _____

2. Problem: _____

   Option A: _____

   Advantage: _____

   Disadvantage: _____

   Option B: _____

   Advantage: _____

   Disadvantage: _____

3. Problem: _____

   Option A: _____

   Advantage: _____

   Disadvantage: _____

   Option B: _____

   Advantage: _____

   Disadvantage: _____

4. Problem: _____

   Option A: _____

   Advantage: _____

   Disadvantage: _____

Option B: _____

Advantage: _____

Disadvantage: _____

Group Evaluation:

Evaluate your discussion. Did everyone contribute? Did you accomplish your task successfully? What additional questions do you have about problem solving? How will you find answers to your questions?

_____

_____

_____

EXERCISE **3.4**

MARIE IS A POOR PROBLEM SOLVER. Read about her problem and think about how she could become a successful problem solver.

I have a big problem this term: my French class. I'm flunking, and I don't know why. I've stopped going to class because it was depressing me to sit there feeling stupid. Now I can forget about how much I hate it, and I can sleep late on Friday mornings, too. I'm angry at the college for having so many requirements for students to fulfill. I'm disgusted at my French instructor, who refuses to speak any English in class. How can I learn if I can't understand what's going on? I passed Spanish in high school, so I know this problem is not mine. It must be their crazy new method of teaching languages. Maybe I should take beginning Spanish again. At least I know I could pass!

1. **What is Marie's problem?**

   _____

   _____

2. **Is Marie self-motivated (internal locus of control) or other-motivated (external locus of control?**

   _____

   _____

3. **What new behaviors could Marie adopt to help her solve her problem?**

   _____

   _____

4. **Write a short plan for Marie to follow this week.**

   _____

   _____

   _____

A student in each of the following scenarios has a problem and has come up with a solution. Based on your understanding of the COPE method, evaluate their plans. If you decide that one or more of the plans may not work, then suggest alternatives that have a better chance of being successful. Do this exercise on your own or with group members.

1. Kevin has been a heavy smoker for ten years. Although he has no physical problems now, his doctor has told him that he should quit smoking to prevent any health problems in the future. Kevin agrees that he ought to quit smoking; after all, his friends who don't smoke are always after him to quit. His family gives him a hard time, too. And it is becoming more and more difficult to find places to smoke. Many restaurants and most public businesses are declaring themselves smoke-free. Kevin has decided to quit cold turkey. Once he's made a decision, he likes to get on with it.

2. Misako attends a community college. It is now time to register for the next term. She knows that she is scheduled to have surgery shortly after midterm. She figures that she will have to miss two weeks of classes. She knows that many instructors will not permit more than two or three absences, so she decides to register for classes and not mention to her instructors her need to be absent. Instead, she hopes that when the time comes, they will be understanding and let her remain in the class and make up the work.

3. Although Raymond started out making Cs in his composition class, his grades are getting worse, not better. His instructor has said that his sentence skills need improvement and has suggested that he go to the writing center for some tutorial help. She said that he should make arrangements to meet with someone once a week or more because sentence skills take time to develop. Raymond went once, and on the next paper he earned a D. He has decided to withdraw from the course because he believes that he cannot pass it.

thinking *ahead* ▶

What practical knowledge have you gained from this chapter that you can use to solve real-world problems? To find out, read the following scenario and complete the items that follow it.

Tyrone's father is a surgeon. He enjoys his work and its financial rewards. He has provided well for his family and has sent three children to college. His older son and daughter are both physicians. Tyrone, the youngest, is a sophomore in college. His family expects him to enter the medical field also. Tyrone has no interest in medicine, but he doesn't want to disappoint his family. After all, they are paying for his tuition. Tyrone's father has mapped out a course of study for Tyrone so that he can complete his required courses during the first two years, leaving the last two years to concentrate on his major. Tyrone's grades are good, but he dreads taking the science courses that will prepare him for medical school. Tyrone is good in math, enjoys working with computers, and knows he would be much happier as a business analyst or a purchasing manager for a large company. He would much rather seek a degree in business administration than in medicine. However, his earning capacity would be greater as a doctor—and his father would be proud. Tyrone doesn't know what to do.

1. **Why is Tyrone having trouble making a decision?**

   _____

   _____

2. **What are Tyrone's alternatives?**

   _____

   _____

3. **Of the alternatives, which do you think best meets the six characteristics of a reachable goal?**

   _____

   _____

4. **What solution can you suggest that would not disappoint either Tyrone or his family?**

   _____

   _____

chapter **re**view

To review the chapter, reflect on the following confidence-building attitudes, complete Concepts to Understand, and practice your new skills at every opportunity.

ATTITUDES TO DEVELOP

- positive thinking
- self-motivation
- personal responsibility

CONCEPTS TO UNDERSTAND

Knowing why you are attending college, learning to set _____, and knowing how to solve _____ will help you to become a more confident student. Students have many reasons for attending college. It is important that the reasons you identify be your own and that you use them to motivate yourself.

(Continued)

A _____ is an outcome, the result of a plan, something you want and are willing to work for. _____ goals take some time to accomplish and may include such things as graduating from college, changing careers, or planning for a child's education. _____ goals are intermediate steps between the initiation of a plan and its outcome—the achievement of a long-term goal. For example, when you have successfully completed a course, you have achieved a _____ goal that will help you reach the _____ goal of graduating from college. Long-term and short-term goals fall into three general categories: _____ goals, _____ goals, and _____ goals.

Success is more likely if you set reachable goals. A reachable goal has six characteristics. A goal is _____ if you can reasonably expect to achieve it given your abilities. A goal is _____ and possible if you know what it takes to achieve it and where to begin and end. For example, it is possible to complete a bachelor of arts program in four years, perhaps even in three years. But a goal of completing the program in one year would be both unbelievable and impossible. To set _____ goals, give yourself a time limit. Keep your goals _____ and _____ by deciding what you want to do and by being willing to change your plans if necessary. _____ goals are fair to all concerned.

As you continue your college education, you will encounter some difficulties. You can successfully overcome these problems and meet your goals if you consistently use a problem-solving approach such as the COPE method. COPE is a four-step plan that starts with a _____ or problem, its causes, and a result. The second step is to think of _____, or possible solutions, to your problem. Third, make a _____ to act on one or more of your options. Your _____ is the final step after you have given your plan sufficient time to work. Be prepared to revise your plan as necessary.

To access additional review exercises, see http://college.hmco.com/success.

SKILLS TO PRACTICE
- setting goals
- solving problems
- developing character-building values

Your Reflections

Your Reflections

Reflect on what you have learned about strategies for setting goals and solving problems and how you can best apply that information. Use the following list of questions to stimulate your thinking and then write out your reflections. Your response may include answers to one or more of the questions. Incorporate in your writing specific information from this chapter.

- Describe something difficult you have achieved. How did you achieve it? Was setting goals part of the process?

- Which of the goal-setting and problem-solving strategies explained in this chapter do you already use? Which ones do you plan to try?

- Review the values listed in Figure 3.3, page 61. Explain the role that one or more of these values plays in the way you solve problems.

- What have you learned from this chapter that you would recommend to a friend, and why?

- Of all the attitudes and skills listed in the chapter review, which do you think will be useful to you at work or in your career?

4

Sharpening Your Classroom Skills

DO YOU ALWAYS arrive on time, prepared for class? Do you attend regularly and take part in all class activities? Did you know that active involvement is the key to successful classroom performance?

BECAUSE MOST EXAMS and class activities are based on information presented in lectures, your ability to listen and take notes is closely linked to your performance in a course. If the lecture method is not your preferred mode of instruction, then you may need to improve or develop listening and note-taking skills that will enable you to gain as much from lectures as you do from other instructional modes.

In many classrooms learning is a collaborative activity. Sharing your ideas with others builds confidence. Moreover, group work, oral presentations, and class discussion are significant parts of the assessment and learning processes. The give-and-take of these activities helps you build the interpersonal skills needed for effective interaction in class as well as in the workplace.

To sharpen your classroom skills, you must make a commitment to learn, take responsibility for the outcome of every course, and be an active participant in all classroom activities. Your critical thinking and study skills key unlocks five strategies for active learning in the classroom.

- Prepare for class.

- Become an active listener.

- Develop a personal note-taking system.

- Learn to make effective oral presentations.

- Participate in class and group activities.

Take the first step toward becoming more actively involved in your own learning process by evaluating your current performance in the classroom: Complete Awareness Check 7.

Awareness Check 7

HOW EFFECTIVE ARE YOUR CLASSROOM SKILLS?

Check yes *if the statement applies to you or* no *if the statement does not apply.*

Yes	No	**Part I: Preparing for Class**
☐	☐	1. I attend class regularly.
☐	☐	2. I usually arrive on time.
☐	☐	3. I use my syllabus, or course outline, to keep up with assignments.
☐	☐	4. I begin studying for tests as soon as they are announced.
☐	☐	5. I always bring my textbook and other necessary materials to class.
☐	☐	6. I do my assignments for every class.
☐	☐	7. I usually know what the instructor expects of me.

Yes	No

Part II: Listening to Lectures

1. I always assume that I can get new information from a lecture.

2. I am able to follow the instructor's ideas.

3. I know what signal words are, and I listen for them.

4. I can ignore most distractions when I am listening to a lecture.

5. I consider students' comments and questions to be part of the lecture, and I listen to them.

6. I keep listening even if I don't agree with the instructor or if I don't understand some part of the lecture.

If you checked no *to any of the statements in Parts I and II, your classroom preparation or listening skills may need improvement.*

Prepare for Class

YOUR FIRST STRATEGY for success in any course is to come to class prepared. Although the following tips may seem obvious, many students sabotage their learning by ignoring them.

Attend Regularly and Be Punctual. Don't miss classes; when you miss a class, you miss instruction. In any course that teaches a sequence of skills, such as a language or math course, you need to attend regularly because each day's lesson is based on previous lessons. If you attend regularly and arrive on time, then you will know what to expect. You will be less likely to show up unprepared for a quiz or an assignment that is due. Punctuality and regular attendance are habits valued not only by instructors but by employers as well.

Use Your Syllabus. The course syllabus helps you keep up with assignments and tests, tells you what topics were covered if you were absent, and summarizes the instructor's requirements. Review it often to keep this information fresh in your mind. Bring it to class every day. Then, if the instructor makes a change or postpones a test, you can note the change directly on the syllabus. Your syllabus is a confidence builder because it gives you a plan to follow.

Bring Textbooks and Other Supplies to Class Every Day. Instructors often call attention to information in the textbook, or they may ask you to do an exercise from the textbook in class. Some instructors lecture on material contained in the book, especially if it's complicated or needs supplementing. If you bring your textbook to class, you will be able to follow along and mark important passages.

Do the Assignments. Assignments provide the practice you need to acquire new skills. They help reinforce ideas and concepts discussed in class. Most important, doing the assignments provides you with a background of information that will help you make sense of future assignments. Also, you may lose points on tests if you are not able to answer questions that come directly from your assignments.

Anticipate the Next Lesson.   Follow two simple steps to anticipate what will be covered in class each day.

1. **Review the previous day's work.** Read your notes from the last class. Review the previous chapter and the assignment, if any. The next class is likely to expand on this information. Reviewing the work from the previous class helps you retain the information and prepare for the next class.

2. **Preview the next day's assignments.** Review your syllabus to determine what will be covered and how it relates to what was covered in the previous class. Formulate some questions in your mind about the topic. Ask yourself, "What do I already know?" Also, skim assigned chapters before reading them to determine whether new words or terms are introduced; then look up the terms and definitions to familiarize yourself with them before doing the reading. Considering past assignments, try to predict what the instructor's approach to the material will be—whether lecture, discussion, or group work—and prepare for class accordingly. Previewing helps you relate new information to your prior knowledge, placing it in a meaningful context.

If you attend class regularly, are punctual, use your syllabus, bring your textbook and other supplies to class, do the assignments, and anticipate the next lesson, you will always know what to expect from your classes, you won't feel lost, and you will be in the proper frame of mind to listen attentively.

Become an Active Listener

YOUR SECOND STRATEGY for classroom success is *active listening*. Since lecture–discussion is the preferred style of many college instructors, you will probably spend most of your class time listening. Listeners fall into two categories: those who are passive and those who are active. *Passive listeners* do more hearing than listening. They are aware that the instructor is speaking, but they aren't making sense of what he or she is saying. Passive listening is characteristic of the external locus of control. For example, passive listeners may expect instructors to motivate them and to interest them in the topic. On the other hand, *active listeners* pay attention to what they hear and try to make sense of it. Active listening is characteristic of the internal locus of control. For example, active listeners are self-motivated, and they expect to find their own reasons for being interested in a lecture topic. Figure 4.1 compares the traits of active and passive listeners. Which kind of listener are you?

To get more out of lectures, become an active listener. Follow these six steps:

1. **Decide to listen.** By deciding to listen, you are strengthening your commitment to learn. Also, by deciding to listen, you are taking an active role instead of waiting passively to receive information.

2. **Listen with a positive frame of mind.** Expect to find something in the lecture that will interest you. Assume that you will learn something useful, that you will expand your knowledge, and that you will increase your understanding of the course.

Figure 4.1 Traits of Passive and Active Listeners

PASSIVE LISTENERS	ACTIVE LISTENERS
Expect a lecture to be dull	Expect to find something in the lecture that interests them
Assume that information in a lecture will not be useful or pertain to their lives	Assume that information in a lecture will be useful—if not now, then later
Look for weaknesses in the speaker's style instead of listening to what the speaker says	May notice weaknesses in the speaker's style but pay attention to what the speaker says
Listen only for main ideas and ignore details and examples	Listen for main ideas and the details that support them
Give in to daydreaming and become distracted	Resist daydreaming and ignore distractions
Tune out when they disagree with the speaker	Keep listening even when they disagree with the speaker
Tune out difficult or technical information; do not ask questions	Try to understand difficult or technical information; ask questions as needed
May doze in lectures if tired	Fight to stay awake if tired
Do not take good notes	Take well-organized notes

3. **Focus your attention on the speaker.** If you keep your eyes on the speaker, you should be able to ignore any distractions that compete for your attention. Keep your mind on the speaker's topic. Do not give in to negative thoughts or feelings about the speaker, the topic, or the speaker's opinions. Your purpose is to learn what the speaker has to say.

4. **Encourage the speaker.** Look interested. Sit straight but comfortably, and make eye contact. Ask questions and comment when it's appropriate. Studies of audience behavior indicate that a speaker who gets positive feedback is encouraged to do an even better job. Your posture and expression can communicate to the speaker that you are listening. Everything you do to encourage the speaker has the added benefit of making you concentrate on the lecture.

5. **Take notes.** Taking notes also helps you concentrate on the lecture. Taking notes activates your tactile sense, as explained in Chapter 2, so that you are more likely to retain the information, especially if you review your notes soon after the lecture. Take notes consistently when listening to lectures and adopt or develop a note-taking system that works for you. (More is said about note taking later in the chapter.)

6. **Decide what is important.** Listen for repeated terms or ideas. Speakers use repetition to emphasize important points. Watch for gestures and facial expressions that may also be used for emphasis. Listen for signal words or phrases. See Figure 4.2 for a list of signal words and phrases and explanations of what they mean.

Figure 4.2	**Signal Words and Phrases**

1. To indicate that another main idea or example follows:

also	furthermore	another
in addition	moreover	

2. To add emphasis:

most important	above all	of primary concern
remember that	a key idea	most significant
pay attention to	the main idea	

3. To indicate that an example follows:

for example	to illustrate	such as
for instance	specifically	

4. To indicate that a conclusion follows:

therefore	in conclusion	finally
consequently	to conclude	so

5. To indicate an exception to a stated fact:

however	although	but
nevertheless	though	except

6. To indicate cause or effects:

because	due to	consequently
since	reason	result
for	cause	effect

7. To indicate that categories or divisions will be named or explained:

types	parts	groups
kinds	characteristics	categories

8. To indicate a sequence:

steps	numbers (1, 2, 3, …)
stages	first, second, etc.

9. To indicate that items are being compared:

similar	different	equally
like	in contrast	on the other hand
advantages	disadvantages	contrary to

Listening for signal words helps you listen for ideas. For example, if an English instructor says, "You can use seven different patterns to organize details in a paragraph," then you should number from one to seven on your paper, skipping lines between, and listen for the seven patterns and the instructor's explanations. If you get to the fifth pattern and realize that you don't have anything written down for the fourth one, then you know you have missed something in the lecture. At this point, you should ask a question.

EXERCISE **4.1**

APPLY WHAT YOU HAVE LEARNED about signal words by doing this exercise with group members. Follow the guidelines for successful collaboration that appear on the inside back cover. Read the following paragraph. Next, identify as many signal words as you can and discuss their meaning in the sentences in which they appear, using Figure 4.2 as a reference. Then discuss and answer the questions. When you arrive at consensus, record your answers and evaluate your work.

Most of us assume that listening is an innate skill. Aren't most people born with the ability to sleep, breathe, see, and hear? But is hearing the same act as listening? Although most of us can hear perfectly well, we are not all good listeners. What, you might ask, are the characteristics of a good listener? First, a good listener makes a commitment to listen. Second, a good listener focuses attention on the speaker. For example, a good listener is not reading the newspaper or watching television while listening to a friend explain a problem. Most important, a good listener is genuinely interested in the speaker and in what he or she says. In conclusion, listening is not something you should assume that you do well. It is a lifelong skill that can be improved with earnest practice and hard work.

1. **What signal words indicate that an example is to follow? What example does the writer give?**

   _____

2. **Write the signal word that indicates that categories or divisions will be explained.**

   _____

3. **Write the signal words that indicate sequence.**

   _____

4. **What does the writer believe is the most important characteristic of a good listener?**

   _____

5. **What is the writer's concluding idea about listening?**

   _____

Group Evaluation:

Evaluate your discussion. Did everyone contribute? Did you accomplish your task successfully? What additional questions do you have about signal words? How will you find answers to your questions?

   _____

   _____

EXERCISE 4.2

FORM A GROUP WITH FOUR or five students. Using the traits listed in Figure 4.1 as a guide, prepare a short demonstration on listening behavior. Let one person in the group be the lecturer. Let other group members demonstrate passive or active listening habits. The group member acting as the lecturer should be able to explain to the class which group members were good listeners and which were not. Practice your demonstration. Your instructor may call on one or more of the groups to present in class.

Develop a Personal Note-Taking System

THE THIRD STRATEGY for classroom success is good note taking. There is no *best* way to take notes. The suggestions offered in this chapter have worked for many students. Experiment with them, and then adapt them to find the style of note taking that consistently gives you good results. Complete Awareness Check 8 before you begin reading this section.

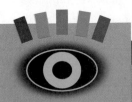

Awareness Check 8

HOW EFFECTIVE ARE YOUR NOTE-TAKING SKILLS?

To see where you need improvement, evaluate your lecture notes from a recent class. Read them over and answer yes or no to the following questions.

Yes	No	
☐	☐	1. Did you date your notes and number the pages?
☐	☐	2. Did you write the course name or number on your notes?
☐	☐	3. Did you write down the topic of the lecture?
☐	☐	4. Did you use 8½" by 11" paper to keep in a loose-leaf binder?
☐	☐	5. Did you take notes with a ballpoint pen?
☐	☐	6. Are your notes easy to read?
☐	☐	7. Is this set of notes in the same notebook as all your other notes for this class?
☐	☐	8. Are your notes organized into an informal outline or other logical format?
☐	☐	9. Are you able to distinguish the speaker's main ideas from the examples that illustrate them?
☐	☐	10. As you read your notes, are you able to reconstruct in your mind what the lecture was about?

If you answered no to any of the questions in the Awareness Check—particularly the last two—then your note-taking skills may need improvement. Try the guidelines that follow for improving your note taking.

Guidelines for Note Taking

- Keep track of your notes by heading your paper with the *date, name of course,* and *lecture topic.* Number consecutive pages. Later, when you study, you'll be able to match up class notes and textbook notes or assignments on the same topic.

- Use standard sized paper—8½" by 11"—that will fit into most notebooks or folders. Small sheets of paper won't hold enough writing and may get lost or out of place.

- Keep the notes for one class separated from the notes for other classes. Use separate notebooks for each class or use dividers to distinguish different sections in one notebook. Some students like to use spiral notebooks. Others prefer to use a loose-leaf binder so that lecture notes, textbook notes, and the instructor's handouts may be taken out of it and reorganized for study purposes.

- Use a ballpoint pen for taking notes. Ink from felt-tip pens blurs and soaks through the paper, spotting the sheets underneath. Pencil smears and fades over time. Many students prefer to use blue or black ink because other colors, such as red or green, are hard on the eyes.

- If you know your handwriting is poor, print for clarity. Illegible or decorative handwriting makes notes hard to read.

- To speed up your note taking, use standard abbreviations but make up some of your own for words or phrases that you use often. Make a key for your abbreviations so you won't forget what they mean. See Figure 4.3 for a list of some common abbreviations. For even greater speed while taking notes, omit the periods from abbreviations.

Figure 4.3	Commonly Used Abbreviations and Symbols
1. equal: =	11. introduction: intro.
2. with: w/	12. information: info.
3. without: w/o	13. department: dept.
4. number: #	14. advantage: adv.
5. therefore: \	15. organization: org.
6. and: +	16. maximum: max.
7. and so forth: etc.	17. individual: ind.
8. for example: e.g.	18. compare: cf.
9. against: vs.	19. association: assoc.
10. government: gov't.	20. politics: pol.

- Copy into your notes anything that is written on the board or on overhead transparencies. Test questions often come from material that is presented in these ways.

- Take organized notes. Use a system such as one of those suggested later in this chapter or devise your own. Make main ideas stand out from the examples that support them. Do not write lecturers' words verbatim. Summarize ideas in your own words so that they will be easier for you to remember.

- As soon as possible after class, review your notes to fill in gaps while the information is still fresh in your mind. The purpose of taking notes is to help you remember information. If you take notes but don't look at them until you are ready to study for a test, you will have to relearn the information. To retain information in your long-term memory, review it frequently.

- If something is missing, compare notes with a classmate or see the instructor.

The Informal Outline/Key Words System

Ideas that are organized in a logical pattern are easier to remember than isolated facts and examples that don't seem to relate to one another. Try this simple, two-step system to improve your note taking.

Draw a line down your paper so that you have a 2½" column on the right and a 6" column on the left. Take notes in the 6" column, using an informal outline. Make main ideas stand out by indenting and numbering the details and examples listed under them. Skip lines between main ideas so that you can fill in examples later or add an example if the lecturer returns to one of these ideas later on. After the lecture, write key words in the right margin that will help you recall information from your notes.

Figure 4.4 shows a student's lecture notes on the topic "Studying on the Right Side of the Brain." The student has used the informal outline/key words system. On the left side of the page, the student has outlined the lecture given in class. Later, on the right side of the page, in the margin, the student has written key words or abbreviations that show at a glance what the lecture covered.

When you use this system, wait to write in the key words until you are reviewing your notes.

The Cornell Method*

Developed by Dr. Walter Pauk of Cornell University, the Cornell method is a note-taking system that has worked for many students. One version of the system involves six steps: *recording, questioning, reciting, reflecting, reviewing,* and *recapitulating.*

Begin by dividing an 8½" by 11" sheet of notebook paper into three sections, as shown in Figure 4.5. Then follow these steps for taking notes from a lecture:

1. **Record** facts and ideas in the wide column. After the lecture, fill in any gaps and neaten up your handwriting, if necessary, so that you will be able to read your notes when you review again.

---

*Walter Pauk, *How to Study in College,* Fifth Edition. Copyright ©1993 by Houghton Mifflin Company. Used with permission.

Figure 4.4   **The Informal Outline/Key Words System**

Study Skills 1620   Sept. 18

Studying on the Right Side of the Brain	
Visual thinking	
1. Use graphic techniques like diagrams, maps, etc. to organize information into a meaningful pattern.	def.
2. Visual learners need to make verbal information "visual" or they will have a hard time remembering it.	reason for using "visuals"
Fantasy	
1. The ability to create and use mental images is another kind of visual thinking.	def.
2. To understand the stages in an organism's life cycle, imagine you are the organism going through the stages.	ex. of fantasy
Hands-on experience	
1. Get involved in a direct experience of what you are learning.	def.
2. Do lab experiments, take field trips, role play, look at or touch objects as they are described. Go through the steps of a process.	hands-on activities
Music	
1. Common belief: music distracts while studying.	
2. Music can accelerate learning.	effect of music on learning
3. Studies show retention improved when students read to music.	
4. Instrumentals that match the feeling or mood of the information to be remembered are the best type of music.	

Figure 4.5 **The Cornell Method: Setting Up the Paper**

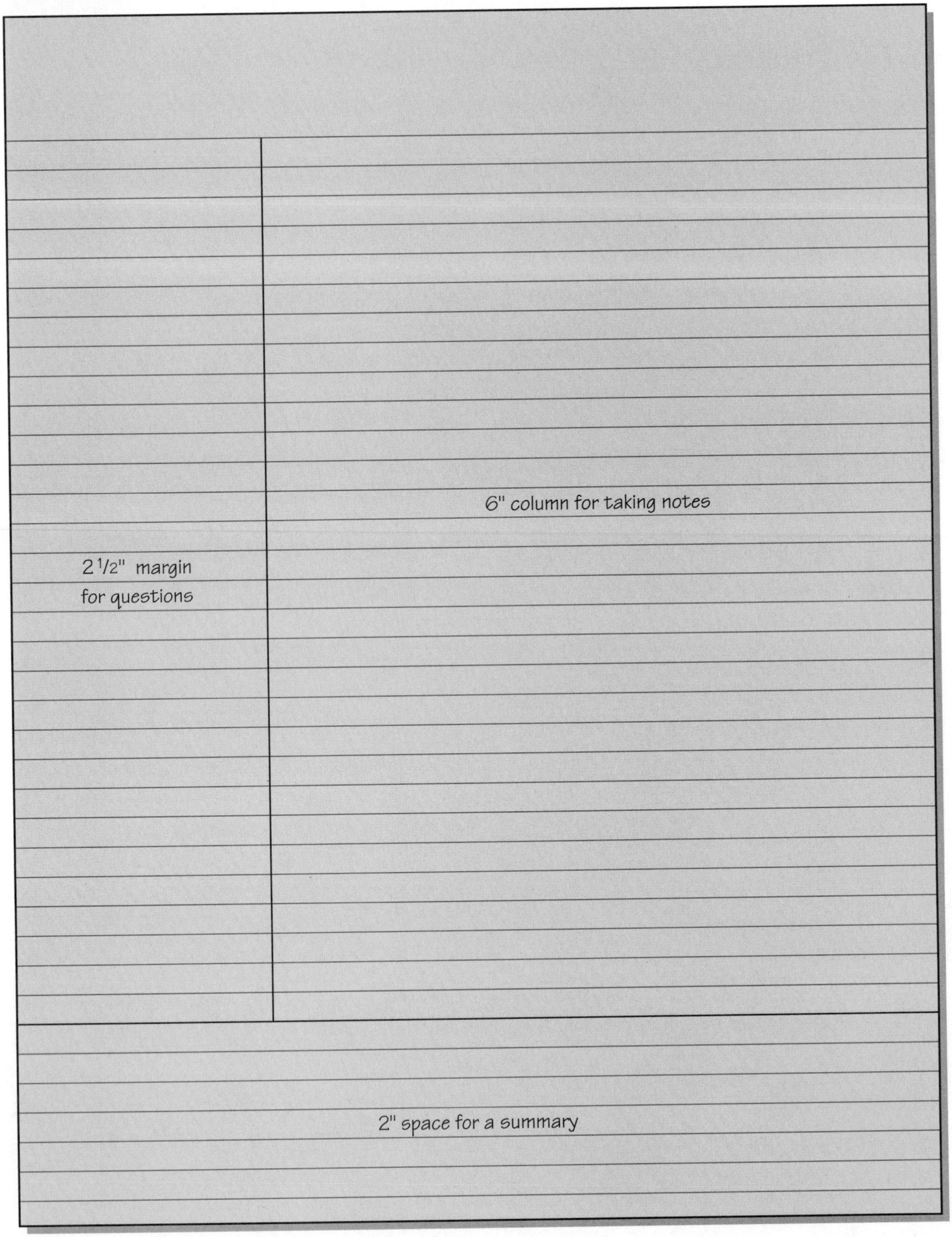

2 1/2" margin
for questions

6" column for taking notes

2" space for a summary

2. **Question** facts and ideas presented in lectures. Write questions about what you don't understand or what you think an instructor might ask on a test. Write your questions in the left margin beside the fact or idea in the wide column. Writing questions helps you strengthen your memory, improve your understanding, and anticipate test questions.

3. **Recite** the facts or ideas aloud from memory and in your own words. If you summarized them in your notes in your own words, then this will be easy to do. If you are an auditory learner, reciting will improve your retention because you will be using listening, your preferred mode. As an awareness check of how much you remember, cover up the wide column of your notes and recite from the key words or questions in the left margin. Recite the key word or question first; then try to recall and recite the whole fact or idea. To check yourself, uncover the wide column and read your notes.

4. **Reflect** on what you have learned from the lecture by applying the facts and ideas to real-life situations. Determine why the facts are significant, how you can use them, and how they expand or modify your prior knowledge.

5. **Review** and recite your notes every day. A good way to begin a study session, especially if you have trouble getting started, is to review your notes. Reviewing reminds you of what you have learned and sets the scene for new information to be gained from the next assignment.

6. **Recapitulate** by writing a summary of your notes in the space at the bottom of your paper. You can summarize what you have written on each page of notes, or you can summarize the whole lecture at the end of the last page. Doing both a page summary and a whole-lecture summary is even better.

Now, clarify these steps in your mind by examining the student's lecture notes shown in Figure 4.6.

Matching Note-Taking Style and Learning Style

What if you are not a linear thinker? What if a 1, 2, 3 order of information does not appeal to you because you don't think that way, and instructors don't always stick to their lecture outlines? You may prefer a more visual style of note taking. Try *clustering*. Start a few inches from the top of the page and write the speaker's first main idea in a circle near the middle of the page. If the speaker gives an example, draw an arrow to another circle in which you write the example. If the speaker presents another main idea, start a new cluster. Figure 4.7 shows an example of the cluster note-taking technique. This student's notes will help her visualize the information she wants to remember. An advantage of clustering is that if the speaker leaves one idea and returns to it later, it is easy to draw another arrow from the circle and add the example. Clustering is a nontraditional note-taking procedure, but if it works for you and if it makes note taking easy and pleasant, then don't hesitate to use it.

Figure 4.6   **The Cornell Method: One Student's Notes**

Literature 2010   Sept. 18

	The Five Elements of Fiction
	1. Plot
How does the	a. Events and setting
plot of the	b. Plot development
story develop?	* conflict
	* complications
	* climax
	* resolution
	2. Character
What is the	a. Dynamic
difference between	* well rounded
a dynamic and a	* motives
static character?	b. Static
	* flat
	* stereotype
	3. Point of view
What are the	a. First person
four points	b. Omniscient
of view?	c. Limited omniscient
	d. Dramatic
How is the	4. Theme
theme of the	a. Meaning or significance
story revealed?	b. Revealed through interaction of five elements
What makes one	5. Style/Tone
writer's style	a. Mood or feeling
distinctive?	b. Choice of words, use of language

The writer uses five elements of fiction—plot, character, point of view, theme and style/tone—to develop the story. Through the interaction of these elements, the meaning of the story is revealed and the reader can understand its significance.

Figure 4.7   Clustering: A Visual Form of Note Taking

Tricky Dicky

Bubba

Name calling

The wimp

Glittering generalities

The most advanced...

Everyone does it!

Bandwagon

Six common fallacies

Transfer

He drives a Mercedes; he must be rich.

Plain folks

Nixon's fireside chats

Clinton's baseball caps

Testimonial

Famous person endorses idea

Sally Struthers "Save the Children"

EXERCISE 4.3

IN THIS CHAPTER YOU HAVE learned three effective ways to organize your notes: (1) the informal outline/key words system, (2) the Cornell method, and (3) clustering. Reread the sections of this chapter that describe these three techniques and then use the following diagram to try clustering. Fill in each circle. Then add arrows and circles to the cluster to complete your notes about the three techniques.

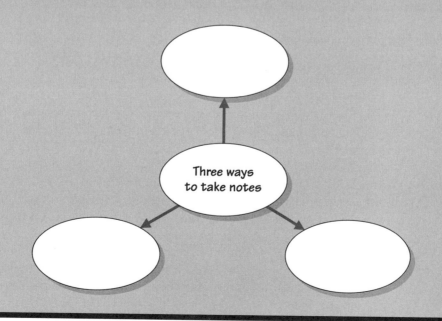

Three ways to take notes

EXERCISE 4.4

PRACTICE NOTE TAKING WITH A classmate. During the next class meeting, both of you should take notes, using your preferred method. After class, compare your notes. Do your notes cover the same information? Are your note-taking styles similar or different? Whose notes are neater, better organized, and more thorough? What have you learned from this exercise that will help you improve your note-taking skills?

CRITICAL THINKING

Interview a senior college student or one who is nearing graduation. Find out how this student's classroom behavior changed over time. During the interview, practice your listening and note-taking skills. After the interview, write a brief report explaining what you have learned. The following is a list of questions to guide your interview.

1. How would you rate your classroom performance in each of these areas: attendance, punctuality, preparation of assignments, participation in class activities?

2. Has your behavior in these areas changed over time, and if so, how?

3. What listening, note-taking, and study systems do you use, and have they changed over time?

4. What is your learning style, and how have you learned to adapt to others' styles?

5. What would you say is your greatest strength as a student?

6. What weaknesses, if any, do you still need to overcome?

7. What advice can you offer students to help them be more successful in the classroom?

Learn to Make Effective Presentations

BEING ABLE TO make an effective oral presentation is the fourth strategy for success in the classroom. A speech course is a general education or liberal arts requirement at many colleges and universities because oral communication is an important academic and career skill. In a speech class you learn how to plan, organize, and make speeches. You also learn how to cope with *stage fright,* the fear of speaking or performing in front of an audience, and the stress that results from that fear. If it has been a while since you took a speech course, or if you have not yet had an opportunity to take one, then the following suggestions may help you prepare yourself for making an oral presentation.

Suppose your literature instructor asks you to give an oral interpretation of a poem you were assigned to read. Or maybe your biology instructor asks you to report to the class about the results of an experiment you performed in the lab. Perhaps a finance professor requests that you analyze and give an oral report on several properties that a company might purchase. You are to explain which purchase would net the company a greater return on its investment. In each case, you would first decide what your *purpose* is. For example, the purpose of your interpretation of a poem might be to explain what you think the writer's theme is. In your report about your lab results, your purpose would be to tell what conclusion you reached as a result of your experiment. In your report to your finance class, your purpose might be to convince class members that the purchase of one of the properties is best for the company.

Once your purpose is clear, you can *plan* and *organize* your speech. Outline your main idea and the details that support it. Recite from your outline several times until you know what you want to say. Try your speech out on a friend or family member and ask for suggestions about how to improve your delivery or how to explain your ideas more clearly. If you think you might forget something, summarize your main idea and details on three-by-five-inch cards. The notes will jog your memory, and holding the cards will give you something to do with your hands.

In general, a good plan to follow in preparing an oral presentation is to use a three-part development:

1. **Tell your listeners what you're going to say.** Introduce your topic. State your purpose and main idea.

2. **Say it.** Support your main idea with details. State the facts, reasons, or examples that explain your opinions. Draw a conclusion from your evidence: Tell listeners why the information you have just given them is important and how they can use it.

3. **Tell them what you have just said.** Briefly summarize your main idea, details, and conclusion.

Make eye contact with the audience; speak loudly enough for those in the back of the class to hear; speak distinctly and watch your pace. If you talk too fast or too slowly, you will interrupt the flow of ideas, and your listeners may have trouble following you.

If you get nervous, try not to focus your attention on your feelings. Thinking about your nervousness will only make it worse, and you may forget what you want to say. Instead, keep your attention focused on the task of making your speech or completing your report. Think about your audience and how they may benefit from the information you are giving them.

Making oral presentations is like any other skill. With practice, you will gain confidence. Being able to express yourself clearly when speaking is an asset in college and in your career. Look upon oral presentation assignments as opportunities to practice and improve your skill.

EXERCISE **4.5**

IMAGINE THAT YOU HAVE BEEN asked to give a three-minute speech on a topic from Chapter 1, 2, or 3 that interests you. Select a topic by looking at the headings in these chapters. Then, using the three-part development plan for oral presentations, plan a speech by answering the questions that follow.

(Continued)

PART 1. TELL YOUR LISTENERS WHAT YOU'RE GOING TO SAY.

1. **What is your topic and purpose? For example, what is the subject, and why have you chosen it?**

   _____

   _____

2. **How will you introduce your topic? For example, how will you interest your listeners in it?**

   _____

   _____

3. **What is your main idea? For example, what do you expect your listeners to be able to understand or do?**

   _____

   _____

PART 2. SAY IT.

1. **What is your evidence? What facts, reasons, or examples support your main idea?**

   _____

   _____

2. **What is your conclusion? For example, why is the information that you've presented important, or how is it useful?**

   _____

   _____

PART 3. TELL THEM WHAT YOU HAVE JUST SAID.

1. **What is your summary?**

   _____

   _____

EXERCISE **4.6**

FIND ONLINE RESOURCES TO HELP you prepare speeches and presentations. Some search words to try are *public speaking, stage fright,* and *oral presentations.* For a summary of the basics of public speaking from Toastmasters International, see http://www.toastmasters.org/tips.htm.

After reviewing these resources and any others that you may find, briefly explain in writing which ones were the most useful. Also be prepared to present your findings orally to the rest of the class.

COMPUTER CONFIDENCE

Use a Computer to Organize Your Notes

Taking notes in class and while you're reading is an important first step toward understanding new material. But the next step is even more important—organizing your notes into a format from which you can study effectively. That's where a computer can make a big difference. Whichever note-taking style you prefer—the informal outline/key words system, the Cornell method, clustering, or a system of your own—using the computer to reorganize your notes offers several advantages:

1. It's easy to move whole blocks of words around to rearrange information into a format that makes sense to you

2. It's easy to add new ideas to your notes as you go along or to combine class and textbook notes to give yourself the most complete coverage of the information.

3. The actual process of typing your notes on the screen improves your memory by engaging your tactile and visual senses.

Many word-processing programs offer easy-to-use outlining features that automatically provide an outline format into which you can type your notes. Or you can create your own outlines by following these simple steps:

1. Open a separate file for each of your courses. Create a name for the file.

2. Try to get to the computer soon after each class, while the lecture is still fresh in your mind. Enter the date and topic of each lecture at the top of a new page.

3. Review your class notes. No matter what note-taking system you're using, this is a good time to focus on the main ideas or key questions. Then type your notes into the computer, using a system. For example, use the boldface function to make main ideas stand out, use tabs to indent details, and set special margins for key words or questions.

4. At this point, you may wish to add comments, insert notes from your reading, or move sections of your outline around. To create a formal outline, insert Roman numerals and uppercase letters to mark major divisions, and move each line so that it aligns correctly. Then insert Arabic numerals and lowercase letters in front of the details and also align them.

5. Print out the final version. Double-space the printed copy so that you will have room to insert additional notes.

Other options for note taking with a computer include using voice-recognition software that allows you to dictate your notes. A hand-held computer is convenient to use between classes to enter a few ideas while on the run until you have time to sit down and review the lecture and organize your notes.

Participate in Class and Group Activities

THE FIFTH STRATEGY for classroom success is to become involved in whatever is happening in class. Contribute to class discussions and ask questions, even if you are reluctant to do so. You may find that other students have similar questions or comments but might be afraid to speak up. They'll be grateful to you for asking. Speaking out in class will give you confidence. In time, you will become less self-conscious. You'll learn to express yourself with clarity and authority, and this skill will serve you well in whatever career you pursue.

When other students do take risks and speak out, give them your full attention. After all, you know how they feel. During a class discussion, maintain eye contact with whoever is speaking and listen attentively. Students soon overcome nervousness when they realize that others are interested in what they have to say.

Make your contribution to small group activities. Try to get something accomplished and follow these rules for polite discourse:

1. **Allow each person equal time to contribute to the discussion.**

2. **Question points of view; do not attack the person asserting a point of view.**

3. **Volunteer to do your part of the work, and follow through.**

4. **If you are a discussion leader, make sure that everyone contributes, keep the discussion focused on the topic, and summarize the group's conclusions at the end of the discussion.**

5. **Whatever your role is within the group, do your part to help the group stay on task. Do not let the discussion degenerate into a social exchange.**

The more involved you are in your classes, the more you will feel at home in the learning community. Sharpening your classroom skills will make you a more confident student.

CONFIDENCE
Builder

Interpersonal Skills for College and Career

When you interact with others in class, especially in small group activities and on collaborative projects, you are building interpersonal skills that will give you an edge in the workplace. The days of isolated workers sitting in their cubicles are giving way to work teams in which work is shared by a group of colleagues, each contributing his or her expertise. At companies such as AT&T and Lockheed Martin much of the work is done in teams, and employees are expected to have the necessary interpersonal qualities and leadership skills. In 1991, the U.S. Department of Labor, through the Secretary's Commission on Achieving Necessary Skills (SCANS), issued a report on the skills students will need to succeed in the high-performance workplace of the twenty-first century. The Department of Labor calls these skills, collectively, "workplace know-how." One of the skill areas cited as being necessary for solid job performance is *interpersonal skills.*

Participating in class and working collaboratively on projects in and out of the classroom have the potential of helping you develop two of the SCANS' interpersonal skills: *working as a member of a team* and *exercising leadership.*

What behaviors promote effective teamwork? The SCANS report lists the following:

- Share the work.

- Encourage others by listening and responding appropriately to their contributions.

- Recognize each other's strengths and build on them.

- Settle differences for the benefit of the group.

- Take responsibility for achieving goals.

- Challenge existing procedures, policies, or authorities—but do so in a responsible way.

How do you exercise leadership within a group? The SCANS report says that competent leaders do the following:

- They make positive use of the rules and values followed by others.

- They justify their positions logically and appropriately.

- They establish their credibility through competence and integrity.

- They take minority opinion contributions into consideration.

In plain language, what do these competencies for participating and leading mean? Simply put, if you are the leader of a group discussion in class, you can make "positive use of rules and values" by making sure that your group follows the guidelines your instructor has given for completing the assignment. As a leader, you "justify" your position "logically and appropriately" by not monopolizing the discussion and by keeping order when things get out of hand. You "establish credibility" by doing your share of the work, and you show "integrity" by seeing that the work gets done. If someone in the group expresses an opinion different from that of the majority of group members, you treat that "minority contribution" fairly and do not dismiss it out of hand.

Suppose that you don't understand the instructions or that you see an easier, better way to accomplish the task than to follow the guidelines you've been given. How do you "challenge existing procedures" responsibly? Discuss your concerns with your instructor, asking in a polite way whether the guidelines can be modified and being willing to proceed as instructed if necessary.

Respect for others and their opinions is the key to effective participation in groups, whether in class or at work. To learn more about SCANS online, go to AltaVista or another search engine and type *SCANS report* as your key word.

HOW WELL DO YOU PARTICIPATE in your classes? Read about three members of a sociology class and see if you find yourself mirrored in their profiles. Then answer the questions that follow.

Bob always sits at the back of the classroom so that he can nap quietly if he has stayed out late the night before. He rarely makes a comment or asks a question. If he doesn't understand something the instructor says, he forgets about it. He's sure that he'll figure the problem out when he does the reading just before the final exam. He would probably forget about it anyway before the exam rolled around.

Sam can't wait to get to class. He has done all the reading, and he has millions of questions to ask. Sam's voice is always the first one heard. His hand is raised many times each class hour, whether there's a lecture or a discussion. Often frustrated, Sam does not listen to either his peers or his instructor. If he did listen, he'd realize that many of his questions had already been addressed. Sometimes Sam is so interested in getting his point across that he interrupts his classmates' remarks, or he attacks them for challenging his views.

Carmen loves sociology class. She enjoys listening to the lecture, but she also enjoys the give-and-take of class discussions. At first, she was hesitant to speak out, but once she became convinced that she could learn a great deal from the questions and comments of her peers, she tried participating. When she leads a discussion, Carmen makes sure that everyone has a chance to contribute, keeps the discussion focused, and summarizes the discussion at its close.

1. **List three negative behaviors that Bob exhibits in class.** _____

_____

_____

2. **How could Bob change his behavior so that he could participate more fully in class?** _____

_____

_____

3. **Why is Sam's behavior negative? How could he change his behavior to participate in a more positive way?** _____

_____

_____

4. **How does Carmen play an active role in class?** _____

_____

_____

5. **Why is Carmen a good discussion leader?** _____

_____

_____

6. **Which of the students seems the most self-motivated (internal locus of control)?** _____

_____

_____

thinking *ahead*

What practical knowledge have you gained from this chapter that you can use to solve real-world problems? To find out, read the following scenario and answer the questions listed after it.

Paulette works for a toy manufacturer. Paulette's supervisor has appointed her to a committee whose function is to brainstorm ideas for new products. Paulette must attend meetings and then report back to her supervisor. Paulette was chosen for this task because creativity and people skills are her strengths.

Although she interacts well with committee members, Paulette has trouble taking notes during the meetings. Her mind wanders during long presentations, and she begins thinking about personal matters. At the end of a presentation, her note pad is either blank or filled with meaningless scribbles. Even when she is listening attentively, Paulette has a hard time deciding what she should write in her notes. As a result, she has difficulty reconstructing what went on during the meeting so that she make her report.

1. What is Paulette's problem?

_____

_____

_____

_____

2. What strategies can she use to solve her problem?

_____

_____

_____

_____

3. How can she use her creativity and people skills to overcome her problem?

_____

_____

_____

_____

4. What else can Paulette do?

_____

_____

_____

_____

chapter **re**view

To review the chapter, reflect on the following confidence-building attitudes, complete Concepts to Understand, and practice your new skills at every opportunity.

ATTITUDES TO DEVELOP

- positive thinking
- consideration for instructors and classmates
- willingness to get involved

CONCEPTS TO UNDERSTAND

The five strategies for successful classroom performance are _____ for class, become an _____ listener, develop a _____ note-taking system, make effective _____ presentations, and _____ in class and group activities.

To prepare for class, do the following things. Attend _____ and arrive on time. Use your _____ to keep up with assignments and bring your textbooks and other supplies to class every day.

Do all assignments and anticipate the next lesson or assignment. Improve your listening skills by becoming an _____ listener. Listen with a _____ frame of mind, focus your attention on the speaker, encourage the speaker, take notes, and decide what is important in a lecture by listening for _____ words and phrases.

To take notes effectively, you need a personal note-taking system. Students have used many such systems successfully. For example, you can use the informal _____ system, the _____ method, or the _____ technique discussed in this chapter. Any of these systems—or one that you adapt from them—will work.

To make an effective oral presentation, have a _____ for speaking on the topic you have chosen. Then plan and organize your presentation by using this three-part development: Tell listeners what you are going to say, _____, and then tell them what you have just said.

Take part in group activities and discussions, and ask questions as needed. Do your share of the work and don't monopolize the discussion. Your involvement in class will help you add to your background of knowledge, which is the framework on which you can build effective listening and note-taking skills.

SKILLS TO PRACTICE

- preparing for and participating in class
- listening actively
- taking good notes
- planning and making oral presentations
- interacting with others

Your Reflections

Your Reflections

Reflect on what you have learned about classroom skills and how you can best apply that information. Use the following list of questions to stimulate your thinking and then write out your reflections. Your response may include answers to one or more of the following questions. Incorporate in your writing specific information from this chapter.

- Of the five classroom skills listed on the first page of this chapter, which are your strongest? Which need improvement? How can you build on your strengths and overcome your weaknesses?

- What relationship do you see between attendance and punctuality in the classroom and in the workplace?

- How has your preparation for classes either led to or prevented your success?

- Which of the strategies explained in this chapter do you plan to try—and how?

- Of the attitudes and skills listed in the chapter review, which do you think will be most useful at work or in your career?

CHAPTER

5

Making the Most of Your Time

HOW OFTEN HAVE you said "I don't have

time to study"? When was the last time

you were able to finish everything you needed to do on time?

How would you like to learn some strategies

that will help you take control of your time

and your life?

MUCH OF LEWIS CARROLL'S *Through the Looking Glass* takes place on a giant chessboard. Alice is a pawn who wants to win the game and become a queen. Choosing a square and trying to hold her position, she finds herself on the other side of the board. Frustrated, she turns to the Red Queen for advice. Explaining the rules of the game, the Red Queen says, "Here it takes all the running you can do to keep in the same place." Do you sometimes feel, like Alice, that you are just running in place, never getting ahead?

What are the factors that make time management difficult? Course requirements, work demands, family responsibilities, and personal needs all compete for your time. Nevertheless, time is a resource you can learn to manage. By taking control of your time now, you can establish efficient work habits that will lead to success in college and in your career. You already possess several keys to effective time management. Use your assessment skills to identify your time-management strengths and weaknesses. Your understanding of learning styles can open the door to your and others' time-management styles. Finally, by thinking critically and using the strategies explained in this chapter, you will be able to manage your time instead of letting time manage you:

- Use the GRAB method to take control.

- Make and follow schedules.

- Avoid procrastination.

How to GRAB Some Time

TO TAKE CONTROL of your time, you must be aggressive, especially if you are a chronic procrastinator—someone who consistently puts off doing difficult, boring, or time-consuming tasks. Unless you live alone, you may have to fight for study time. Talk honestly with family members about your goals. Ask for their suggestions. Make it clear that their support, cooperation, and encouragement will increase your chances for success. Talk plainly to roommates about your and their study needs and arrange your schedule accordingly. Above all, be candid with yourself about your own time-management issues. Time will slip away from you unless you GRAB it and hold tight (see Figure 5.1).

Goal

To GRAB study time, **set a goal.** What do you want to do? Would you like to set aside a block of time each day for completing your assignments? Would you like to have Tuesday and Thursday evenings free for study? Do you want to set aside one afternoon a week, in the library, to write drafts of essays for your composition class? The goal is up to you; it should be a reachable goal, one you can reasonably expect to achieve. The time limit you set should be one you can live with. For more information on how to set reachable goals, see Chapter 3.

Responsibilities

Determine your responsibilities. To manage time, you must first determine what your responsibilities are. Do you live alone? If not, then you have responsibilities to those with whom you live. Do you work? If so, then you have obligations to

Figure 5.1	How to GRAB Some Time
G GOAL	Set a goal.
R RESPONSIBILITIES	Determine your responsibilities.
A ANALYSIS	Analyze where your time goes.
B BALANCE	Balance work, class, study, and leisure time.

your boss and coworkers. As a student, you have course requirements to meet. All of these responsibilities—which may include child rearing, cooking, cleaning, working, and studying—somehow have to be met. Sharing household tasks with family members will leave you more time for study. By considering your roommate's needs, you can work out a study schedule that is mutually agreeable. Your employer may be willing to adjust your hours to accommodate your course schedule. Enlist the aid of family members, roommates, your boss—whoever is in a position to help you reach your goals. With a little effort, you can manage your time so that you can meet all your responsibilities.

Analysis

Analyze where your time goes, and you may be able to find a more efficient way to use your time. What are the fixed times in a typical day for you? **Fixed times** include the hours you spend working, attending classes, and traveling to and from each activity. These are the time slots that may be difficult or impossible to change. For example, if you are an athlete, then your fixed times will include

Your fixed times may include special activities or classes that meet during the same hours each week.

© Ron Sherman

practice and participation in games or events. If you are a parent, then your fixed times may include driving children to and from school and to other regularly scheduled activities. If you are working full-time and attending college part-time, then your fixed times include the hours you spend in classes and at work. For many students, regular exercise warrants a fixed time in their schedules. **Flexible times** include the hours you spend doing such things as sleeping, eating, watching television, and studying. You can choose when you do these activities and how much time you spend on each.

Balance

To manage your time effectively, **balance work, class, study, and leisure time** through scheduling. *A schedule is a structure that you impose on the events of one day, week, semester, quarter, or any other block of time you choose. A schedule is a plan for getting things done; it is a commitment you make that reminds you of your goals and helps you stay on track. Since it is* your *commitment, you are free to revise, change, or terminate your schedule at any time.* To achieve balance among work, class, study, and leisure, you must first determine how much time you presently spend on these activities. Complete Awareness Check 9 to assess your use of time.

Awareness Check 9

WHERE DOES YOUR TIME GO?

Estimate the number of hours you spend each week on the following activities. When you are finished, subtract your total hours from 168, the number of hours in a week. How much time is left? How can you use this time to reach your goals?

Activity	Hours per Week
1. Attending classes	_____
2. Working	_____
3. Sleeping	_____
4. Dressing, showering, etc.	_____
5. Traveling to and from work, college, etc.	_____
6. Studying	_____
7. Eating	_____
8. Watching television	_____
9. Engaging in leisure activities	_____
10. Caring for family	_____

11. Cleaning and doing laundry   _____

12. Socializing   _____

13. Attending athletic practice   _____

14. Surfing the Internet   _____

15. Other   _____

                                    Total =   _____

                    168 Hours minus Total =   _____

Now answer the following questions:

1. On which activity do you spend the least amount of time?

_____

2. On which activity do you spend the most time?

_____

3. Is the amount of time that you spend studying producing the grades you want?

_____

4. Overall, are you satisfied with the way you spend your time? Why or why not?

_____

5. If you could make some changes, what would they be?

_____

After completing the Awareness Check, you may find that you have some surplus time during the week. You might use this time either for scheduling additional study hours as needed; for setting aside a block of regular, consistent study time; or for completing a task or activity you did not think you had time to do. Schedules can make your life easier, not harder, because they help you organize your time.

Scheduling Your Time

SCHEDULES PUT YOU in control of your time and your life. Your schedule is the result of the inward decision you make to control events instead of letting external circumstances control you. **Semester** or **quarter calendars, weekly schedules,** and **daily lists** are three time-honored plans that have helped thousands of students become better time managers. Build confidence in your ability to manage your time by trying out each of these plans.

The Semester or Quarter Calendar

A calendar for the current term allows you to see at a glance what you need to accomplish each month in order to complete your course requirements. A semester is about sixteen weeks long, a quarter about ten weeks long. If your college is on a semester system, you probably attend different classes on alternate days: Monday, Wednesday, and Friday or Tuesday and Thursday. On the quarter system, however, you may attend some classes every day. The system your college uses will determine what your calendar will look like and how you will be able to schedule the rest of your time around your classes. To make a complete semester or quarter calendar, you need the following three items:

- **Your college calendar,** which is printed in the college catalog or can be found on your college's web site.

- **A syllabus,** or instructor's outline, for each course.

- **A calendar,** one you either buy or make yourself, that contains squares big enough for you to record information.

Use your semester or quarter calendar as a quick reference to remind you of such things as upcoming tests and the due dates of important assignments. Keep the calendar on your desk, on a wall above your desk, or on a bulletin board where you will see it every day when you sit down to study. Always have two months visible so that by the last week of the current month, you will also be aware of what's ahead in the next month. Follow these steps to make your calendar:

1. Enter the following information in the appropriate squares: when classes begin and end, college holidays and those that coincide with your religion or culture, registration and final exam times, and any other important dates or deadlines such as midterm exams or degree application times. Your college's catalog or web site may contain most of this information.

2. Review the instructor's **syllabus** that you received for each course. The syllabus, or course information sheet, may list test dates and major assignments such as essays, research papers, or projects that are due throughout the term. Some instructors do not plan very far ahead. They may wait to announce test dates several days beforehand. If that is the case, you will want to update your calendar as you receive this information.

3. Enter any other information, event, or activity you want to include. For example, if you plan to attend sports events or concerts, fill in those dates on the calendar. If you take part in any regularly scheduled activities such as sports practice and club or organization meetings, add them to your calendar.

4. Be sure to leave enough space in each square. You may have to list more than one item under each date.

Be creative with your calendar. Make planning your semester or quarter an enjoyable activity. Either purchase a calendar that you find attractive or make your own. Use different colored inks or marking pens for each kind of information you enter. If you type your calendar on the computer, add some graphics. Figure 5.2 shows one month from a student's calendar for a typical semester or quarter.

Figure 5.2	**One Month in a Student's Semester or Quarter**

December						
Sunday	Monday	Tuesday	Wednesday	Thursday	Friday	Saturday
			1	2	3 Comp. essay due	4 First day of Hanukah
5 2 p.m.–4 p.m. Charity walk/run	6 Dentist appt. 4:00 p.m.	7 Hum. paper due	8 Concert 8:00 p.m.	9	10 Comp. 1 final 10:00 a.m.	11
12	13 Alg 1 final 8:00 a.m.	14	15 Psych. final 7:00 p.m.	16	17 Hum. final 10:00 a.m.	18
19	20	21	22 College closed: Dec. 20–Jan. 3	23	24	25 Christmas
26	27	28	29	30	31 New Year's Eve	

Your Weekly Schedule

The main purpose of the weekly schedule is to help you plan your study time. By scheduling your study time and making a commitment to stick to your schedule, you will be giving studying the same importance that you give to working or attending classes. Without a schedule, you may begin to study only when you have nothing else to do, at the last minute before a test, or late at night when you are tired. If you are a procrastinator, a weekly schedule may provide the extra motivation you need to get your work done. Your schedule is your commitment to learn. Figure 5.3 is an example of a student's weekly schedule.

This student, Lloyd, has fixed times for classes and church attendance. He has flexible times for his other regular activities. In the time remaining, he has allotted the same block of time each day for studying. He has made a commitment to treat studying like a job. If Lloyd sticks to his schedule, then, over time, studying will become a habit for him. When he sits down to study at his regular time, he will be able to get to work quickly and to give his assignments maximum concentration. During some weeks Lloyd may need additional time to study for a test or to

Figure 5.3   Lloyd's Weekly Schedule

	Sunday	Monday	Tuesday	Wednesday	Thursday	Friday	Saturday
6:00 – 7:00	Sleep	Run, Dress, Eat				→	Sleep
7:00 – 8:00	Sleep	← Transportation to class →					Sleep
8:00 – 9:00	Sleep	Algebra class	Study in library	Algebra class	Study in library	Algebra class	Eat, Run
9:00 – 10:00	Run, Dress	Comp. 1	French 1	Comp. 1	French 1	Comp. 1	Study
10:00 – 11:00	Eat, Trans. to church	Biology class	Biology lab	Biology class	French lab	Biology class	Study
11:00 – 12:00	Church	Lunch/ Trans.	↓	Lunch/ Trans.	↓	Lunch/ Trans.	Lunch
12:00 – 1:00	Trans. church to home	Home		Home		Home	
1:00 – 2:00	Lunch	Study	Study	Study	Study	Study	
2:00 – 3:00	Clean apartment						
3:00 – 4:00	Free	← Laundry, other chores →					Leisure
4:00 – 5:00	Free					→	or study
5:00 – 6:00	Free					→	May go
6:00 – 7:00	Dinner					→	out later
7:00 – 8:00	↑					→	
8:00 – 9:00	Study or					→	
9:00 – 10:00	Watch TV					→	
10:00 – 11:00						→	
11:00 – 12:00	↓					→	
12:00 – 1:00	Sleep						→

complete an especially lengthy assignment. On these occasions he can use some of his "free" hours for more studying. What if Lloyd decides to take a part-time job? Then he will have to modify his fixed, flexible, and free times. Lloyd's schedule puts *Lloyd* in control of his time and his life.

As you experiment with making schedules, keep in mind that for maximum performance, many experts recommend at least two hours of study time for every hour spent in class. For a class that meets three times a week, this would mean six hours of studying per week. Thus, if you are taking five three-hour courses, and you want to do your best, you would need to schedule thirty hours a week of study time. If you are a working student, you may have difficulty finding that much time to study. To reach your goals, you may be forced either to take fewer courses or to reduce your working hours.

If the ratio of study time to class time seems high, remember that it takes a lot of time and effort to acquire knowledge and to learn skills. However, you may spend less time studying subjects that are easy for you than you spend studying difficult ones.

EXERCISE **5.1**

CREATE A SEMESTER OR QUARTER calendar. Either buy a calendar or make copies of the template in Figure 5.4 for each month in your semester or quarter. Also see http://college.hmco.com/success to download copies of the calendar. Write in the month and each day's date on each calendar page; then staple the pages together. Look again at Figure 5.2, and then enter the following information:

1. **When classes begin and end, holidays, final exam dates**

2. **The registration date for the next semester or quarter**

3. **Test dates and dates when major assignments are due**

4. **Dates of activities or events that you want to participate in or attend**

5. **Any other dates or deadlines you want to remember**

A Daily List

Keep a daily list of things to do and appointments to keep. Nearly everyone makes lists: grocery lists, appointment lists, errand lists. As a student, you need to make lists, too—when to return library books, specific study tasks you must complete, counseling appointments, and so on. Consult your lists frequently and check off items as you complete them. A list is a motivational aid that reminds you to stay on track. Each item you complete and check off brings you closer to achieving your day's goals, boosting your confidence.

Figure 5.4   **Calendar Template**

	Sunday	Monday	Tuesday	Wednesday	Thursday	Friday	Saturday

EXERCISE **5.2**

MAKE A WEEKLY SCHEDULE. SEE Figure 5.5 for the template that accompanies this exercise or download copies of the template from http://college.hmco.com/success. If you prefer, use a word-processing program to make your own schedule template, either by setting up a table or by using your program's graphics. Programs differ; therefore, if you need more specific instructions, either see your instructor or consult with someone in your college's computer or media center. To fill in your schedule, follow these directions:

1. **Fill in your fixed-time activities. These are the things you must do at scheduled times—for example, working and attending classes.**

2. **Fill in your flexible-time activities. These are the things you need or want to do that you can schedule at your own discretion.**

3. **The squares remaining are your free times. Schedule a regular time each day for studying.**

4. **Be sure to schedule some time for leisure activities.**

5. **Fill in every square.**

Figure 5.5   **Weekly Schedule Template**

	Sunday	Monday	Tuesday	Wednesday	Thursday	Friday	Saturday
6:00 – 7:00							
7:00 – 8:00							
8:00 – 9:00							
9:00 – 10:00							
10:00 – 11:00							
11:00 – 12:00							
12:00 – 1:00							
1:00 – 2:00							
2:00 – 3:00							
3:00 – 4:00							
4:00 – 5:00							
5:00 – 6:00							
6:00 – 7:00							
7:00 – 8:00							
8:00 – 9:00							
9:00 – 10:00							
10:00 – 11:00							
11:00 – 12:00							
12:00 – 1:00							

Some people make lists on little scraps of paper. Others use fancy note pads, small spiral-bound notebooks, daily planners, or appointment books which they buy in bookstores or office supply stores. (If you buy a daily planner or appointment book, be sure to get one with squares that are big enough to hold several items or one that includes a separate note pad.) Whatever you use for making your daily lists, make sure it is a convenient size and keep it handy.

If you have a personal computer, you might want to invest in an electronic calendar. Several programs allow you to keep records of important dates and ap-

---

EXERCISE **5.3**

REVIEW YOUR RESPONSES TO AWARENESS Check 9, which is near the beginning of this chapter. Notice how many hours per week you estimated that you spend on each of the activities listed. For one week, keep track of the *actual* hours you spend on those activities. Write down the actual amounts of time as you spend them (*not* later that day, or you could easily end up estimating your time again). At the end of the week, write your original time estimates and the exact hours you spent on the following lines; then complete the lists and answer the question.

Activity	Estimated Time	Actual Time
1. **Attending classes**	_____	_____
2. **Working**	_____	_____
3. **Sleeping**	_____	_____
4. **Dressing, showering, etc.**	_____	_____
5. **Traveling to and from work, college, etc.**	_____	_____
6. **Studying**	_____	_____
7. **Eating**	_____	_____
8. **Watching television**	_____	_____
9. **Engaging in leisure activities**	_____	_____
10. **Caring for family**	_____	_____
11. **Cleaning and doing laundry**	_____	_____
12. **Socializing**	_____	_____
13. **Attending athletic practice**	_____	_____
14. **Surfing the Internet**	_____	_____
15. **Other**	_____	_____

1. **List the activities in which you spent more time than you had estimated.**

_____

_____

_____

2. List the activities in which you spent less time than you had estimated.

_____

_____

_____

3. How can you use this new information to revise your weekly schedule?

_____

_____

_____

_____

pointments on your computer and to set up your calendar in a variety of formats. When you turn on your computer, for example, the calendar could tell you the day's date and list your schedule for the day. In some programs, you can instruct the computer to beep to remind you of an appointment.

Keeping a daily list can be a quick and easy way to start planning your time effectively. Your daily lists should include whatever you want to do or whatever you need to remember that you might otherwise forget. Figure 5.6 shows a student's list for one day.

Figure 5.6   **A List for One Day**

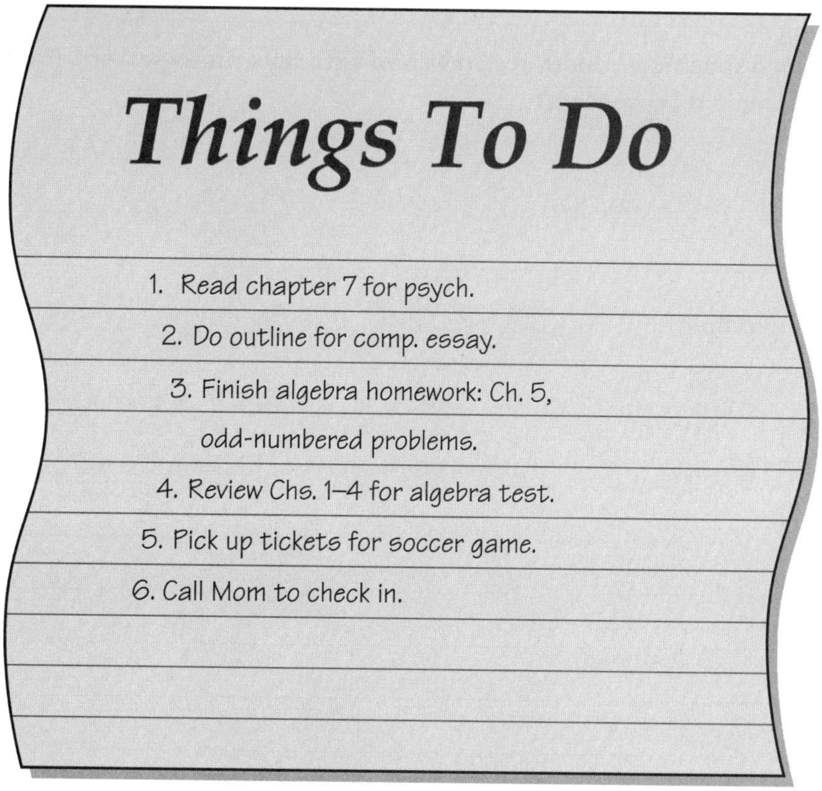

Things To Do

1. Read chapter 7 for psych.
2. Do outline for comp. essay.
3. Finish algebra homework: Ch. 5, odd-numbered problems.
4. Review Chs. 1–4 for algebra test.
5. Pick up tickets for soccer game.
6. Call Mom to check in.

EXERCISE **5.4**

APPLY WHAT YOU HAVE LEARNED about schedules by doing this exercise with group members. Follow the guidelines for successful collaboration that appear on the inside back cover. Discuss the following questions. When you reach consensus, record your answers on the lines provided. Then evaluate your work.

1. **What are your experiences with making and following schedules? Which group members have used schedules, and which have not?**

_____

_____

_____

2. **What are the advantages and disadvantages of making daily, weekly, and semester or quarter schedules?**

_____

_____

_____

3. **Which type of schedule do you find most useful, and why?**

_____

_____

_____

4. **Discuss a specific problem you have had with time management. How could you use schedules to overcome this problem?**

_____

_____

_____

Group Evaluation:

Evaluate your discussion. Did everyone contribute? Did you accomplish your task successfully? What additional questions do you have about making and following schedules? How will you find answers to your questions?

_____

_____

_____

_____

_____

_____

Special Challenges for Commuters

Unlike the resident student, you need to build travel time into your schedule. The time you spend traveling to and from campus or from campus to work to home leaves less time for studying and other activities. You may also need to transport your children to and from school. Because it is easy to underestimate the time it takes you to get from place to place, give special consideration to travel time as you plan your schedule and select courses.

Adding college courses and study time to an already busy schedule is another challenge. You may be tempted to meet it by scheduling all your classes on one or two days. Although this may seem like a good idea at the time, you may encounter one or more common problems. Suppose you schedule all your classes on the same day. If you are absent one day, then you will miss *all* your classes for the whole week. Also, papers, tests, and other assignments for those classes will always be due on the same day. Instead of having a paper due on Monday, several math problems due on Wednesday, and a test on Thursday or Friday, you will have to turn in the paper and the problems and take the test all in one day. Spreading your classes over two days is not much better; you still may have several assignment deadlines or tests on the same day.

What happens at the end of the one or two days when you attend class? For one thing, you are probably exhausted and have so many other things to do that you don't or can't take time to review your notes from each class or begin doing the assignments. Also, you may postpone the work until the night before your classes meet, leaving you only enough time to do a portion of the work. You may even skip one or two assignments, thinking you'll catch up later. This almost never happens. One- or two-day schedules often lead to scheduling classes back to back, which may seem like another good way to save time. Unfortunately, when you attend one class right after another, you don't have time to absorb and process the information covered in the previous class. You set yourself up for *information overload,* a condition in which the material explained in one class gets confused with that covered in another.

Ideal schedules are those that spread classes and study times over the whole week and that alternate class periods with free periods. During your free periods, you can either review notes from your previous class or do some last-minute review for a test you must take in the next class. Because you have free time between classes, you must remain on campus. This puts you in a good position to form a study group that you'll meet with at a regular time or to set up a standing appointment with a tutor if you are having difficulty in one of your classes. You may find that by scheduling classes over the whole week, you are actually *saving* time. This can happen because it's easier to schedule study time around one or two classes a day and still meet your other obligations than it is to try to pack in some study time after having attended four or five classes. However, if you absolutely have to attend classes on a two-day schedule because of work or other obligations, at least try to schedule a free hour between classes.

Time Management and Learning Style

Chapter 2 explains that your body's reactions affect your learning style. For example, you probably have an optimum time of day when your concentration seems to be at its peak, and you are most productive. But being a morning person or a night person isn't just a preference, nor do you have a choice about it.

You have a biological clock that regulates your internal rhythms, telling you when to eat, when to sleep, and when to get up and get moving. The time of day when your temperature is highest is what determines whether you are an "early bird" or a "night owl." Since you can't control fluctuations in your body's temperature, you may as well take advantage of them. Do important activities that require thinking and concentration during your optimum time of day. Try to schedule your classes, especially ones that you expect to be difficult, at the time of day when you are most alert. If you have to take a class at a time when you know you will be working at a disadvantage, try these suggestions:

- When you feel yourself getting drowsy, take a few deep breaths.

- Change your position every few minutes: cross and uncross your legs, sit up straight, and make other adjustments in the way you are sitting.

- Eat a snack such as a handful of raisins or a piece of fruit before you go to class. This will raise your blood-sugar level and your body temperature, making you feel more alert.

- Take deep, rhythmic breaths to get more oxygen into your bloodstream.

EXERCISE **5.5**

WRITE A SHORT ESSAY IN which you explain how your present schedule of classes and study times either does or does not conflict with your learning style and personal habits. Consider which classes require the most work, which assignments need greater concentration, your optimum time of day, and whether your schedule permits you to eat regularly and to get enough rest. What are your schedule's strengths and weaknesses? How can you improve your schedule next semester or quarter? Give your essay a title.

Try these suggestions whenever you must study at a time when you are tired. In addition, when you are at home, prop up your feet to increase the blood flow to your brain.

Time Management and Reading

One of the big differences between high school and college is the amount of reading assigned. Whether you are a recent graduate or an older student, you may be frustrated by the number of pages per week that each instructor assigns. A common complaint you will hear from students of all ages is "Each of my instructors must think his or her class is the only one I have."

Nevertheless, the reading has to be done. Are there any short cuts? No. Reading takes time. The more difficult the reading, the more time it takes. However, you can learn to read more efficiently. Try these strategies:

- Determine the time you will need for reading.

- Schedule your reading time.

• Develop active reading habits and study skills so that you do not waste time.

To calculate your reading time, follow the steps given in Figure 5.7. For example, suppose you have been assigned a fifty-page chapter from your biology text. The assignment is due at the next class meeting. You have determined that it takes you two hours to read twenty-five pages from this book. Sometime between now and the next class meeting, you should schedule four hours of reading time for biology.

Active reading habits include underlining, making notes in the margins of your textbooks, outlining, and other activities such as using a reading system and organizing information for study—strategies explained in Chapters 7 and 8. These strategies lead to concentrated review and may eliminate the need for re-reading entire chapters. In fact, re-reading is an inefficient way to study and one you should avoid. If you take the time to read, mark your text, and make notes, you may be able to shorten your review time. If you think that you have missed something, you can always re-read just those sections of a chapter that contain the information you need.

Figure 5.7   **Calculate Your Reading Time**

1. **Choose three consecutive textbook pages that contain mostly print.**

2. **Time yourself on the reading of these three pages.**

3. **Jot down your starting time in minutes and seconds. When you have read three pages, jot down the time and subtract your starting time to get the total reading time. Divide the total time by 3 to get the time that it takes you to read one page.**

4. **To get the time needed to complete a reading assignment, multiply the number of pages by your time per page. Divide by 60 to get the number of hours and minutes it will take you to finish your reading.**

Example: You have twenty pages to read. How long will it take you?

Here are the results of your initial calculation:

Starting time: 3:00
Finishing time: 3:18

Subtract starting time from finishing time:

$$\begin{array}{r} 3{:}18 \\ -3{:}00 \\ \hline 0{:}18 \div 3 = 6 \text{ minutes per page} \end{array}$$

Multiply the number of minutes per page times the number of pages in the assignment and divide by 60:

$6 \times 20 = 120 \div 60 = 2$ hours (time needed to read twenty pages)

CONFIDENCE
Builder

Time-Management Tips for Student Athletes

College takes a physical and mental toll on student athletes. Self-discipline and the use of effective time management techniques can help to alleviate this.

College challenges student athletes physically. The hours spent practicing, weight training, competing, and traveling to and from sports events leave these students physically exhausted. As a result, they are often too tired to participate fully in classes, remain attentive during lectures, or study with maximum concentration. Exhaustion also may lead to poor eating and sleeping habits which sap students' energy, making study even more difficult.

In addition to the physical toll, student athletes may also pay a mental toll. For one thing, these students are under pressure to earn good grades on which their scholarships and their eligibility to play depend. Also, negative stereotyping in the form of taunts ("dumb jock") and lowered expectations on the part of some instructors and classmates may lead to depression and a loss of self-esteem in all but the most confident students.

What we all need to remember is that every student has strengths and weaknesses, and on any college sports team, as wide a range of abilities will be represented as in any other area of campus life. Nevertheless, the student athlete who *is* underprepared for college work carries a double burden: the need to develop academic skills and the need to resist being dragged down by others' negative attitudes toward him or her.

If you are a student athlete, follow these time-management tips to meet your physical and mental challenges so that you can be successful in your sport and in your academic program. If you are not an athlete, pass on the tips to a friend who is and be supportive of his or her efforts to succeed.

- Use daily lists, weekly schedules, and semester or quarter calendars to manage your time. Remember that if you don't manage time, time will manage you.

- Although it is too late to do anything about this term's classes, you can plan ahead for next term. Keep track of where your time goes and when you are most alert, and use this information to build your dream schedule next term.

- Put studying first. You can't maintain eligibility without grades, so schedule regular study time. If your coach requires you to attend group study sessions, great! If not, form your own study group. Be sure to include one or more non-athletes in your group so that different perspectives are represented. Schedule a meeting time for your study group and follow through on your schedule.

- Arrange your schedule so that you have regular meal times and get adequate rest. If you don't, exhaustion will overtake you.

- If you have weaknesses in any basic skills (reading, writing, mathematics), take any required courses in these subjects as soon as possible. Schedule regular meetings with a tutor if necessary. It's more efficient to take care of basic skills *now* than to risk getting more and more behind. As you build skill, your grades will improve, and with improved performance comes confidence.

- Use *all* your time. Write information for studying on 3"×5" note cards that you should carry with you every-where. While waiting in lines, between classes—anywhere you have extra time which you might otherwise waste—review your notes. In other words, be efficient in your use of time.

- Other people's negative attitudes and stereotypical thinking may be difficult to overcome, but you can control how you respond to them. Let nothing stand in the way of your own success. Arrange your schedule so that you are able to do the studying and skill building needed to ensure successful classroom performance. Sched-uling time for adequate rest and proper nutrition will keep you alert and ready to participate in class. Be punc-tual and prepared, and you may change a few minds about the seriousness of student athletes.

To pursue this topic further, do an online search using these key words as a starting point: *college sports, student athletes and study skills, time management and sports.*

Procrastination

PROCRASTINATION **MEANS NEEDLESSLY** postponing tasks until some fu-ture time. Although procrastinating once in a while may not hurt you, if you delay studying and put off doing important assignments too often, you will sabotage your efforts to succeed. Complete Awareness Check 10 to gauge your tendency to put off tasks.

If you budget your studying time wisely, you will have more time for leisure activities.

© Bob Daemmrich/Stock Boston

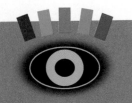

ARE YOU A PROCRASTINATOR?

To find out whether procrastination is keeping you from getting your work done, put a check beside the statements that apply to you.

- ☐ 1. I put off doing an assignment if it seems too difficult.
- ☐ 2. I put off doing an assignment if completing it will take a lot of time.
- ☐ 3. I put off studying if I don't like the subject.
- ☐ 4. I put off studying if I'm not in the mood.
- ☐ 5. I put off writing an essay if I don't know how to begin.
- ☐ 6. I put off studying for a test if I don't know what the test will cover.
- ☐ 7. I put off studying if I get hungry.
- ☐ 8. I put off studying if I am too tired.
- ☐ 9. I put off studying if I don't feel well.
- ☐ 10. I put off studying if there is something else I'd rather do.

All the items of the Awareness Check describe common tactics students use to avoid studying. To build confidence, you need to understand when and why you procrastinate and to fight your tendency to delay getting started.

Why Do People Procrastinate?

Ann has to write a research paper for her composition course. The paper is due in six weeks. She thinks she has plenty of time, so for the first two weeks, she doesn't even think about the project. That leaves her only a month in which to choose a topic, do her research in the library, make an outline, and write the paper. It takes her another week to select a topic, but when she gets to the library, she finds that several of the books she wants have been checked out. By the time Ann decides on another topic and compiles her research materials, she has only one week left to complete the paper. She *does* hand it in on time, but she knows it's not her best effort. She doesn't like to write anyway and is not expecting to receive a very good grade. "Next time," she swears, "I'll get started sooner." But next time Ann will probably procrastinate again because that is her pattern of behavior. She doesn't like to do difficult or lengthy assignments and will put them off until the last minute. Like many students, Ann procrastinates for one of four common reasons. Perhaps you also procrastinate for one of these reasons:

- Your tasks seem difficult or time-consuming.
- You have trouble getting started.

COMPUTER CONFIDENCE

Use the Computer to Save Time

Effective time management is crucial to success in college, especially when it comes to writing papers. For many students, paper writing is the most time-consuming part of any course. How about you? Does the process of planning, researching, drafting, revising, editing, and rewriting seem endless? Do you find yourself waiting until the last minute to get started? If so, try using a computer. You'll be surprised at how efficient your planning and writing will become and how much better your results will be.

Using a computer for writing assignments is a good idea for several reasons. A computer lets you make changes almost instantly. You can move words, sentences, and even whole paragraphs in seconds. A computer gives you a neatly printed draft whenever you want one, quickly and painlessly. Some word-processing programs check your spelling, grammar, and writing style. Using a computer simplifies the mechanics of writing so that you can concentrate on expressing your ideas.

Before you start writing, use a computer to organize your notes. Suppose you have taken notes from several books and magazines. If you enter those notes on disk, integrating them into a coherent outline will be easy, and using your outline may help you write a logically organized paper. (See Computer Confidence, Chapter 3, for more information about outlining.)

Whenever you use a computer to write a paper, follow these steps to make sure that you don't accidentally "lose" your work:

1. Use the "save" command frequently. Save every five or ten minutes. Save every time you complete a page. And save whenever you leave the computer, even if you will be away for only a few minutes. Remember: Save it; don't lose it!

2. Give your files easily recognizable names that clearly indicate the project and its stages of development—for example, the file name *ENG2DR1* might stand for "English class, paper number two, first draft." Date each file so that you can quickly and easily find the most recent one. Write the file name and date on a label you attach to your disk.

3. Before you revise a draft, copy it in case you want to refer to your original version. Renaming each draft automatically saves all your drafts in separate files. At the end of every writing session, print out a paper copy of your new work. This "hard copy" is always useful for revisions. If you have a hard copy, and something goes wrong with your disk, you will still have your work.

4. Keep backup disks of all of your work. At the end of every writing session, copy your completed work onto a backup disk. Remember to store your disks carefully.

- You lack motivation to do the work.

- You are afraid of failing.

Putting off difficult or time-consuming assignments makes them even harder to do when you actually get started and further ensures that you won't be able to do your best because you will not have enough time. However, a task may be less difficult than you think if you break it down into segments that you can handle during short periods of time. If you have trouble getting started on an assignment, or if you waste a lot of time before sitting down to study, then you may be using avoidance tactics. Why are you avoiding what you have to do? Perhaps you aren't interested in the subject, or perhaps you'd simply prefer to be doing something else. You may be insufficiently motivated to perform the work. You may not see a direct connection between the assignment and your goals or your overall grade in the course. Or you may be afraid of failure. If you believe that you will not get a good grade—no matter what you do—you may delay getting started on an assignment. Complete Awareness Check 11 for more insight into why you procrastinate.

Awareness Check 11

WHAT IS YOUR ATTITUDE TOWARD STUDYING?

Read all of the following study situations and imagine that they apply to you. Put a check in the column that best describes how you feel about each one; then add up your checks. An explanation of your results follows.

Positive	Negative	Study Situation
☐	☐	1. A term paper is due at the end of the term.
☐	☐	2. Midterm exams are next week.
☐	☐	3. You have major tests in two classes this week.
☐	☐	4. In one of your classes, the final exam will determine whether you pass or fail.
☐	☐	5. You are in a self-paced math course. You have a list of assignments and several tests to complete by semester's end.
☐	☐	6. You have a sixty-page chapter to read in your psychology text for tomorrow's class.
☐	☐	7. You have a speech to prepare for your speech class.
☐	☐	8. You have a five-hundred-word essay to write for your composition class.
☐	☐	9. You have final exams to study for in all of your classes.
☐	☐	10. You are taking an anatomy course. You must learn the names of all the bones in the body.

Totals: Positive _____   **Negative** _____

All of these study situations represent tasks that are difficult or time-consuming. Look at your totals in each column. In general, based on this exercise, what do you think about difficult or lengthy assignments? Specifically, if you checked negative *for items 1 and 8, perhaps writing is difficult for you, and you avoid getting started for that reason. If you checked* negative *for items 2, 3, 4, and 9, perhaps you avoid studying for tests because you have test anxiety or are afraid that you will fail. See Chapter 12 for some suggestions to ease test anxiety. If you checked* negative *for item 5, maybe the self-paced learning situation seems overwhelming, and you need the structure of a classroom setting, in which the instructor sets the pace for you. If you checked* negative *for item 6, it could be that the length of a reading assignment affects the way that you approach it. Perhaps you'd be more motivated to start sooner if you divided the reading assignment into smaller segments with breaks in between. If you checked* negative *for item 7, perhaps you don't like giving speeches, can't think of what to say, or are afraid you will get nervous and do a poor job. The sooner you start writing your speech, and the more time you give yourself to practice it, the more confident you will feel about your ability to do a good job. If you checked* negative *for item 10, perhaps you avoid starting assignments like this one because the number of items you have to learn and remember seems like more than you can handle. One of the memory techniques suggested in Chapter 11 may make it easier for you to get started.*

How to Beat Procrastination

To avoid procrastination, change your behavior. If you procrastinate when assignments are too difficult or too long, or if you have trouble getting started or lack the motivation to do the work, then instead of focusing on your feelings about the assignment, focus on the advantages of completing it on time. If you get started right away, you will have the advantage of enough time to do your best. You may even complete the assignment with time left over to do something else. However, if you wait too long to begin, then you won't be able to do your best, or you may not finish at all. Fear of failure is sometimes the result of not knowing what to do. If you are not sure about what is expected of you, then you may not know how to begin the assignment. To help you overcome the fear of failure and get started, try using these tips that have worked for many students:

1. Break a large assignment or project into smaller units of work that you can complete in one sitting.

2. Plan rewards for yourself for completing each part of the assignment. Take a break or do something you enjoy.

3. Schedule enough time for completing a long assignment. Set a goal to spend a certain amount of time working each day until the assignment is finished.

4. Get organized. Your attitude toward studying will improve if you have an orderly work area with everything you need at your fingertips—books,

pens and pencils, paper—so that you will be ready to begin the moment you sit down.

5. If you put off assignments because you don't know where to start or aren't sure how to do the work, find out what you need to know. Make an appointment with your instructor. Explain the difficulty you are having and ask for advice. If you have started the assignment, show your instructor where you are having trouble. Or talk to someone in the class. If you missed a lecture or have gaps in your notes, your friend might be able to fill you in.

6. Assume an attitude of confidence, and you will be confident. Instead of thinking, "This is too difficult" or "I'll never finish this," think "I can do this if I get started right now" or "There's a lot of work to do, but if I can do a little bit at a time, I'll be finished before I know it."

Learning to manage time and avoiding procrastination require some effort. Do not be discouraged if your first efforts are unsuccessful. Try to pinpoint your reasons for procrastinating. Identify your avoidance tactics and try to eliminate them. Experiment with schedules until you come up with a plan that works for you. With determination, you will take control of your time and your life—and you will reach your goals.

Your Study Place

Managing your time well also means choosing a quiet place to study. If you are a resident student, you probably do most of your studying in your room or in the library. If you are a commuter, chances are you do the majority of your studying at home. In either case, you probably have to fight distractions, and the best way to do that is to schedule your study time when and where you are least likely to be disturbed.

Your study place should be comfortable, quiet, well lighted, and supplied with everything you need to study.

© Bonnie Kamin/PhotoEdit

CRITICAL THINKING

If you procrastinate only now and then, doing it may not hurt you, but if you regularly put off tasks that you know you should be doing, you are in for trouble. Chronic procrastinators make excuses for their procrastination that are really "cop-outs" or evasive tactics that they use to deflect responsibility for their procrastination from themselves. The following is a list of the top ten excuses students make for not studying or for not completing assignments. The list is adapted from Edwin C. Bliss's list of the top forty cop-outs in *Getting Things Done*, a book that explains why people procrastinate and how to avoid doing it.

Read the list. How many of these cop-outs have you used? How many have you heard other students use? Choose three of them and explain why they are invalid. What advice would you give to students who use these excuses? What suggestions can you make to help them avoid procrastinating?

1. It's not due yet.

2. I work better under pressure.

3. I don't feel like doing it now.

4. It's too difficult.

5. I really mean to do it, but I keep forgetting.

6. I don't know where to begin.

7. It's boring.

8. I don't really know how to do it.

9. I don't have all the materials I need.

10. I probably wouldn't do a very good job anyway.

Adapted and reprinted with the permission of Scribner, a Division of Simon & Schuster from *Getting Things Done* by Edwin C. Bliss. Copyright ©1983 by Edwin C. Bliss.

If you are a commuter, set up a study area in a quiet part of your home. Your study place doesn't have to be elaborate. A desk or small table in your bedroom or in a guest room will do. Avoid studying in bed because you will probably fall asleep. Avoid places in high-traffic areas such as the kitchen or family room. Not only will you be distracted, but your family may also conclude that your studying is not serious business and that you won't mind being interrupted. Having a study area away from the family and the noise of the TV and children's play—a place where you do nothing but study—sends a subtle message that you are treating studying like a job and do not want to be distracted.

Let your family know that you need quiet time to do your work. Schedule a regular time for studying at home and make studying a routine. Soon your family will get used to the idea that when you are in your study place, you are unavailable except in case of emergency. If you can plan your study time for when your children are asleep or when no one else is at home, so much the better.

To help fight procrastination, outfit your study place with everything you might need to get the job done: pens, pencils, paper, a dictionary, a good desk lamp, and whatever other supplies you will need. When you come in from class, go immediately to your study place and unload your books. Then they will already be there waiting for you when you are ready to study.

If you are a resident student, set up a study area in your part of the room. Put your desk against a wall, away from a window or door if possible, and keep the door closed while you are studying. Then you won't be tempted away from your books by whatever is going on outside the window or in the hallway. Like the commuter, you should avoid studying in bed. Like the commuter's family, your roommate and friends across the hall are your temporary "family" and therefore a source of distractions. Early in the term, work out mutually agreeable study times with your roommate. For example, one of you might study while the other is in class. On the other hand, you may want to schedule some of your studying so that you can work together or both study at the same time.

thinking *ahead*

What practical knowledge have you gained from this chapter that you can use to solve real-world problems? To find out, read this scenario and answer the questions that follow it.

Marsha wants a career in advertising. She'd like to work for a big company in a major city. Marsha has done well in her courses in art and advertising and believes that she has the skills necessary to mount a successful ad campaign. In fact, her sketches and designs have won several contests and awards. She made an appointment with a career counselor to find out what additional skills would prepare her for her chosen career. The career counselor told her the following:

Much of the work done in businesses today is accomplished as team projects. A project manager oversees the work, breaking it down into segments for which each member of the project group is responsible. A successful project begins with setting goals both for achievement of the project's purpose and for its completion on time. People who come into the workplace lacking goal-setting and time-management skills are at a disadvantage. Through goal setting and time management, people can direct and change the courses of their lives—and most important to employers, they can get the job done.

"Wow," thought Marsha. "I figured I'd be working alone most of the time." Although Marsha sets goals, she often has trouble reaching them because she does not manage her time effectively and sometimes hands in assignments late. Also, she has had limited experience working with a team. "What can I do?" she asked.

1. **What are Marsha's strengths and weaknesses in terms of her preparedness for her career?**

   _____

   _____

2. **How will her strengths help her in her career?**

   _____

   _____

3. **What can she do to overcome her weaknesses?**

   _____

   _____

4. **If you were Marsha, would you continue to pursue your goals, or would you change your career plans? Explain your answer.**

   _____

   _____

   _____

   _____

chapter review

To review this chapter, reflect on the following confidence-building attitudes, complete Concepts to Understand, and practice your new skills at every opportunity.

ATTITUDES TO DEVELOP

- commitment
- self-confidence
- positive attitude toward studying

CONCEPTS TO UNDERSTAND

Time management and procrastination present major problems for many students. Managing your time effectively and beating procrastination call for aggressive action. *You can GRAB time by following four steps:* First, set _____ and give yourself a time limit to reach them. Second, determine your _____ to the important people in your life and find ways to involve them in your plans to reach your goals. Third, _____ where your time goes so that you can find more efficient ways to use it. Finally, _____ your fixed, flexible, free, and study times by making and following schedules.

Semester or quarter calendars, weekly schedules, and daily lists can help you remember important dates, deadlines, assignments, events, and appointments. Make out a _____ or _____ calendar early in the term so that you can see at a glance what you have to accomplish each month. Use your _____ schedule to help you keep up with weekly assignments and plan reviews for tests. Your _____ list can be a reminder of all the things that you need to do during the day that you might forget—phone calls you need to make or appointments you must keep, for example. Schedules help keep you organized and on track.

People procrastinate for four common reasons that may also apply to you. Your tasks seem difficult and time-consuming; you have trouble getting started; you lack motivation to do the work; you are afraid of failing. Avoid _____ by understanding the reasons why you delay performing required tasks and by changing the behaviors that may contribute to the problem.

To access additional review exercises, see http://college.hmco.com/success.

SKILLS TO PRACTICE

- managing your time
- making and following schedules
- avoiding procrastination

Your Reflections

Your Reflections

Reflect on what you have learned about making the most of your time and how you can best apply that information. Use the following list of questions to stimulate your thinking; then write your reflections. Your response may include answers to one or more of the questions. Incorporate specific information from this chapter into your writing.

- What are some of the obligations and responsibilities that compete for your time?

- Are you able to manage your time effectively? Why or why not?

- Do you procrastinate? If you do, what are your reasons for procrastinating? What can you do to keep from procrastinating?

- What relationship do you see between managing your study time and managing time in other situations?

- Of all the attitudes and skills listed in the Chapter Review, which do you think will be most useful at work or in your career?

6

Maintaining Your Health and Well-Being

DO YOU EAT sensibly, exercise regularly, sleep soundly, and manage stress effectively? Are you in control of your emotions and your relationships, or do they control you? Did you know that your health and well-being can help or harm your academic performance?

ONE OF THE values of a college education is that it exposes you to a diversity of students and ideas. It offers you a chance to develop socially, culturally, and intellectually—to become a well-adjusted person. *A well-adjusted person is one who has achieved a balance among his or her physical, emotional, and social needs.* Some students are not managing their lives as well as they could. Other students' emotional and physical well-being are out of balance. Some may place excessive emphasis on their friends' and family's needs and neglect their studies. Still others may be a little too conscientious, neglecting the importance of social relationships and leisure-time pursuits.

Your physical self is linked with health, diet, fitness, and stress management. Your emotional self involves your feelings, your degree of satisfaction in life and career, and your locus of control—your source of motivation—all keys to success in college. Your social self derives from your relationships and your behavior. This chapter explains what you can do to keep your physical, emotional, and social selves in balance:

- Stay healthy.

- Control your emotions and adapt to change.

- Improve your interpersonal skills.

- Manage your sex life.

Health, Well-being, and Success in College

HEALTH AND WELL-BEING can affect your ability to do well in college. If your health is poor, if you have troubled relationships, or if you lack confidence and self-esteem, then your mind will be occupied with these problems, and you will not be able to give studying and classes your full attention. If you are excessively preoccupied with doing well in college and neglect your health, then again you may create problems for yourself that will eventually affect your ability to succeed.

Getting an education is not all tests, lectures, and assignments. If you are a young college student, you are also learning how to live and work effectively for the rest of your life, and you can take advantage of unique opportunities for establishing good health habits, building self-esteem, and forming close friendships. If you are an adult learner, college is another responsibility you are adding to the ones you already have. Your health, relationships, and self-esteem may be put to the test as you struggle to cope with the challenges of being a student.

College is the place, and now is the time for you—no matter what your age—to break any habits that may be ruining your health or limiting your performance, and to establish new habits that may enhance performance and prolong your life.

Staying Healthy

HEALTH IS A basic need. If your body doesn't work, your mind can't function. Health, good or bad, is rarely something that just happens; it is partly the result of a person's choices and actions. If your health is good, then you want to keep it that way. If your health is poor, then you must do all you can to improve it. The four questions that follow embody four goals of healthful living that can lead to

Awareness Check 12

ARE YOU LEADING A BALANCED LIFE?

Check the statements in each part that describe you.

Part I: Your Physical Self

☐ 1. I exercise regularly, three times a week or more.

☐ 2. I feel that I am getting enough sleep most nights.

☐ 3. As far as I know, I eat a balanced diet.

☐ 4. I limit my intake of foods that are high in fat, salt, and sugar.

☐ 5. I feel well most of the time.

☐ 6. I believe that I am not under a great deal of stress.

☐ 7. When I do have stress, I am able to manage it.

☐ 8. I am neither overweight nor underweight.

☐ 9. I do not smoke.

☐ 10. I do not abuse alcohol, caffeine, or other drugs.

Part II: Your Emotional Self

☐ 1. Basically, I am a confident person.

☐ 2. Generally speaking, I am happy.

☐ 3. When I do feel angry or depressed, I can get over it quickly and go on with my life.

☐ 4. My outlook for the future is positive.

☐ 5. I am rarely, if ever, overcome by nervousness, stress, or anxiety.

☐ 6. Overall, my self-esteem is high.

☐ 7. For the most part, I believe that I am in control of what happens to me.

☐ 8. I am not a fearful person by nature.

☐ 9. I am able to take criticism.

☐ 10. I can cope with change.

Part III: Your Social Self

☐ 1. It is fairly easy for me to make friends.

☐ 2. I have several friendships that mean a lot to me.

(Continued)

□   3. I am not uncomfortable if I am at a party where I don't know many people.

□   4. People would probably not describe me as shy.

□   5. I welcome opportunities to meet new people.

□   6. I am a good listener.

□   7. I can also contribute to a conversation.

□   8. Most of the time I get along well with the significant people in my life.

□   9. I understand and accept my responsibilities in a sexual relationship.

□   10. I believe I am assertive about what I want without being overbearing.

□   11. If a friend points out a fault that I have, I don't take offense; instead, I try to change my behavior if I agree with my friend.

All of these statements are positive ones, so if you have checked most of them, you may be managing your life successfully. The statements are grouped into three parts, reflecting the physical, emotional, and social aspects of your health and well-being. Therefore, fewer checks in one section could indicate a need for greater balance in that part of your life. Of course, the Awareness Check is an informal survey that does not begin to cover all of the possible aspects of adjustment, but your responses should give you a starting point for improving your health and well-being.

improved brain functioning. Think about your life and your habits; then, mentally answer the questions *yes* or *no.*

1. **Do you eat nutritionally sound, balanced meals?**

2. **Are you physically fit?**

3. **Are you able to manage stress?**

4. **Do you avoid the use of harmful substances?**

This chapter provides a brief overview of some ways you can maintain good health.

Eating Sensibly

A nutritionally sound, balanced diet is one that includes more fish and poultry than red meat, plenty of fruits and vegetables, whole grains in the form of bread or cereal, and dairy products. A balanced diet contains a variety of foods. It also contains more carbohydrates (starches and sugars) than protein and less fat than either carbohydrates or protein. A fast-food meal of a hamburger, french fries, and a soft drink, for example, is not a balanced meal because it contains too much fat. A more balanced meal would consist of broiled lean meat (chicken or fish), two cooked vegetables or a cooked vegetable and a salad, rice or other carbohydrates, and a piece of fruit for dessert (see Figure 6.1).

Your social well-being and physical well-being are just as significant as your academic abilities in leading a successful life. College provides unique opportunities for enjoying recreational activities and making lasting friendships.

© Bob Daemmrich/Stock Boston

Not only should you eat balanced meals, but you should also eat at regular intervals spaced throughout the day so that your brain is continually supplied with the nutrients it needs to function properly. Skipping breakfast, for example, or going into an exam hungry can interfere with your concentration and memory function and make you feel drowsy and less alert. Your brain responds to high and lows in your blood sugar levels. When you haven't eaten, the level of glucose in your blood is low, and your mental alertness is diminished.

Glucose is a sugar best synthesized from proteins and fats. Eating a candy bar before a test will temporarily raise the level of glucose in your blood, but the burst of energy you get from it will be short lived and will leave you feeling sluggish. Instead, eat balanced meals three times a day with snacks in between. A piece of fruit, which is high in fructose (another sugar), or a cup of yogurt is a good high-energy snack.

What can you do to maintain a healthful diet while you are in college? Try these suggestions:

1. Schedule your classes and other activities so that you have time for three meals a day.

2. Eat balanced meals. You may be able to get a nutritious meal in your college's cafeteria. A variety of vegetables is usually available, and you can select your own combination of foods. If you live off campus, select foods according to the guidelines in Figure 6.1.

3. Avoid rich, high-calorie snacks. If you get hungry between meals, eat an apple or another fruit, carrot or celery sticks, or unbuttered, unsalted popcorn. For an energy boost, try low-fat yogurt or a few unsalted nuts instead of sugary or salty snacks.

Figure 6.1	Nutrition Chart: Guidelines for Good Eating

GUIDELINES	FOODS	REASONS
Eat some of these foods every day.	Fruits, vegetables, whole grains, bread, cereal, dairy products (low-fat milk, cheese, yogurt)	To achieve a varied, balanced diet that supplies enough energy and essential nutrients for optimum brain functioning
Increase carbohydrate intake to 67% of your total daily calories.	Fruits, vegetables—especially starchy vegetables such as broccoli, corn, and cauliflower—nuts, whole grains	For maintaining energy throughout the day
Reduce protein intake to 8% of your total daily calories.	Lean meat, fish, chicken, eggs, peas, and beans	For the growth and repair of tissue and to help fight infections
Limit fats to no more than 25% of your total daily intake.	Butter, mayonnaise, other fats and oils, eggs, rich desserts, fatty meats, whole milk and milk products	To reduce risk of high blood pressure, heart disease, and diabetes

4. If you live off campus, go home for lunch or bring your lunch. Be in control of what you eat.

5. If you go to parties, go easy on the snacks and alcoholic drinks. You may not know this, but alcohol converts to sugar in the bloodstream and is stored as fat. Apart from its other dangers, too much alcohol can make you gain weight, and it can also interfere with your body's absorption of essential nutrients.

6. Don't make a habit of skipping meals. Fatigue, fuzzy thinking, and diminished concentration are among the problems this habit can cause.

7. If you are overweight and would like to reduce, see your doctor. He or she will help you select an appropriate weight-loss program.

8. Exercise regularly; it will increase your level of fitness, make you feel positive and energetic, and help reduce stress. If you are trying to lose weight, combining a sensible diet with exercise will speed up the process and keep the weight off.

9. Put food in perspective. Eat for good health. Don't eat because you feel depressed, because you want to celebrate, or as a social event.

10. Drink eight to ten glasses of water a day to aid the digestive process, help eliminate wastes and toxins from your body, and supply needed moisture to the tissues.

EXERCISE **6.1**

FIND OUT WHAT YOU EAT and whether your diet is as balanced and healthful as it could be. Keep a record of what you eat for one week; then determine ways to eat more sensibly if necessary. For example, if you discover that most of your calories are coming from fats, decrease your intake of fatty foods such as butter, cheese, ice cream, margarine, salad dressings, luncheon meats, or other meats rich in fat, and increase your intake of whole grains, fruits, vegetables, lean meats, fish, and poultry. Keep recording your meals and attempting to adjust what you eat until you achieve a balanced diet.

Make copies of this chart so that you can record what you eat throughout the day. (If you wait until evening, you may forget what you've eaten.) To download copies of the chart, go to http://college.hmco.com/success.

	Sunday	Monday	Tuesday	Wednesday	Thursday	Friday	Saturday
Breakfast							
Lunch							
Dinner							
Snacks							

Improving Fitness

Exercise has many benefits; fitness is just one of them. Regular exercise strengthens your heart, improves circulation, and helps reduce your risk of cardiovascular illness or death from a heart attack or stroke. Exercise can make you strong and able to withstand other diseases, and it can also relieve stress. In addition, it helps you lose weight and improves your appearance.

© Jim Whitmer

Walking is one of the simplest forms of aerobic exercise. Just twenty minutes of brisk walking every day can make a significant difference in your fitness level.

The best exercise is aerobic. *An aerobic exercise lasts for a minimum of twenty minutes during which your heart rate is elevated and your muscular activity is continuous.* You should not do aerobic exercises without checking your pulse frequently and without first receiving instructions on how to perform the activities. Overstressing your heart can have serious, even fatal, effects. "No pain, no gain" is a dangerous myth. "FIT" is a much better guideline.

F = Frequency	How often you exercise—three times a week is the generally recommended starting frequency
I = Intensity	Your target heart rate, based on your age and present level of fitness
T = Time	The amount of time you spend exercising—start with fifteen minutes or less, depending on your age and condition, and then gradually increase the time as you are able

Exercise is great for you if you do it correctly. An excellent place to get started is in your college's athletic department. Courses and individual counseling may be available at a lower cost than you are likely to find at one of the commercial health clubs or spas, and may even be offered free of charge. If you don't have time for exercise that requires a change of clothes or a special place or type of equipment, try walking. You can walk anywhere; just twenty minutes a day of brisk, uninterrupted walking greatly reduces your risk of heart problems and also improves your overall level of fitness. Here is a list of aerobic activities, some of which you may already be doing:

Aerobic dancing

Rowing

Swimming

Bicycling

Running

Walking

Jumping rope

Managing Stress

Some stress won't hurt you. In fact, you should expect to experience stress now and then. For example, it is normal to feel a little anxious before getting up in front of a group to speak. You want to do your best, and you may be wondering whether you will be able to remember everything you want to say. Once you get started, this anxiety should quickly pass as you begin to focus your attention on giving the speech. It is also normal to feel a little anxiety on the day of an exam. But once you have the exam in front of you and get down to the business of taking the test, the anxiety should pass. *Real stress is unrelieved anxiety that persists over a long period of time.* Stress is especially harmful if you are unable to manage it. Unrelieved stress can weaken you physically so that you become vulnerable to

Find a way to take a break and lose yourself when you are experiencing a great deal of stress. Hobbies, sports, and friendly conversations can provide relief from pressure or worries.

© Howard Dratch/The Image Works

disease, and it can impair your ability to think clearly so that your performance in class and at work suffers.

Many warning signs can tell you if your stress is getting out of control. Look at the brief list that follows and see whether you have any of these common symptoms of stress. The more of these symptoms that you have, the more likely it is that you need to learn some strategies for coping with stress.

Depression	Loss of pleasure in life
Difficulty falling asleep	Increase or decrease in appetite
Extreme tiredness, fatigue	Muscular aches for no apparent reason
Feelings of anger or resentment	Stomach or intestinal disturbances
Frequent absence from work or classes	Sweaty palms
	Tension headaches
Impatience	Test anxiety
Inability to concentrate	

Many students find adjusting to college and meeting course requirements extremely stressful, especially if they are also working, raising a family, or trying to cope in an environment in which they feel out of place. Some students are chronically anxious about tests, and their nervousness prevents them from doing their best. Test anxiety is a special kind of stress related to testing situations. Chapter 12 explains test anxiety and how to overcome it. It is important that you find ways to manage stress so that you can reach your goals and enjoy yourself in the process. Try the following tips for managing stress.

Ten Stress Beaters

1. **Be realistic.** You know what you can and cannot do, what is within your power to change, and what you can't do anything about. Don't waste energy worrying about matters that are out of your control. Instead, use your energy to alter those situations that you have the power to change. Unrealistic goals, perfectionism, and believing you have to do everything right the first time will set you up for failure. Be reasonable about what you expect of yourself, and don't be afraid to make mistakes.

2. **Exercise tensions away.** When you are under stress, your muscles tense involuntarily. You may have noticed the tightness in the back of your neck and across your shoulders that often precedes a headache. Exercise has a natural calming effect that is accompanied by a positive feeling. For example, you may have heard about or experienced "runner's high," the feeling of euphoria and the sudden burst of energy runners get after they have been running for a long time.

   To help you relax, try the desktop relaxation technique and the chair-seat relaxation technique explained in Chapters 9 and 10. Also try this simple deep-breathing technique for calming yourself in any situation: Breathe slowly through your nose, filling your lungs. Then slowly exhale through your mouth. As you take ten deep breaths in this manner, think to yourself: "I am relaxed; I am calm."

EXERCISE **6.2**

FIND AN EXERCISE PROGRAM THAT works. Choose a form of exercise that you enjoy and can easily fit into your schedule. Try out some of the aerobic exercises listed on page 141; then use the following chart to summarize and comment on your experiences. You can also download the chart from http://college.hmco.com/success. The chart will help you determine which type of exercise works best for you and why.

Type of exercise	Aerobic dancing					
Time of day	7:00 p.m.					
Amount of time spent	1 hour					
Reaction	I went to an aerobics class with a friend, and I liked it so much I decided to join too.					

3. **Learn to say no.** For whatever reason, many of us have difficulty saying *no* when someone asks us to do something, even if we don't have the time or desire to do it. When you are under stress because of work, family, course requirements, and other obligations, the last thing you need is to take on more responsibilities. When someone makes demands on your dwindling time, think carefully about how you feel. Ask yourself, "Do I really want or need to do this?" If the answer is "No," don't be afraid to say so. If you have trouble saying *no,* you may need to become more assertive, as explained later in this chapter. If you are interested in assertiveness training, consult your counseling department. Check the newspaper for an

announcement of a workshop or request one through your student activities office. You could also check your campus bookstore, the library, or the Internet for information on the topic.

4. **Ask for help.** Some problems may be more than you can handle by yourself, so you may need to seek financial, medical, or some other type of help or advice. Some problems may look a lot worse than they are until you talk to someone about them and get a different perspective. If you are the kind of person who hates to ask for help, try to get over this attitude. Many times we worry needlessly and cause ourselves even more stress by living with problems that we consider unsolvable when asking for help and getting it might bring immediate relief.

5. **Learn to deal with negative people.** People who display negative attitudes, a pessimistic outlook on life, and a constant state of nervousness can make you experience negative feelings that add to your stress. If you can eliminate negative people from your life, do so. If they are friends or family members, try to counter their negative remarks with positive ones of your own. When they do behave in a more positive way, comment on what you like about their behavior, thereby positively reinforcing a behavior that you want them to continue.

6. **Lose yourself in activity.** When you are under stress, engage in some activity that causes you to lose all track of time. During those moments, you can forget your worries and experience happy, calming feelings. Reading, playing a sport, and spending time pursuing a hobby or special interest are all activities in which you can lose yourself.

7. **Treat yourself.** Do something nice for yourself, especially when you are under stress. Buy yourself a present. Go out to dinner or see a movie you've been meaning to see with a friend whose outlook is positive.

8. **Get your life in order.** You've probably been meaning to do this anyway. If you are off schedule or behind in your courses, if your room or your house is a mess, and if you keep postponing a trip to the dentist, then it is no wonder that you are feeling stressed out. Resolve to get organized. Make out a new study schedule that includes time to catch up on work you've missed. Make a list of all the other tasks that need doing; then tackle them one at a time. Don't worry if it takes you a while to get organized. After all, it took a while to get off schedule.

9. **Make a wish list.** We all have a tendency to say to ourselves, "If only I had the time, I'd do _____." How would you complete this sentence? Make a list of all the things you'd do if you had the time. When stress has become more than you can handle, and you have to get away for a while, do one of your wish-list activities.

10. **Help someone else.** It's no secret that doing something for someone else can make you feel good and can take your mind off what is worrying you. Take the opportunity to help a friend who has a problem. Helping your friend find a solution may give you ideas for ways to solve one of *your* problems. If you know someone who is having trouble in a course you are taking, offer to study with him or her. The things you do for others not only help them but also have a positive effect on you.

Are You Spending Too Much Time on the Net?

With most college campuses being wired, a new student health issue has surfaced: Internet addiction. Cruise by your college's computer lab at any time of day, and you are likely to see all stations occupied. What are these students doing? Some undoubtedly are researching and writing. Many, however, are playing games and visiting chat rooms. Though harmless in themselves, when taken to extremes, these activities can put students at risk for failing grades and failed relationships. College counselors are troubled by the attrition rate of students whose misuse of the Internet has disrupted their lives and curtailed their education.

A person who uses the Internet obsessively to the point of losing self-control suffers from *Internet addiction*. Four types of addictive online behavior are *cybersexual addiction*, which involves visits to adult chat rooms and pornography web sites; *cyber-relationship addiction*, whereby online friendships become more important than real-life relationships with friends and family members; *net compulsions* such as online auctions, trading, and compulsive game playing; and *information overload* resulting from obsessive web surfing or prolonged database searching.

Why do people become addicted to the Net? Cyberspace is a virtual community in which one can escape from reality and the complexities of real-world human relations. In cyberspace, people can create new identities, concealing their real names, ages, personalities, and socioeconomic status. The intimacy that develops between friends who meet in chat rooms is, therefore, an illusion. Real intimacy comes from closeness with another. But cyber-relationships are, by their nature, at arm's length.

Who is at risk? The same risk factors that apply to drug and alcohol use apply to Internet addiction. Depression, anxiety, or lack of self-confidence and self-esteem may cause people to seek relief in the stimulating world of cyberspace. People who have abused drugs, alcohol, or tobacco may have an increased susceptibility to Internet addiction.

What can you do? As with any other activity that has a potential for abuse, use caution. Have a purpose for using the Internet and schedule your online time so that it doesn't interfere with your other activities. Use the Internet as a research tool or for an occasional game, but don't let it become a substitute for social interaction. Email, too, can get out of hand if reading and sending messages consumes too much of your time or if you use email not as a convenience but rather as a way to keep the people closest to you at a distance. If you are concerned that your Internet use may be excessive, seek help.

The Internet is a helpful tool for researching and fact finding; it can also be a pleasant distraction similar to watching a movie or a favorite TV program. But when your Internet use becomes obsessive, it may also become addicting. Watch for these warning signs:

(Continued)

- Internet activities are on your mind more often than not.

- The amount of time you spend on the Net has gradually increased.

- After deciding that you were spending too much time on the Net, you tried to stop or cut back but were unsuccessful.

- Just the thought of limiting your Internet time makes you feel anxious or depressed.

- Friends, family members, or others close to you have expressed concern about the amount of time you spend on the Net.

- You often turn to the Net for relief from stress, life's problems, or feelings of depression.

Do four or more of these warning signs apply to you? If so, you may be spending too much time on the Net.

To explore this topic further, see the following web sites for a list of resources, including an online test for Internet addiction that you can take: www.netaddiction.com and www.virtual-addiction.com.

EXERCISE **6.3**

ADDICTIVE BEHAVIOR—WHETHER IT INVOLVES binge drinking, smoking, overeating, using drugs, or surfing the Net to excess—interferes with your health and undermines your performance. If you are struggling with an addiction, or if someone you know is, research the addiction online. Find out what support groups may be available and what other useful information exists. As a starting point, use *addiction* as one of your search words and the name of the behavior or substance in which you are interested. If your topic is "Internet addiction," try the suggestions in this chapter's Computer Confidence. Then share what you find with the rest of the class.

Avoiding Harmful Substances

When it comes to drugs, both legal and illegal, it's best to take a realistic approach. What are the facts and misconceptions surrounding alcohol, tobacco, caffeine, and illegal drugs such as marijuana and cocaine? What are the risks and perceived benefits of using one or more of these substances? Arming yourself with knowledge enables you to deal with issues of substance use and abuse on your own terms.

Tobacco. Smoking places you at risk of getting lung cancer, heart disease, and a host of other illnesses, according to the American Cancer Society, the American Lung Association, the American Heart Association, and many other health organizations and professionals. Because second-hand smoke poses similar risks for nonsmokers, smoking is now prohibited or limited in all public buildings, many restaurants, and other establishments. Public awareness about the dangers of smoking has increased, and a growing social stigma against smoking prevails. All states have laws prohibiting the sale of tobacco products to minors. Those are the facts.

A misconception some people have is that they can quit smoking whenever they want to. According to a report issued by the Surgeon General of the United States several years ago, nicotine is as addicting as the illegal drug heroin. If you smoke, ask yourself this question: What is this habit doing for me? If, after considering the risks and benefits, you decide to quit, ask your doctor to suggest a smoking cessation program.

Caffeine. How many students do you know who can't face the morning without a cup of coffee? How many students need caffeine to keep them going throughout the day or to keep them awake during late-night study sessions? Here are the facts about caffeine: It is present in coffee, tea, chocolate, some soft drinks, and certain over-the-counter drugs. When used in moderation, caffeine reduces drowsiness and increases energy. When abused, caffeine can produce anxiety and tremors, and may aggravate certain conditions such as heart disease and high blood pressure. Caffeine can be addicting: an abrupt decrease or cessation of use produces withdrawal symptoms such as headaches and jitters, but one or two cups a day may produce few if any negative side effects. As you weigh the benefits and risks of using caffeine, consider two alternatives to morning coffee: switch to decaffeinated or manage your time so that you get enough rest, eliminating the need for a caffeine boost.

Illegal Drugs. What is the allure of drugs such as marijuana, cocaine, heroin, amphetamines, and LSD? They stimulate the brain's pleasure centers, generating feelings such as alertness, euphoria, or relaxation. But the "high" users get is short-lived and may be followed by feelings of depression or anxiety. Because these drugs are both psychologically and physically addicting, abuse can lead to a habit that is extremely hard to break. Because the drugs are illegal, the Food and Drug Administration has no control over their manufacture. As a result, they may be produced in unsanitary conditions and may contain toxic additives that increase users' health risks.

Some students who have experimented with illegal drugs have experienced few, if any, ill effects. But some have become addicted, some have died of overdoses, some have been sexually assaulted while under the influence, and others have served jail terms and have had their academic careers and future prospects forever curtailed as a result. Keeping these facts in mind, ask yourself whether the short-term benefits students may think they are getting from drug use are really worth the considerable risks involved and their long-term consequences.

Alcohol. We have saved this drug for last because its use and abuse are of greatest concern to college students. Because binge drinking on college campuses, alcohol abuse at campus social events, and alcohol-related deaths and other incidents during Spring Break get a lot of media attention, it's easy to get the impression that "everybody does it." The reality is that many college students do not drink, and many who do drink do so responsibly. But for others, alcohol abuse has resulted in dangerous behavior—and even death. Because students are often pressured to drink in social situations and because the opportunities to abuse alcohol are readily available, your best defense is knowledge.

Why do students drink? Psychologists and other professionals cite several reasons. For one thing, children of alcoholics and children who grew up in homes where alcohol was used at family occasions may be more prone to use alcohol. Also, some experimentation with "the forbidden" is a normal part of growing up. Drinking, for some students, is a rebellious act through which they establish their independence. Third, despite the risks of drinking, some students turn to alcohol to relieve stress or to escape unpleasantness. Peer pressure is another reason. Students may feel that they must drink in order to be accepted. Finally, the media and the campus atmosphere exert powerful influences. The media are filled with images that make drinking seem glamorous. Beverage companies sponsor social events that make alcohol consumption by young people seem normal, average. Social organizations on campus, Greek organizations in particular, may sponsor events that revolve around drinking. Too often, college administrators look the other way, ignoring the underage drinking that may be occurring on campus.

What is binge drinking? Although light drinking may pose few health risks, binge drinking is dangerous. Ingesting four or five drinks in a short time period constitutes binge drinking. This behavior can result in injury, illness, and even death from alcohol poisoning. Binge drinking has negative academic effects as well, impairing performance and judgment.

What are your choices? As a student, you must make your own decisions about alcohol use. You don't have to drink, but if you choose to, know the risks. Know the difference between light-to-moderate drinking and abusive or binge drinking. Consider also your religious beliefs and personal values. Be aware of legal limits and campus policies regarding alcohol use and make ethical choices. If you do drink, the following guidelines may help you drink safely and responsibly.

- **Know what you're drinking.** It's easy for someone to slip a drug into a drink and easy for someone to spike a drink with more alcohol than you had intended to consume. Therefore, do not accept a drink from anyone. Get your own drink.

- **Time your drinking.** Don't drink too much too fast. Drink slowly, making one or two drinks last at least an hour.

- **Do not drink on an empty stomach.** Eat or nibble while drinking. Eating slows the absorption of alcohol into the bloodstream.

- **Opt out of drinking games.** Games such as chug-a-lug contests are risky because they introduce too much alcohol into your system too rapidly.

- **Say "No" when you've had enough.** A simple *no* is all you need to say to refuse a drink. You don't owe anyone an explanation.

- **Do not drink and drive.** If you and your friends are out drinking, let someone who has not been drinking be your designated driver. Do not drive drunk, and don't ride with a driver who is.

Choosing not to drink is a valid option. If you make this choice, you can still attend parties and other social events where alcohol is consumed without participating in drinking. Take someone with you who is also a non-drinker. In addition, choose other, positive ways to find escape, relaxation, excitement, and pleasure. For example, plan activities with your friends that involve physical and mental stimulation. Attend sports events, take bicycle or hiking trips, go to the beach for a day of surfing and sunning, or go to a movie. Solitary pursuits that provide escape, adventure, and excitement include reading; writing poems, essays, and stories; and learning a new hobby, craft, or sport. For example, you might enjoy taking a course in creative writing or drawing.

Like everything else, deciding whether or not to drink is *your* choice. In this behavior, as in all others, by being informed and by making responsible choices, you are taking control of your life.

EXERCISE 6.4

HOW PREVALENT IS DRINKING ON your campus? Take this informal survey to gather information about your own habits and assumptions. Do not identify yourself on the survey. Your instructors will compile all students' answers and report back to the class.

To take the survey, read each question and circle your answer.

1. **Do you drink?**

   a. never   **b. occasionally**   **c. regularly**

2. **How many drinks do you have in a week?**

   a. none   **b. 1 or 2**   **c. more than 1 or 2**

3. **When are you most likely to drink?**

   a. at social events   **b. on special occasions**

   c. with meals   **d. whenever I'm with friends**

4. **How many drinks do you usually have at a social event or during an evening spent with friends?**

   a. 1 or 2   **b. 2 to 5**   **c. more than 5**

5. **Have you ever engaged in binge drinking?**

   a. never   **b. occasionally**   **c. regularly**

6. **Have you ever engaged in drinking games?**

   a. never   **b. occasionally**   **c. regularly**

7. **To the best of your knowledge, how prevalent is binge drinking among the students on your campus?**

   a. not prevalent at all   **b. somewhat prevalent**   **c. quite prevalent**

8. **In general, what would you estimate to be the percentage of students on your campus who drink regularly?**

   a. fewer than 50 percent   **b. about 50 percent**   **c. more than 50 percent**

9. **Do you believe that a student on your campus has to drink in order to be accepted or to have a social life?**

   a. not at all   **b. in some cases**   **c. definitely**

(Continued)

10. **Based on your own experience, how would you describe college students' drinking behavior?**

    a. **Most students do not drink.**

    b. **Most students engage in light-to-moderate drinking.**

    c. **Most students drink to excess.**

11. **How does drinking behavior on your campus compare to that on other campuses?**

    a. **There is less drinking among students on my campus.**

    b. **About the same amount of drinking occurs among students on my campus as on others.**

    c. **Students on my campus drink more than students on other campuses.**

12. **If you are out with friends, how likely is one of you to abstain from drinking so that he or she can be the designated driver?**

    a. **not likely**   b. **somewhat likely**   c. **very likely**

13. **How much underage drinking do you see at campus events or other social events at which college students are present?**

    a. **hardly any**   b. **some**   c. **a great deal**

14. **Among the students on your campus, how much pressure is there to engage in drinking?**

    a. **none**   b. **some**   c. **a great deal**

15. **Do you know anyone on your campus who has been involved in one or more of the following while drinking (circle all that apply)?**

    a. **acquaintance rape**   b. **an automobile accident**

    c. **a serious injury**   d. **unsafe sexual activity**

16. **Do you know anyone on campus whose drinking has led to one or more of these outcomes (circle all that apply)?**

    a. **missed class or was late**   b. **scored poorly on a test**

    c. **failed to hand in course work**   d. **had a loss of memory**

Your Emotions

ALTHOUGH YOU MAY be faced with a situation you cannot change, you *can* change how you feel about it. For example, if you are having trouble getting along with a roommate, you may be losing study time because of arguing or worrying about the problem. Soon your grades will suffer if you can't resolve your differences and get back on schedule. Obviously, you can't change your roommate's behavior, but you can change your feelings about that behavior. You can decide not to let it get to you. Focus your attention on doing well in your courses. Concentrate on meeting every requirement, completing every assignment, and preparing for every test. Do most of your studying in the library or some other place away from your roommate. Try to resolve your differences, but if you cannot, make the best of the situation until you can make other living arrangements. Avoid getting into arguments and say to yourself, "I am in charge of my feelings, and I will not let my conflict with my roommate interfere with my success in my courses."

Similarly, if you are an older student who lives off campus, you may have a family member or friend who tries to undermine your efforts to be successful by making such comments as "You'll never make it" or "You shouldn't put yourself through this." Negative comments like these don't have to upset you. Your emotions belong to *you*. People cannot control how you feel unless you give them that power.

Understanding Your Feelings

To begin taking control of your emotions, determine what causes you to feel one way or another. Begin by listening to yourself think and talk. Are your thoughts and words dominated by statements that begin with *they, he, she,* or *you*? Do you often make statements such as these?

You make me angry because you don't listen to what I say.

She doesn't care how I feel.

He really hurt my feelings.

They make it hard for me to get the schedule that I want.

She gave me a D on that paper, but I deserved better.

When you make statements like these, you place all the blame for your feelings on someone else. You place yourself at the mercy of others' whims. If they choose to, they can make you feel great. If they choose to, they can make you feel awful. You never know where you stand with people, and consequently, your self-esteem is undermined.

Chapter 1 explains locus of control as a factor that influences your motivation. *Locus of control* is a psychological term that describes where you place responsibility for the control of your life's events. For example, if your locus of control is *external,* you expect someone or something to motivate you. If your locus of control is *internal,* you are self-motivated. Locus of control may also explain, in part, *what* controls your feelings. Externally motivated students tend to blame others for the way they feel. Internally motivated students are more likely to examine their own behavior to find the source of their feelings.

One way to take control of your emotions is to replace any statements of feeling that begin with *they, he, she,* or *you* with statements that begin with *I.* You will then be able to determine what actually caused the feeling. For example, here are the same statements you read before, but the word *I* has replaced the first word, and the statement has been altered to shift the cause of the feeling to the person making the statement:

I get angry when I think you're not listening to what I say.

I believe she doesn't care how I feel.

I feel hurt by some of the things he does.

I find it hard to get the schedule that I want.

I made a D on that paper, but I could have done better.

Pretend for a moment that you made these statements. Notice how you have accepted responsibility for the feelings. For example, by accepting that the D is the grade that you earned, you are likely to do better next time. But if you blame someone else for the D, then you are off the hook and have no control over your future in the course. Similarly, if "they" are not responsible for your schedule, then you must determine what actions you should take to get the schedule you want. This kind of thinking puts *you* in control of the situation.

For example, in the first three statements, you accept responsibility for your feelings that seem to result from others' actions. The value of doing this is that it opens a discussion about behavior you don't like without blaming the other person. For example, if it turns out that your friend really doesn't listen, doesn't care how you feel, or does things that hurt you, then you must decide what you are going to do about the situation. You have to decide whether it is worthwhile to try to improve the relationship or to end it. In either case, you open the way for communication rather than for more arguments and bad feelings.

Leading a Purposeful Life

When you control your emotions and accept responsibility for your feelings, you increase your chances for happiness and decrease your chances for disappointment. A sense of well-being results from having goals to reach and making plans to achieve them. As explained in Chapter 3, setting reachable long-term and short-term goals will give you a purpose for attending college, completing your tasks at work, and realizing your dreams and plans. When your purpose is clear, you are more likely to schedule your time, follow through on your plans, and avoid procrastination.

If your life seems to lack purpose, examine what you are doing in your courses, at work, or at home. Ask yourself, "Why am I doing this?" Answers may not come right away, but when they do, they may remind you of your goals or indicate a need to make some changes in your life. This knowledge will give you a renewed sense of purpose.

Accepting the Need for Change

Negative feelings, a sense of helplessness, and lowered self-esteem result when something you are doing isn't working out, but you are afraid to make a change. An unhappy wife or husband may continue without help in a relationship that makes both partners miserable because one or the other is afraid of the changes that counseling might require. A person who has been offered a new and better job or a transfer to a higher-paying job out of state may turn down the offer because he or she fears change. You may keep working on a research paper—even though you may realize that you have chosen an unworkable topic—because you don't want to start over. If you are "test anxious," you may avoid seeking help because you believe that the problem will go away or that there is nothing you can do about it. Trying to avoid change by ignoring a problem can be self-destructive. Negative feelings breed more negative feelings, encouraging the mistaken belief that a bad situation can only get worse.

Accept the need for a change when it becomes clear that you have done all you can do in a situation that is not working. Acceptance is the hard part. Once you're committed to making a change in your life, exploring your options and deciding what to do next can be fun and challenging.

CRITICAL THINKING

As explained earlier in the chapter, accepting the need for change is one way to control the emotional feeling of helplessness you get when something isn't going well. When you accept the need for change, you make a positive choice either to act or to feel differently about a situation. But what about the unwelcome event in your life that forces a change upon you that you did not choose? The result is stress, and unless you can adapt to both the desired and the undesired changes in your life, the stress will go unmitigated and will become a threat to your health and well-being. Listed next are some stress-producing changes that can upset the balance of a person's health and well-being. How many of these changes have affected you within the last year or past six months? Write about what you are doing to adapt to these changes or write about another change or event that may be the source of stress in your life. Then explain what you are doing to cope with the change.

Death of a spouse or partner

Death of a parent

Death of other close family member

Divorce

Unwanted pregnancy

Major injury or illness (self)

Major injury or illness (family member or partner)

Loss of a job or financial support

Breakup of a relationship other than marriage

Serious argument with someone

Legal problem

Academic difficulties, probation

Relocation of residence

EXERCISE 6.5

IN THE FOLLOWING STATEMENTS, THE pronouns *they, he, she,* and *you* suggest that the people making the statements are not taking responsibility for their feelings and behavior. Rewrite each statement so that the focus is on the person making the statement. Replace any pronouns with the first-person pronoun *I* and change any other wording as needed.

1. You didn't tell us that we had to do the exercises.

_____

_____

_____

(Continued)

2. **Why can't I have an override? They told me that the department chairperson would let me in the course even though it's full.**

_____

_____

3. **You are not paying attention to me.**

_____

_____

4. **She gets on my nerves.**

_____

_____

5. **He is never in his office when I try to see him.**

_____

_____

EXERCISE **6.6**

LIKE MOST PEOPLE, YOU PROBABLY have times in your life when you feel disappointed, depressed, angry, frustrated, lonely, incompetent, or unloved. Like many people, you may tend to blame others for making you feel this way. In fact, no one needs to have that much power over you if you assume responsibility for your own well-being. Complete the statements that follow to remind yourself of what you have and the things that make you feel good. Think about these positive qualities and accomplishments whenever you lack confidence.

1. **My finest character trait is** _____.

2. **My favorite possession is** _____.

3. **My closest friend is** _____.

4. **I am proud of myself for** _____.

5. **I feel happiest at home when I** _____.

6. **I feel most comfortable at work when I** _____.

7. **The course in which I am doing my best is** _____.

8. **Something I enjoy doing by myself is** _____.

9. **A skill I have mastered very quickly is** _____.

10. **One thing I can really do well is** _____.

11. **On my next vacation I will** _____.

12. **One of my plans for the future is** _____.

CONFIDENCE Builder

Emotional Intelligence—Another Way of Being Smart

Why do some highly intelligent people fail? Why do some whose IQs are not so high still manage to do well? What makes one person moody and another person more even-tempered?

Emotional intelligence, or EQ, may be the answer. Daniel Goleman, author of *Emotional Intelligence,* draws on Howard Gardner's theory of "personal intelligences," Peter Salovey's definition of "emotional intelligence," and the research of many others to explain why your EQ may be more important than your IQ.

According to Goleman, "IQ contributes about 20 percent to the factors that determine life success, which leaves 80 percent to other factors." One of those factors is emotional intelligence: the qualities that enable you to control your emotions instead of letting them control you. For example, you could have the IQ of an Einstein and still find yourself on academic probation if you could not control your emotions that make you want to party instead of study. What exactly is emotional intelligence, and can it be developed? Goleman says it can. Emotional intelligence adds up to *character,* and it includes these qualities:

- **Self-motivation.** You alone are responsible for paying attention, maintaining concentration, and relieving yourself of boredom.

- **Persistence.** Following through on schedules and commitments, living up to obligations, and continuing to make progress despite temporary setbacks will help you to achieve your goals.

- **The ability to control impulses and delay gratification.** Now and then we all do things on a whim or "in the heat of the moment." But some people let passion rule, with disastrous results: the student who drinks too much, has unprotected sex, or acts first and thinks later. To control your impulses, you have to think ahead to the consequences and ask yourself, "Is it worth it?"

- **The ability to regulate moods.** How fast can you bounce back from disappointment and frustration? Do you allow yourself to be overcome by sadness, anxiety, or anger? Constantly giving in to your emotions produces stress that has harmful physical and mental effects. If your inclination is to say, "But I can't help how I feel," think again. The answer is to know yourself. Learn to recognize what your feelings are and what causes them. When you know *why* you are depressed, for example, you can figure out what it will take to eliminate the cause.

- **Empathy.** *Empathy* is another word for *caring,* and it is a valuable interpersonal skill. People who are empathetic have a high degree of self-awareness that enables them to sense the feelings of others. They are able to put themselves in another's place so that they can tell what he or she wants or needs.

- **Hope.** You have to believe that things will get better, that life is basically good, and that with hard work and persistence, you will achieve your goals. Without hope, it is unlikely that you will have either the will or the self-discipline to make a plan and follow it through.

Do you see a connection between Goleman's emotional intelligence and the internal locus of control? Remember that internally motivated people take responsibility for their own successes and failures. They manage their lives, as opposed to allowing life's circumstances to manage them. Goleman's qualities of self-motivation and persistence are also characteristic of the internal locus of control.

To pursue this topic further, see Goleman's book *Emotional Intelligence* or do an online search using these key words as a starting point: *emotional intelligence* and *Daniel Goleman.*

Your Interpersonal Skills

THE MOST INFLUENTIAL people in your life may include your parents, your spouse or other intimate partner, your children, your roommate, and your friends. You depend on these people for many things, and they depend on you. Your relationships with these people can span the entire range of emotions, from great happiness to extreme disappointment. What makes a relationship succeed or fail? Educators, philosophers, psychologists, writers, and many others have explored this question. Perhaps you have also explored it. Though each relationship is based on a complex system of need satisfaction, and though each type of relationship has characteristics that distinguish it from other types, five interpersonal skills that you can develop will lead to more satisfying relationships.

Listen. Give all of your attention to the people you are with. Spend an equal amount of time listening and talking. In this way you will be sharing your ideas, but you will also be giving others an opportunity to share theirs. Listen actively and make eye contact. Show interest by asking questions and commenting on what is being said. Encourage people to explain their opinions; then listen without judging. Respond by giving your opinions. When you are not sure what the other person means, paraphrase (restate) and preface your remarks with "Did I hear you say . . . ?" or "Did you mean that . . . ?"

Converse. Don't "hold forth"; don't deliver long, rambling monologues; and don't interrupt. A conversation is an interchange of ideas and opinions. Remember to listen 50 percent of the time and to talk 50 percent of the time. Avoid making critical or judgmental remarks. If talking with you is unpleasant, people will avoid conversation, believing that they won't be understood or appreciated. A breakdown in communication is the first sign that a relationship is in trouble. When people are asked what they like most in a relationship, a frequent answer is "Someone I can really talk to."

Have Fun. Create opportunities to have fun together. Make a mental list of interests you have in common with each of your relatives and friends, and plan trips or outings that focus on those interests. Or plan an adventure with someone. Go someplace new or try out a sport or activity together that neither of you has ever done before. When you discover a new activity that you both enjoy, set aside time to pursue it together. And make sure that you don't change or cancel plans at the last minute.

Be Supportive. You know how you feel when you have a problem, and the person you turn to for help lets you down. You know how you feel when you come home from work excited about some small but important accomplishment, and the person you were hoping would share this excitement acts uninterested. Don't be that kind of person. Encourage others' dreams. Share each triumph and disappointment as if it were your own. Don't assume someone you love knows you care; let your feelings show.

Being supportive is especially important in a diverse learning community or workplace in which people of different cultures and backgrounds share assignments and tasks. Being supportive means respecting others' opinions and being receptive to new ideas.

Be Assertive. Being assertive means being able to ask for what you want. It also means not giving in to people who try to make you do something you don't want to do. But don't confuse assertiveness with aggressiveness. *Aggressive behavior* is rude, domineering, and intimidating. *Assertive behavior* is polite but strong and independent. Being assertive means *standing up for your rights without denying the rights of others.* As an assertive person, you have the right to express your feelings and opinions, to ask for what you want, and to say *no.* At the same time, you must respect the fact that others have the same rights.

Few college students are truly aggressive, and far more students are passive than assertive. Being passive is taking the easy way out by letting other people make decisions for you. If you're at a party, and someone pushes another beer on you when you don't want it, do you take the beer so that you won't seem unsociable? If you don't want another beer, say so assertively and mean it: "No thanks, I've had enough." If you're a mother who comes in from classes to find dishes stacked in the sink and laundry piled up by the washer, do you start rinsing the dishes and sorting the clothes? Only if that's what you *want* to do. You should make it clear to your family that you need some help. Getting them to share the problem and its solution rather than demanding their help increases your chances of success.

Assertive behavior is responsible behavior. When you are assertive, you accept responsibility for what you will or will not do and for the consequences of your actions. Aggressive people, on the other hand, are irresponsible because they attempt to get what they want by intimidation. This approach may lead to outright refusal or a fight, a consequence the aggressor may not have intended. Aggressive people are less likely to predict or control the outcome of events than assertive people are because they don't take into account others' feelings or reactions. Passive people are also irresponsible because they give control over their lives to others.

As a college student, the more assertive you become, the more likely you are to be successful. As an assertive person, you will ask questions, seek out information, and be able to express clearly to your instructors what you do not understand and what help you need from them.

EXERCISE **6.7**

APPLY WHAT YOU HAVE LEARNED about interpersonal skills by completing this exercise with group members. Remember to follow the guidelines for successful collaboration that appear on the inside back cover. Read the following scenario and, using the questions as a guide, discuss how Jack and Bonita could improve their relationship. When you arrive at consensus, record your answers on the lines provided. Then evaluate your work.

Jack was exhausted. He had three college courses on Mondays and worked the lunch shift at the cafeteria. Then he had to rush to pick up his girlfriend Bonita at her part-time nursing job. Today Bonita seemed particularly disgruntled. "I hate the hospital. I hate my supervisors," she said. "I just want to be home practicing my guitar."

"Your supervisors work hard all day, too," Jack snapped.

(Continued)

"Why don't we stop for coffee on the way home?" asked Bonita.

Jack sighed and answered, "Not today. I have a paper to finish. And maybe you should spend some time on those job applications."

Bonita turned her back and looked out the window.

1. At what point could Jack have listened more actively to what Bonita was saying?

_____

_____

2. What could Jack have said to start a positive conversation with Bonita?

_____

_____

3. How could Bonita have been supportive of her boyfriend?

_____

_____

4. How could Jack and Bonita have spent time together before going home to do their work?

_____

_____

Group Evaluation:

Evaluate your discussion. Did everyone contribute? Did you accomplish your task successfully? What additional questions do you have about interpersonal relationships? How will you find answers to your questions?

_____

_____

EXERCISE **6.8**

THE FOLLOWING IS A LIST of behaviors typical of assertive people. Put a check beside those that are typical of you. For any behaviors that you did not check, summarize on the lines that follow why you would or would not feel comfortable engaging in those behaviors.

Assertive people:

☐ **1. Turn down invitations without feeling guilty**

☐ **2. Politely refuse offers of food or drink if they don't want it**

☐ **3. Do not let themselves be talked into doing something that goes against their values**

☐ **4. Make choices and decisions based on what they think is the right thing to do**

☐ 5. **Have little difficulty saying *no***

☐ 6. **Reserve the right to express their opinions while respecting others' rights to do the same**

☐ 7. **Reserve the right to change their opinions**

☐ 8. **Are not afraid to speak up, ask questions, or seek information**

☐ 9. **Are not afraid to make mistakes or to take action to correct them**

☐ 10. **Do not feel compelled to share others' feelings, beliefs, or values that go against their own**

_____

_____

_____

_____

Making Friends

COLLEGE OFFERS THE opportunity to build new relationships and to test old ones. Your well-being depends, in part, on the relationships you are able to establish and maintain. When you are new in college, you may have trouble meeting people at first, but don't be discouraged. Many students are in the same situation as you are, and they are just as eager to make friends. In the student center or cafeteria, resist the temptation to sit by yourself. Join a group at a table and introduce yourself. Offer to exchange phone numbers with one or two people in each of your classes so that you can compare notes if one of you should be absent. Participate in as many campus activities as you can. You will meet people who share your interests, which is the basis of any long-lasting relationship. If you live in a residence hall, introduce yourself to the students living on either side of you and across the hall. Invite someone to go home with you one weekend. As you extend these offers of friendship to others, you will find them responding to you with similar offers of their own.

Friends offer support and companionship and are an important part of your college experience.

© Richard Lord/PhotoEdit

EXERCISE **6.9**

COLLEGE OFFERS A VARIETY OF situations and settings for meeting new people. But college students often spend hours in solitary studying and miss out on or ignore many opportunities for socializing. Imagine that you are a new transfer student at your college and don't know a soul. How would you go about meeting new people? Using your student handbook, college newspaper or web site, student bulletin, and posted flyers as resources, list places and situations for meeting new people. Find examples in the following three categories.

1. Academic activities

_____
_____
_____

2. Social events

_____
_____
_____

3. Recreational activities

_____
_____
_____

Are you the kind of person who meets new people easily, or do you take a long time to "warm up" to someone? Think about the three newest friends in your life. Describe where and how you met these people. Can you draw a conclusion about what kinds of situations you find most conducive to meeting new friends? Write your conclusion in one or two sentences.

Friend 1:_____
_____

Friend 2:_____
_____

Friend 3:_____
_____

Conclusion:_____
_____
_____
_____

Your Sexuality

SEX TAKES A relationship to a new level of physical and emotional intimacy. Whatever your sexual orientation, you probably want the same thing that most people want from an intimate relationship: mutual acceptance, trust, respect, and—given the prevalence of sexually-transmitted disease (STD)—honesty about past relationships. Although some people may profess a desire for recreational sex or sex without emotional intimacy or commitment, the truth is that sex is rarely, if ever, "just physical" for both people involved. Sexual behavior carries with it emotional issues of self-esteem, self-respect, and self-confidence. Moral values and ethics, too, play an important role. In fact, the kind of person you are and your character—or lack of it—are revealed in the way you handle *all* your relationships. Here are some guidelines to follow:

- **Don't rush sex.** If you become physically involved with someone for whom you don't feel real affection, you will probably suffer a loss of self-esteem.

- **Listen to your feelings.** Anxiety before sex, guilt afterwards, and a lack of desire or pleasurable feeling at any point along the way signal that something is wrong.

- **Stand by your values.** Don't let someone pressure you into any type of sexual activity if you don't want it or if it goes against your morals, and

In an intimate relationship, you should expect to give and to get acceptance, trust, and respect.

© Jim Whitmer

Figure 6.2	Contraceptive Methods and Their Effectiveness Rates	

METHOD	EFFECTIVENESS RATE
Oral contraceptive	97–99%
Intrauterine device (IUD)	94–98
Condom	90
Diaphragm	80–95
Cervical cap	80–90
Spermicidal creams, foams, jellies	75–80
Natural family planning (refraining from sexual intercourse during a woman's period of ovulation)	80
Coitus interruptus (withdrawal before ejaculation)	80

don't pressure others. Sexual activity should be mutually desired by both partners. Anything less is sexual harassment or acquaintance rape.

- **Practice safe sex.** Take precautions to avoid pregnancy and disease. Either of these can limit your possibilities for the future. Figure 6.2 lists contraceptives and their effectiveness rates, which are based on consistent use according to directions. Remember that no birth control method, short of abstinence, is 100 percent effective. To guard against STDs, condoms offer some protection, but, again, they are not 100 percent reliable. Your risk of contracting an STD increases with the number of sexual partners you have had. If you and your partner are honest about past relationships, you will both be in a better position to make a wise decision about whether to become sexually involved.

Understanding Acquaintance Rape

Acquaintance rape is forced sexual intercourse involving people who know each other. Studies done on campuses place the percentage of women who may become the victims of rape or attempted rape before they graduate at anywhere from 15 to 35 percent.

In any discussion of acquaintance rape, you need to keep in mind three things. Rape is a crime, no matter who is involved. A person who forces sexual intercourse on an acquaintance is just as guilty of a crime as someone who sexually assaults a stranger. Second, a person has a right to say *no* to sex at any point during a date or in a relationship, regardless of any previous sexual activity that may have occurred. Finally, because alcohol lowers inhibitions, acquaintance rape may be more likely to occur in situations where one or both parties involved may have had too much to drink. The following guidelines should serve as a first step toward acquaintance rape prevention:

- **Set standards for sexual conduct.** Decide how far you will go both physically and emotionally before getting involved with someone.

- **Communicate with each other.** Talk with each other about your expectations. Don't expect your partner to read your mind. Sex is too important to leave to chance.

- **Stand your ground.** If you don't want to respond to someone's sexual advances, your responsibility is to be assertive. Say *no* and mean it. Don't be hesitant, and don't back down. Even if you *do* want to have sex, your responsibility is to listen when your date says *no* and to believe that *no* means *no,* even if your date's nonverbal signals seem to say *yes.*

- **Treat each other with respect.** You have a right to your opinions and should trust your feelings. When something feels wrong, it probably is. Demand respect from your partner. At the same time, respect his or her choices as well. Don't let sexist notions or social pressures determine your behavior. Stick to your standards.

If you are a victim of rape, realize that you are not at fault and that you have options. Seek help immediately. Get medical attention. Do not shower, douche, or change clothes. Then call the police. To help yourself cope with the aftereffects of sexual assault—which may include nightmares, depression, mood swings, feelings of guilt or shame, and various physical symptoms—call a rape crisis center.

Dealing with Sexual Harassment

Sexual harassment is any kind of unwanted teasing, touching, or inappropriate remarks. Sexist jokes, sexist remarks, unwanted touching, or unwelcome requests for sexual favors are forms of sexual harassment and are inappropriate behaviors in any relationship. Your college probably has a policy on sexual harassment, which may be stated in a pamphlet, student handbook, or college catalog or on a web site. Your college may have a designated advisor or other official on campus who deals with sexual harassment issues and complaints.

Once sexual harassment starts, it will probably continue until you demand that it stop. Dropping a course to get away from an offending professor or changing your major because you are the recipient of sexist remarks and behaviors are ineffective ways of coping with sexual harassment. Instead, you should speak up at the first sign of sexism and confront the harasser by making it clear that you want the behavior to end. Don't keep sexual harassment to yourself. Talk to an advisor or report the behavior to the person at your college who handles complaints of sexual harassment. Make sure you have kept a record of the date, time, and place where the harassment occurred and of those people present who can act as witnesses.

Sexual harassment is everyone's problem, and creating a friendly, nonsexist environment is everyone's responsibility. Speaking out against sexism is one way students can let professors and each other know that sexism has no place in the classroom or on the campus.

thinking *ahead*

What practical knowledge have you gained from this chapter that you can use to solve real-world problems? To find out, read this scenario and complete the items that follow it.

After high school, Wes attended a technical college, where he prepared for a career in the building industry. He now works for a company that makes cabinets. Lately, he has begun stopping off at a bar after work with two of his buddies. At first, he had one or two beers, then went home to his family. Evenings were a special time when Wes and his wife would play with their children, feed them dinner, and put them to bed. Then Wes and his wife could spend time together.

But recently his after-work drink with the guys has been getting out of hand. Now Wes has several beers, stays later and later, and is missing dinner and playtime with his family. His wife is angry and says so, which makes Wes angry. He snaps at her and the kids. To compound these problems, he often wakes up with a hangover.

Wes knows he must do something. Not only is he afraid of losing his family, but he also worries about driving under the influence. He'd like to stop going out after work, but he wonders how the guys would feel. Would they think he's a wimp? Would his abstinence affect his relations at work? He needs the job and likes the company and his coworkers. What can Wes do?

1. State Wes's problem as you see it.

_____

_____

_____

2. What are Wes's options?

_____

_____

_____

3. What are the advantages and disadvantages of these options?

_____

_____

_____

4. What solution would you recommend, and why?

_____

_____

_____

chapter review

To review the chapter, reflect on the following confidence-building attitudes, complete **Concepts to Understand**, and practice your new skills at every opportunity.

ATTITUDES TO DEVELOP

- personal responsibility
- willingness to change
- willingness to seek help

CONCEPTS TO UNDERSTAND

Your health and well-being are within your power to control, and they affect your ability to do well in college. Successful adjustment depends on achieving a balance among your _____, _____, and _____ needs. This chapter suggests ways to maintain good health and increase your well-being.

To become healthy and stay healthy, choose a _____ diet that includes a variety of foods and is low in _____. Become physically fit following a fitness program you can live with that includes _____ exercises such as running or swimming. Learn to manage _____ by first determining what circumstances and conditions make you feel stressed, then by trying the stress beaters suggested in this chapter. Avoid using harmful substances such as illegal drugs, alcohol, nicotine, and caffeine.

To increase your well-being, learn to take control of your _____ by understanding your feelings, leading a purposeful life, and accepting the need for change. To improve your relationships, try these five strategies:

1. _____ to your friends and important others.
2. Converse and have fun with them.
3. Be _____ of them.
4. Take advantage of the opportunity college offers for making new friends.
5. Be _____ about what you want.

Protect yourself by making good decisions about sexual behavior. Practice safe sex, reduce your risk of date rape, deal assertively with sexual harassment, and avoid unwanted pregnancy.

To access additional review exercises, see http://college.hmco.com/success.

SKILLS TO PRACTICE

- making wise choices about health
- controlling your emotions
- interacting with others
- being assertive

Your Reflections

Your Reflections

Reflect on what you have learned about maintaining your health and well-being and how you can best apply that information. Use the following list of questions to stimulate your thinking; then write your reflections. Your response may include answers to one or more of the questions. Incorporate in your writing specific information from this chapter.

- Are you leading a balanced life? Are your physical, emotional, and social selves in balance? Explain.

- Do you have any harmful habits that need changing? If so, what self-improvement goals will you set?

- Of the interpersonal skills on pages 156–157, which is your strongest? Which needs work?

- What relationship do you see between your EQ, as explained on page 155, and your locus of control?

- Of the attitudes and skills listed in the chapter review, which do you think will be most useful at work or in your career?

Creating Your Study System

IS YOUR STUDYING hit or miss? Do you

have trouble deciding what to study

or how much time to spend studying? Did you know

that having a system, especially one that you

adapt to your learning style, can take the

guesswork out of studying?

THE KEYS TO creating your study system are twofold: You need to develop appropriate study skills and to use your learning style. If you have trouble getting started when you sit down to study or have trouble staying with it once you have started, then you probably don't have a reliable *study system* that you consistently use. Studying with a system can transform a burdensome chore into a pleasant task. You can adopt a proven system such as SQ3R, which is explained in this chapter, or you can devise one to fit your learning style and courses.

As explained in Chapter 2, not everyone learns in exactly the same way. As you experiment with study systems, remember that you may prefer a certain learning mode—such as *visual, auditory,* or *tactile*—and that your study system should allow you to use your favorite mode. If you see yourself as a visual learner, for example, your study system may include making diagrams or charts of information you want to remember. Also, your system will work best if you study at the time of day when you are most alert and if you study in your preferred learning environment.

Moreover, a system that you use for college reading and study can be adapted to any workplace learning situation that requires you to read, remember, and use information to develop reports or complete projects.

This chapter explains several strategies that will help you create your study system:

- Identify and use the common parts of textbooks and chapters as convenient study aids.

- Experiment with proven study systems such as SQ3R.

- Devise your own system to meet course requirements or specific learning tasks.

EXERCISE **7.1**

AS A PREREADING EXERCISE, DISCUSS your current study methods with a partner. How do you study from textbooks? How do you review for tests? Do you have a study system? What is one aspect of your studying that you would like to improve or change? Share your thoughts with the rest of the class.

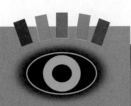

Awareness Check 13

ARE YOU USING YOUR TEXTBOOKS EFFICIENTLY?

Part 1

Can you identify and use the parts of a textbook? Match the textbook parts in Column A to their functions in Column B.

Column A

1. _____ title page
2. _____ copyright page
3. _____ contents
4. _____ introduction
5. _____ glossary
6. _____ index
7. _____ appendix
8. _____ bibliography

Column B

A. contains supplementary material

B. lists topics, terms, names of people, and their page numbers

C. tells when a book was published

D. lists chapter titles, main headings, and page numbers

E. lists author's sources or references

F. tells author's purpose for writing the book

G. identifies title, author, and publisher

H. contains terms and definitions

Part 2

Can you identify and use the common parts of most textbook chapters? Match the chapter parts in Column A to their functions in Column B.

Column A

1. _____ title
2. _____ introduction
3. _____ heading
4. _____ visual aid
5. _____ summary
6. _____ questions and exercises

Column B

A. restates and condenses author's ideas

B. helps explain or illustrate

C. identifies overall topic covered

D. used for review or skill practice

E. identifies section topic or main idea

F. states author's purpose and gives overview

Part 3

Yes	No

Do you have a study system? Respond yes or no to the following statements.

1. When I sit down to read or study, I often have trouble getting started.

2. My studying is hit or miss. I don't have any set way to study; I do it when and if I have time.

3. I underline or highlight when I read.

4. I know how to tell what is important in a chapter.

Check your answers to Part I: 1. G, 2. C, 3. D, 4. F, 5. H, 6. B, 7. A, 8. E. The answers to Part II are 1. C, 2. F, 3. E, 4. B, 5. A, 6. D. In Part III, if you checked yes for statement 1 or 2 and no for statements 3 and 4, you will benefit from learning how to use a study system.

SQ3R: The Basic System

IT'S EASY TO see why students who don't read textbook assignments make poor grades. It may be a little harder to see why students who do read all assigned material may still not make the grades they want. There is a big difference between reading and studying. You can't merely read a chapter from first word to last and expect to retain the information. You must read *actively* by underlining, making notes, asking questions mentally, and then looking for the answers. Studying with a system guides your reading so that you can find the information you need to complete assignments and prepare for tests.

Perhaps you've heard of SQ3R. Developed by Francis P. Robinson in 1941, SQ3R is a classic system that is still in use. Millions of students have successfully used SQ3R's five steps, or a variation of them, to improve their reading and studying. Before reading the detailed explanation of each step, see Figure 7.1 for an overview of the system.

Survey

A *survey* is a quick review or brief overview of an entire textbook or a single chapter. You can survey a textbook in about ten minutes, and you need do it only once to determine what it covers and what helpful aids it contains. This knowledge will help you begin your courses with confidence. Surveying also has a practical advantage beyond the classroom. You can survey *any* book that you are thinking of

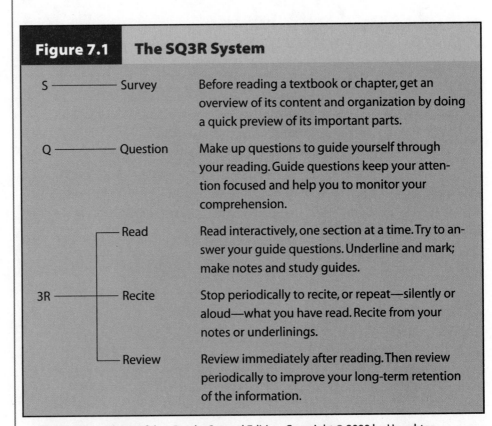

Figure 7.1	The SQ3R System
S —— Survey	Before reading a textbook or chapter, get an overview of its content and organization by doing a quick preview of its important parts.
Q —— Question	Make up questions to guide yourself through your reading. Guide questions keep your attention focused and help you to monitor your comprehension.
3R —— Read	Read interactively, one section at a time. Try to answer your guide questions. Underline and mark; make notes and study guides.
Recite	Stop periodically to recite, or repeat—silently or aloud—what you have read. Recite from your notes or underlinings.
Review	Review immediately after reading. Then review periodically to improve your long-term retention of the information.

Carol C. Kanar, *The Confident Reader,* Second Edition. Copyright © 2000 by Houghton Mifflin Company. Reprinted by permission.

buying. To survey a work of fiction, read the title and the plot summary to get an idea of what it is about. The plot summary appears on the back of a paperback or inside the jacket of a hardcover book. Read any comments from reviewers to find out what they think of the book. Read the first paragraph to see if the author's style and subject matter arouse your interest. Your survey will help you determine whether you want to read the book. You can also survey books online at sites like http://www.amazon.com or http://www.barnesandnoble.com

Surveying also has a practical application in the workplace, where a significant amount of information processing occurs. Surveying an article or other printed matter is a quick way to assess its importance or usefulness.

How to Survey a Textbook. Survey a textbook one time only—as soon as you buy it—before the first chapter is assigned. Then you can start the class with

Figure 7.2	**How to Survey a Textbook—Features and Purposes**	
TEXTBOOK FEATURE	**PURPOSE**	**HOW TO SURVEY**
Title Page	Lists title, author, publisher	Look at the title. Ask yourself what the book is about. Find out what you can about the author's qualifications, such as his or her college affiliation or degrees.
Copyright Page	Tells when book was published	Look at the copyright date to see how recent the book is and how many editions there have been. (If the book is in its second edition, it has been updated once.)
Introduction (Preface, To the Student)	Tells author's purpose and audience	Read the introduction to find out why the author wrote the book, for whom, and what the author expects readers to learn. The author may also explain how to use the book.
Table of Contents	Lists parts and chapters	Look over the contents to see what topics are covered. Be thinking about how these topics relate to your course.
Glossary	Lists special words, terms, and definitions	Look for a glossary. If there is one, you should use it for looking up words and terms to learn any special meanings the writer wants you to know.
Appendix	Contains material that supplements topics covered	Look for an appendix to see what additional materials the author has included.
Bibliography	Lists sources the author consulted to write the book	Look for a bibliography. You may need to refer to it later if you need more information.
Index	Lists author's topics alphabetically and their page numbers	Look at the end of the book for the index and use it when you need to find a topic quickly.

Carol C. Kanar, *The Confident Reader,* Second Edition. Copyright © 2000 by Houghton Mifflin Company. Reprinted by permission.

an advantage: You will already know what topics the course is likely to cover. You will also have determined which of the eight common parts your textbook has and how they may be useful to you. For example, if you are taking a biology course and you find out by surveying your textbook that the book has a glossary, then you know that you will be able to save time while studying. It is much quicker and easier to look up specialized terms in a glossary than in a dictionary. Also, glossary definitions fit the author's use of terms within the context of a book's subject matter.

To survey a textbook, examine its parts in the order in which they appear as you leaf through the book from beginning to end. Figure 7.2 on page 171 lists features common to most textbooks, their purposes, and how to survey them. See also Figures 7.3 and 7.4, which illustrate these common textbook parts: title page, copyright page, preface, and table of contents.

How to Survey a Textbook Chapter. Survey a chapter before you read it for the first time. Then resurvey chapters that you are reviewing for a major exam. Resurveying material that you have not read for a while will refresh your memory.

| Figure 7.3 | **Sample Title Page (left) and Copyright Page (right)** |

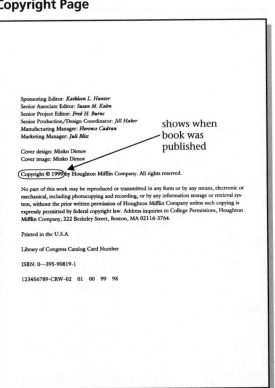

Barry L. Reece and Rhonda Brandt, *Effective Human Relations in Organizations,* Sixth Edition. Copyright © 1996 by Houghton Mifflin Company. Reprinted by permission.

Figure 7.4   **Sample Preface (left) and Table of Contents (right)**

Preface

PREFACE

TO THE STUDENT

The purpose of this textbook is to introduce you to the basic facts and principles of chemistry. Chemistry is a vital and dynamic science. It is of fundamental importance not only to all the other sciences and modern technology but also to any explanation of the material things around us. Consider these diverse questions. What is the environmental role of ozone in the earth's atmosphere? What is responsible for the red color of Io, one of Jupiter's moons? And finally, how can we see inside the brain of a patient without doing harm? All of these questions involve chemistry, and they are just some of the questions you will explore in your reading of this text. I hope I have piqued your curiosity. In your study of general chemistry, you will discover many things, but ultimately you will find that there is so much more to learn and that it is exciting to discover and to question.

The challenge to any author of a general chemistry text is to present a solid understanding of the basic facts and principles of chemistry while retaining the excitement of the subject. I feel strongly that the way to do this is by constantly relating the subject matter to real substances and problems in the real world. We begin the study of chemistry with the discovery of the anticancer activity of a bright yellow substance called cisplatin. We use this discovery to illustrate the introductory ideas presented. In Chapter 2, we start by looking at sodium (a soft, reactive metal) and chlorine (a pale green gas) and the reaction between them to produce sodium chloride (ordinary table salt). Each of these substances is quite different, and the reaction, which is shown in an accompanying photograph, is a dramatic example of the transformation that occurs when substances react. With this vivid picture in mind, we go on to explain substances and chemical reactions in terms of atomic theory. In each chapter, wherever we introduce basic principles of chemistry, we keep close contact with the world of real chemical substances and their everyday applications.

Table of Contents

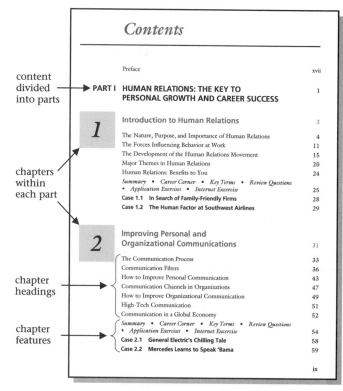

chapters within each part

chapter headings

chapter features

left: Darrell Ebbing, *General Chemistry,* Fifth Edition. Copyright © 1993 by Houghton Mifflin Company. Used with permission.

right: Barry L. Reece and Rhonda Brandt, *Effective Human Relations in Organizations,* Sixth Edition. Copyright © 1996 by Houghton Mifflin Company. Reprinted by permission.

Your chapter survey will not take long, it will focus your attention, and it will help you determine a purpose for reading. To survey a chapter, examine its parts in the order in which they appear. Figure 7.5 lists the parts of most chapters and a purpose for surveying them. (For more detailed information on how to read graphics such as tables, charts, and diagrams, see Chapter 14.)

Surveying helps you make assumptions about what a chapter covers. It is a prereading activity that focuses your attention on a topic. By relating the topic to what you already know, you prepare yourself for the next step in the SQ3R system: asking questions to guide your reading.

Question

During your chapter survey, as you read each heading, turn it into a question. The heading of a section identifies the topic covered in that section and may serve as a clue to the author's main idea. For example, three questions you could ask about

Figure 7.5	**How to Survey a Chapter—Features and Purposes**	

CHAPTER FEATURE	**PURPOSE**	**HOW TO SURVEY**
Title	Tells you what topic the chapter covers	Read title to activate your background knowledge on the topic and create a context for reading.
Objectives or Goals	Tell what the author expects you to learn	Read goals or objectives, if any, to focus your attention on what you need to find out.
Introductory Material	Tells you the author's purpose and central idea	Read first paragraph or introductory section to determine the author's central idea—what the whole chapter explains.
Major Headings and Subheadings	Tell how the central idea is broken down	Read headings and subheadings to reveal the author's organization and major support for the central idea.
Graphic Aids	Illustrate topics or ideas that need clarification	Look over charts, graphs, diagrams, photos, and other visuals.
Key Words and Terms	Call attention to key ideas and concepts	Look for boldface or italicized words or terms. Some may be printed in color or in a different typeface.
Summary	Gives an overview of the author's central idea and supporting information	Read the summary, if there is one, so that you know what to look for when you read the chapter.
Questions or Problems	Ask you to apply concepts or to practice skills covered in the chapter	Read over the questions or problems at the end of the chapter to see what the author expects you to be able to do with the information you have learned.

Carol C. Kanar, *The Confident Reader,* Second Edition. Copyright © 2000 by Houghton Mifflin Company. Reprinted by permission.

the heading "Concentration" are "What is concentration?" "How can I improve my concentration?" and "Why is concentration important?" The "what" question asks you to read for a definition. The "how" and "why" questions stimulate you to think critically about the value of concentration and how to improve it.

Turning headings into questions guides your reading so that you can find important details and examples. Later, as you read each section carefully, try to find the answers to your guide questions. You may discover that some of your questions are off the topic; but even if they are, you will win. Right or wrong, your questions can help you follow the author's ideas and correct errors in your comprehension.

EXERCISE **7.2**

BORROW A TEXTBOOK FROM A friend who is taking a course that you plan to take. Survey the textbook from beginning to end and then respond to the following items.

Book Title: _____

Name of Course: _____

1. **Can you tell from the title whether the book is an introductory text or an advanced text? Explain your answer.**

_____

_____

_____

2. **How current is the information in the text? In what part of the book did you find your answer?**

_____

_____

_____

_____

3. **What is the author's purpose? In what part of the book did you find your answer?**

_____

_____

_____

_____

4. **Where are chapters listed? Write the title of a chapter whose topic interests you.**

_____

_____

_____

5. **Does the book contain a glossary? If so, on what page does it begin?**

_____

_____

_____

6. **Does the book contain a bibliography? If so, on what page does it begin?**

_____

_____

_____

COMPUTER CONFIDENCE

Survey to Save Time on the Net

Surveying is an important prereading step not only for textbooks but for *any* reading you might do. Surveying before reading on the Internet is yet another practical application of this essential prereading strategy. Whether you are reading your email or researching a topic on the Web, surveying is a time-saving first step that will help you sift through irrelevant data to find desired information quickly.

Survey Email

Log on to the Internet and start your mail program. Any new messages are usually listed by date and time, along with the subject lines of their message headers. Survey the subject lines to determine which messages may be urgent and which ones can wait. Then you can decide which messages to read first, saving the rest for a more convenient time.

Survey Web Sites

As an information-gathering and communication tool, the World Wide Web provides access to resources located throughout the world's libraries, universities, and research institutions. You can browse these resources in search of books, periodicals, and other materials. Because resources are so extensive and because not all Internet connections provide access to the Web, tools such as *search engines* and *web indexes* can help you find information quickly.

A *search engine* is a program that collects and indexes information from web pages, allowing you to search the indexes by topic. Using a search engine, you can generate a list of resources on a topic of your choice, survey the list, and select possible sites to visit. To use a search engine, follow these steps:

1. Choose an engine such as AltaVista or Yahoo and go to its web site.

2. Select a few *key words* that describe or relate to your topic.

3. Type your key words in the appropriate area on the engine's web page.

4. Click on *Search* or *Enter*.

These steps will generate a list of web sites that relate to your topic. The list may be extensive, depending on your topic, and some of the sites listed may be better than others. By surveying the list, you should be able to select the sites most likely to provide the information you need. If none of the sites seem appropriate, ask to see additional pages that match your key words or start over using new key words.

EXERCISE **7.3**

TO PRACTICE SURVEYING WEB SITES, try the following two browsing activities. Then discuss your results with the rest of the class.

1. **Many people have web sites and home pages. Find someone on the Net. Choose a person who interests you: an athlete, an entertainer, a senator or representative, an artist, or an author. Survey the information that is available on the person of your choice, read what interests you, and write a brief summary of it. If you need help getting started, see your instructor or visit your college's computer or media center.**

2. **Most colleges and universities have web sites. A university's home page is a directory to the information available on the site. Find the home page of a university of your choice; then survey the home page to find out what information or courses are offered to help students improve their learning and study skills. If the institution you chose has no such information or courses, try another one. Report your findings to the rest of the class.**

EXERCISE **7.4**

THE PURPOSE OF THIS EXERCISE is for you to practice surveying a textbook chapter with group members. Follow the guidelines for successful collaboration that appear on the inside back cover. Your tasks are as follows: Select a chapter to survey from Part 2 of *The Confident Student*. Each person must survey the chapter and write answers to items 1–7 within a time limit of ten minutes. Let one group member serve as timekeeper. Discuss your answers, resolving any differences of opinion to arrive at consensus. Your best answers should be recorded on a separate sheet of paper to be handed in along with the group evaluation.

Chapter Title: _____

1. What are the chapter goals or objectives? _____

_____

_____

_____

2. According to the introductory section or paragraph, how will the information contained in this chapter help you? _____

_____

_____

_____

(Continued)

3. List three major headings and turn each one into a question to guide your reading.

Headings   Questions

_____   _____

_____   _____

_____   _____

4. How many visual aids are there? What kind?

_____

_____

5. List two key words or terms that you should remember.

_____

_____

6. List a major point that is emphasized in the summary.

_____

_____

7. What skill or topic is covered in the first exercise?

_____

_____

Group Evaluation:

What have you learned about surveying? Is surveying a strategy that you will use? Why or why not? Did your group complete its tasks successfully? What improvements can you suggest? How will you find answers to your questions?

_____

_____

Read

Read slowly and carefully, concentrating on one section at a time. Don't worry about how long you take. Although you may wish you could read faster, it takes time to absorb new ideas. Do not skip unfamiliar words or technical terms. If you can't infer their meanings from context, look them up in the book's glossary or in a dictionary. Then, be sure to reread the sentence in which each new word appears to make sure that you understand it. Carefully examine each diagram, chart, illustration, table, or other visual aid. Often, ideas that are hard to understand when you first read about them are easier to comprehend in a diagram or other graphic.

After reading, try to determine the main idea of the section. Summarize this idea in a marginal note that will aid your recall when you review. Read through

Before you sign up for a course, visit the campus bookstore to survey the text the instructor has chosen. This will enable you to see what the course will cover and whether the level of the material is suited to your background and skills.

the section again and underline the main idea and key details or examples. If you have difficulty deciding what is important, see Chapter 13 for a complete explanation of how and what to underline or highlight.

If a section seems particularly technical or complex, you may have to read it more than once. You may also have to restate the author's ideas in your own words to get the information into your long-term memory. Chapter 8 explains how to make study guides to aid your recall.

Making notes, underlining or highlighting, and constructing study guides are essential steps of active reading. They help you think critically about what you read, they make studying a productive activity, and they enhance memory.

Recite

Recitation is an essential aid to memory. After reading a section, try to state—aloud or silently—the important ideas covered in that section. If you find this hard to do, you probably have not understood the section and need to reread it. However, if the important ideas stand out, then you are probably comprehending what you read. Reciting not only increases your memory's power; it also helps you monitor your comprehension.

Review

Review a chapter immediately after reading it. One quick way to review it is by resurveying the chapter. Go over any notes you made in the margins and see if they still make sense to you. Reread any underlined or highlighted passages. Also, review a chapter before you take a test. It is a good idea to review a chapter at least once between your first reading and your last pre-test review. With practice, you will discover how often you must review a chapter in order to keep the information in your long-term memory.

EXERCISE **7.5**

THE SQ3R READING AND STUDY system is taught at most colleges and universities, either in reading courses or in student success courses. Find out more about SQ3R online. Use these key words as a starting point: *SQ3R, study skills,* and *study systems.* See also http://college.hmco.com/success.

CONFIDENCE
Builder

Be Proactive About Studying

Stephen R. Covey, author of *The Seven Habits of Highly Effective People,* says that people are either proactive or reactive in their responses to life's circumstances. *Proactive* people take initiative and accept responsibility for what happens to them. *Reactive* people lack initiative; instead of taking responsibility for what happens, they blame other people or outside events. The first and most important of Covey's seven habits is to *be proactive.* Being proactive means being in control of how you feel, what you think, and what you do. Being proactive means accepting responsibility for your own success or failure. Being proactive also means choosing your actions, accepting the consequences, and modifying your behavior as needed to achieve success.

When it comes to studying, are you *reactive* or *proactive*? Language is a key. The language of reactive people, according to Covey, relieves them of responsibility. For example, if you say, "I can't make a good grade in that class," then you are saying that you are not responsible. Rather, someone or something is preventing you from making good grades in the class. If you say, "I don't have time to study" instead of managing your time, you are allowing the factor of limited time to control you. If you say, "I have to study," then you mean that you are not free to choose this action; instead, someone or something is forcing you to do it.

To be proactive about studying, you must first take control of your language. The following is an example of how language can either limit or expand your horizons. When you say, "I can't make a good grade in that class," you convince yourself that there is no reason to try. As a result, you give up. You stop studying. The belief that you can't make a good grade becomes a self-fulfilling prophecy. But if you become proactive and instead say, "I choose to make good grades in that class," then you realize that grades are the result of your own decisions and your own effort. You can then accurately assess what your strengths and weaknesses are and choose appropriate study systems or strategies that will get you the results that you want.

The following chart lists reactive statements about studying and their proactive counterparts. Use the chart to assess your own language. Ask yourself, "Am I reactive or proactive?" Then take steps to modify your language and behavior as needed.

Reactive Statements	Proactive Statements
I don't have time to study.	I can make time for studying.
I have to study.	I can choose whether, when, and how to study.
I must pass this test.	I will study and do my best to pass this test.
I'm just no good at math.	I can improve my math skills.
I can't understand this chapter.	I will use a study system to understand this chapter.
My instructor gave me a B on the test.	I earned a B on the test.

How does Covey's advice, *be proactive*, relate to locus of control? Those who have an external locus of control are *reactive* because they expect others to motivate them. Those who have an internal locus of control are *proactive* because they are self-motivated. How does proactivity relate to goal setting, time management, and problem solving? In every case, the proactive response of selecting a desired outcome and taking the steps necessary to achieve it puts *you* in control of your life and learning. With control comes confidence and increased self-esteem.

To pursue this topic further, do an online search using the key words *Stephen R. Covey, Seven Habits of Highly Effective People, motivation,* and *values.*

CRITICAL THINKING

Think about the courses you are taking, the difficulty level of the textbooks, the types of tests and assignments required, and the problems and successes you have had in meeting course objectives. Then select one course. Devise a plan that will help you be proactive about learning the kinds of information taught in that course. Summarize your results in writing.

Devising Your Study System

NO ONE HAS discovered the best way to learn because no system works for everyone all the time. What is best for *you*—what helps *you* read, study, and remember information—depends on your learning style. Commitment and consistency are the study attitudes that lead to success in college. Finding a study system that works, making a commitment to learn, and using your system consistently are much more important than which particular system you use. Also, don't expect instant improvement. Give your system time to work, be persistent, and improvement will come. Most study systems are variations on the basic one, SQ3R. Try SQ3R first and see if it works for you. Or use it as a starting point to create your own study system by varying the steps to fit your preferred way of learning and the material that you need to study.

For Mathematics Courses

Add a *practice* step for solving problems. In math courses you learn mathematical operations and procedures. To master them, you must practice, so doing the practice exercises in your math textbook is an essential part of studying for the course. Before you start a new assignment, review the previous one since each new skill or concept builds on previously learned skills or concepts. Don't attempt to do the exercises in a new chapter until you have first read the chapter and studied the example problems.

Your *review* step in a math course should include a review of mathematical terms. Math has a specialized vocabulary. Every chapter in a math textbook is filled with new terms to learn. In fact, terms and definitions often appear in bold type, italics, or a special color. As you read a chapter, make a list of terms and definitions. When you study, review your list. Many students who have done well in math courses say that learning the language of math has been an important key to their success.

Your studying for a math class will be most productive if you do it as soon after the class meets as possible, while explanations are still fresh in your mind.

For Science Courses

Add a *draw* step to supply a visual mode for getting information into your long-term memory. Make your own diagrams of processes and concepts such as reproduction and food chains. Draw organisms and label their parts. Your diagram of a complex process may be easier for you to remember than a list of the steps would be. When you recite, describe processes and state principles in your own words. If your preferred mode of learning is auditory, recitation will be an important step for you. You'll find it easier to retrieve your own words from memory during an exam than to recall someone else's words that you have memorized. Make flash cards of specialized terms to recite from and review.

For Literature Courses

Expand the recite and review steps of SQ3R to include *interpret, evaluate,* and *write.* In a literature course you must interpret the theme of a story, the meaning of a poem, or the development of a character, and you must evaluate the worth or literary merit of what you have read. Put your thoughts in writing to prepare for papers and essay exams. Underlining and marking your book can help you remember the characters and events of a story or a novel. Mark words and phrases that identify characters or suggest a theme. Write plot summaries of stories. Make flash cards of important literary terms. Write a brief statement of your interpretation of a poem's meaning. While reading literary criticism, summarize in your own words the critic's evaluation of the story, poem, or novel. Then write your own evaluation of the significance of the literary work that you are studying.

For Foreign Language Courses

As in math courses, *practice* exercises are an essential part of studying a foreign language. Exercises help you learn new words, verb conjugations, and parts of speech. They also provide practice in using words in different contexts so that you can develop your skill in forming sentences and translating from one language to another. Follow a regular study routine. Review the previous chapter, read the new chapter, and then do the practice exercises as soon as possible after your class has met. Spend a lot of time reciting new words and meanings and drilling yourself on verb conjugations through all the tenses. To the *review* step of SQ3R, add making flash cards for terms and conjugation charts for verbs. Recite from these and use them to review for tests.

For Social Science Courses

When you underline and mark during the *read* step, focus on theories and principles of behavior and research findings that support a certain theory. Make charts to compare theories and recite from your charts.

Other ways to vary SQ3R may take into account whether you prefer to study alone or with someone else and whether you prefer visual, verbal, auditory, or tactile modes of learning. For example, if you prefer to study with someone, do your surveying, questioning, and reading on your own but recite and review with a study partner. If you prefer auditory modes of instruction, tape the material you want to review—a list of vocabulary words and definitions, for example—and then listen to the tape. If you prefer visual modes of learning, make charts, diagrams, and illustrations for review. If taking notes from textbooks and outlining information that you need to remember are strategies that work for you, by all means, use them. You will have to resort to these strategies if you are studying from library books or materials your professor has put on reserve.

As part of your review for any course, *connect* and *reflect.* Make connections between what you already know and what you have learned. How does what you are learning add to or change what you already know? Reflect on ways in which you can use new information or apply it in different contexts. For example, use the research and writing skills acquired in a composition class to write papers and compile reports due in other classes. Use the information learned in one course as a source of topics for writing papers in other courses. The interpersonal skills that you learn in a business course may improve your relations with others at work. The skills learned in an accounting course may help you improve the way you keep track of your spending. Through connection and reflection, you can personalize what you have learned, making the information your own so that you are less likely to forget it.

Once you have settled on a study system that works, use it consistently. Knowing that you have a study system will make you feel confident that you can learn and remember. Also, if you are like many students and have trouble getting started when you try to study, a study system will provide the starting point you need. Figure 7.6 is a summary of ways to vary the SQ3R study system to meet specific course needs. It shows that surveying, questioning, and reading, reciting, and reviewing are essential for studying every subject. Variations in the system can be made in the way you apply the steps or in the addition of a step. As you become more comfortable using a study system, you will think of many more variations. Some of them may be better for you than those suggested in this chapter because they will be based on your learning style.

Figure 7.6	How to Vary the SQ3R Study System	

COURSE	WHAT TO STUDY	YOUR SYSTEM
Math	Sample problems and exercises	Add a *practice* step for solving problems.
Literature	Elements of fiction: plot, characters, point of view, theme, style, and tone	Expand *recite* and *review* to include *interpret, evaluate,* and *write.*
Science	Facts, processes, and principles	Add a *draw* step to illustrate principles and processes.
Foreign languages	Words, meanings, pronunciations, and tenses	Add flash cards and conjugation charts to your *review* step.
Social sciences	Theories and principles of behavior and the people who developed them	Add underlining and marking to the *read* step; make charts to compare theories and record data.

EXERCISE **7.6**

DO YOU KNOW WHAT TO study for your courses? List the courses that you are taking and the kinds of information that you are expected to learn. To help yourself with this exercise, look at the assignments you have been doing for these courses and at your old tests.

Course

Information

Now, find the type of information you listed in the "What to Study" column in Figure 7.6. Look at the "Your System" column for ways to build the best study system for yourself.

EXERCISE 7.7

READ THE NEXT ASSIGNED CHAPTER in one of your textbooks and try out the SQ3R study system. When you have finished, answer the following questions.

Yes   No

☐   ☐   1. **Did surveying the chapter before reading it give you an idea of what the chapter would cover?**

☐   ☐   2. **Were you able to formulate questions from the headings to guide your reading?**

☐   ☐   3. **Did you find answers to most of your questions as you read each section?**

☐   ☐   4. **After doing the reading, did you know what to underline?**

☐   ☐   5. **Did you make any marginal notes?**

☐   ☐   6. **Did you find any material that would be easier to understand if you were to diagram it to make it more visual?**

☐   ☐   7. **After reciting and reviewing, did you have a thorough understanding of the information contained in the chapter?**

☐   ☐   8. **Did you vary the SQ3R system? If so, how and why?**

☐   ☐   9. **Given your learning style, is SQ3R an effective system for you? Why or why not?**

☐   ☐   10. **How can you adapt SQ3R to fit your learning style?**

thinking *ahead*

What practical knowledge have you gained from this chapter that you can use to solve real-world problems? To find out, read this scenario and complete the items that follow it:

To support himself while attending college, Samuel works as a research assistant at a local newspaper. His job is to research a topic, read relevant articles and reports, and then summarize them for his boss. Samuel has good library and Internet skills, so he has no trouble finding the information he needs. However, reading the articles is difficult for him. Samuel loses interest in some of the topics, and he always has trouble remembering what he has read. He spends a lot of time rereading material, so it takes him forever to get his work done. He is worried that his college assignments may suffer as a result. "You need a reading system," said a friend of his. "Why?" asked Samuel. "Reading is reading."

1. What is Samuel's problem?

_____

_____

_____

_____

2. What are Samuel's strengths?

_____

_____

_____

_____

3. Which of Samuel's strategies seem to be ineffective?

_____

_____

_____

_____

4. What strategies would you suggest that Samuel try and why?

_____

_____

_____

_____

chapter review

To review the chapter, reflect on the following confidence-building attitudes, complete Concepts to Understand, and practice your new skills at every opportunity.

ATTITUDES TO DEVELOP

- commitment to learning
- consistency of effort
- willingness to persist

CONCEPTS TO UNDERSTAND

Making graphic aids of material that you want to remember is especially helpful if your preferred learning style is _____. Remember, too, that the best study system is one which you create that takes into account the characteristics of your _____ _____ and the kind of information you need to remember.

Depending on how you use them, your textbooks can be either indispensable tools or dead weight in your backpack. To get the most out of your textbooks and their individual chapters, become familiar with their common parts, and _____ them before you begin to study.

Use textbook parts to help you find information you need. For example, look up a topic in the _____ quickly and easily instead of wasting time flipping through the pages of the text to find it. Use the parts of a chapter to form questions in your mind to guide your reading.

In addition to knowing how to use your books and how the information they contain is organized, you need a study system to help you understand and remember what you read. _____ is only one of many systems. The best system for you is one that works, whether you adopt someone else's or create your own.

To access additional review exercises, see http://college.hmco.com/success.

SKILLS TO PRACTICE

- using textbook and chapter study aids
- using the SQ3R system
- creating your own system

Your Reflections

Your Reflections

Reflect on what you have learned about study systems and how you can best apply that information. Use the following list of questions to stimulate your thinking; then write your reflections. Your response may include answers to one or more of the questions. Incorporate in your writing specific information from this chapter.

- Evaluate the study system you now use. What works, what doesn't work, and why?

- What is your most demanding course? What have you learned from this chapter that will help you improve the way you study for that course?

- Are you taking a course that is not covered on pages 182–183? How can you adapt SQ3R to meet the needs of this course?

- How do you plan to use this chapter's information to create your most effective study system?

- Of all the attitudes and skills listed in the chapter review, which do you think will be most useful at work or in your career?

8

Organizing Information for Study

DO YOU STUDY efficiently by reviewing the most important information? Do you know that you can make study guides that condense and organize information in meaningful ways? Do you realize how convenient it is to study anytime, anywhere, using your own study guides?

MEMORIZING LISTS OF facts, concepts, and other important information may not be the most effective way to study. For example, you could memorize the definitions of the terms *id, ego,* and *superego,* but would that help you understand Freud's theory of personality and how the id, ego, and superego interact to affect human behavior? Would learning only the definitions of Freud's terms help you to explain how Freud's theory compares to other personality theories or what the limitations of his theory are? Probably not.

One good way to study Freud's theory is to make a chart that lists his components of personality, a brief explanation of each, and an example showing how each affects behavior. In making such a chart, what have you done? You have restructured the information in a format that gives it meaning. Your chart is called an *organizer,* of which there are many types.

Diagrams, charts, and other organizers have three advantages. First, they condense information into smaller, meaningful chunks that are easier to remember than an author's exact words. Second, they help you visualize relationships among ideas. Third, the process of deciding what is important and choosing the best organizer for your purpose builds organizational and decision-making skills essential for success in college and career.

This chapter explains how to make six types of organizers for efficient and productive study:

- Concept or information maps
- Comparison charts
- Time lines
- Process diagrams
- Informal outlines
- Branching diagrams

Awareness Check 14

HOW WELL DO YOU ORGANIZE INFORMATION FOR STUDY?

The following Awareness Check will help you determine whether you are getting all the information you can out of your textbooks and using it effectively for studying, remembering, and recalling what you have learned. Check the statements that apply to you.

- [ ] 1. Part of my textbook study includes making some type of study guide to help myself remember important information.

- [ ] 2. I rarely, if ever, outline chapters or make study guides.

- [ ] 3. When I make notes from textbooks, I don't copy the information directly; I put it into my own words.

- [ ] 4. If I make notes, I usually copy directly from the text.

☐ 5. I have tried or heard about information maps and other ways of organizing information.

☐ 6. I am not aware of ways to organize information. I study by rereading textbook chapters or reviewing my lecture notes.

☐ 7. I can usually decide what is important in a chapter, and that is what I study.

☐ 8. I have difficulty deciding what is important in a chapter, so I try to study all of it.

☐ 9. Overall, I would say that my method of studying from textbooks is effective.

☐ 10. Overall, I think that my method of studying from textbooks needs improvement.

If you checked mostly odd-numbered statements, you probably are already using an effective method of organizing information from textbooks. If you checked mostly even-numbered statements, you may want to try some of the helpful organizers suggested in this chapter. Although no one of them is necessarily better than the others, you may discover one that works best for you.

CONFIDENCE Builder

Attitudes for Study

Reading and studying take time; there are no shortcuts, only efficient study techniques. To make the most of your study time, use proven strategies and develop the confidence-building attitudes of commitment and persistence. What are these attitudes, and what do they have to do with studying?

Commitment A commitment is a pledge. For example, in marriage, a couple pledge to love one another. Similarly, people who pledge their money and time to support a cause are committed. In academic terms an *attitude of commitment* means a willingness to pledge your time and effort to reach your goals. For example, if you are committed to success, then you will adopt the behaviors that promote success such as regular attendance, sufficient preparation, and studying. Commitment also involves desire. Therefore, if you know what you want and how to get it, and you are willing to set goals, then you have the attitude of commitment.

Persistence Persistence is *the willingness to sustain effort over time, even in the face of difficulty.* Remember when you learned to ride a bicycle or drive a car? These skills took time to master. But no matter how many times you fell off the bike or how many times you had to practice parking and backing up the car, finally you learned to ride or drive. Finally, you got your license. That took persistence. Moreover, you were committed to learn because you *desired* having those skills and the freedom they would give you. In academic terms, an attitude of persistence means a willingness to try out new strategies and to practice new skills as often as necessary until mastery is achieved. Persistence means not giving up in the face of failure but instead analyzing your mistakes to see what

(Continued)

went wrong, then trying again. Through commitment and persistence, you can take control of your learning. Here are seven suggestions:

1. Choose success. Commit yourself to the idea that you will succeed.

2. Be self-motivated. Think about why you are in college. Look to the future. Where do you want to be in five years? What is your dream job or career? Let your desires be your motivators.

3. Set goals. Dreams don't come true without planning and effort. Set long-term goals (complete requirements for my major), set short-term goals (attain a 3.0 GPA this semester; earn an A on this assignment), and make plans to reach them. Commit yourself to the plans and follow through.

4. Remember that each day, each assignment or each test brings you closer to achieving your goals. Make them all count. Put forth your best effort.

5. Try out the strategies that you are learning. They won't do you any good if you read about them and then forget about them. For SQ3R or any study system to work, you have to use it consistently so that it becomes second nature. When surveying before you read becomes a habit, when you read with a pencil or other marker in your hand, and when you take time to review after *every* time you read, you will see your understanding grow and your memory increase. Like SQ3R, making organizers is an *active* process that involves you in learning. The value of both of these methods is that they involve all your concentration, making it less likely that a part of your brain will be on vacation while you are attempting to study.

6. Don't give up. Suppose you have made a bad grade, or you think you aren't making progress. Perhaps more practice is needed, or perhaps you need to try a new strategy. Seek help and be persistent.

7. Turn to your learning community. You are not alone. Other students are experiencing the same successes and failures that you are. Form a study group. Find out from others what works and doesn't work for them. Then revise your plans or methods as needed. Remember, *you* are in control.

The attitudes of commitment and persistence also have a workplace connection. Being committed to a company's goals and being persistent in your efforts to reach them make you a valued employee. To pursue the topic of attitudes and how they affect your academic, personal, and career goals, do an online search using these key words as a starting point: *interpersonal skills, pillars of character, positive thinking, self-efficacy.*

Concept or Information Maps

UNLIKE AN OUTLINE, which is a *linear*, or sequential, listing of main ideas and supporting details, a concept or information map is a *spatial*, or visual, breakdown of a topic that may not be sequential. But like an outline, a map breaks down the information from general to specific concepts or ideas. If your learning style is visual, you may prefer information maps to outlines. To construct an information map, first identify the topic and write it in a box. Identify the ideas that relate to the topic and write them in connecting boxes to show their relationship to the topic.

Read the following paragraph. Then study the concept map shown in Figure 8.1.

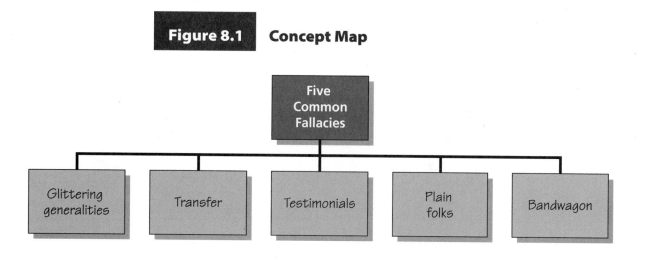

Figure 8.1   Concept Map

*Television advertisers use five common fallacies, among others, to manipulate viewers' attitudes toward their products and to get them to buy. **Glittering generalities** are words and phrases that make viewers respond favorably to a product. Phrases such as "no preservatives," "low fat and cholesterol," or "97% fat free" associated with food products make people believe they're getting something that is healthful. **Transfer** is a fallacious type of reasoning whereby a product is related to an idea or activity with which the reader is likely to identify. Restaurant commercials are a good example of transfer. Families are shown having a good time in a restaurant, or a young couple is depicted in a romantic cafe. Viewers are supposed to get the idea that if they eat at these restaurants, they will become like the happy families and couples in these ads. Many advertisers use **testimonials** of famous people to endorse their products. A film star advocates the use of one brand of shampoo. A sports celebrity endorses a company's athletic shoes. Some advertisers use **plain folks,** people the audience can identify with, to sell products; others encourage viewers to jump on the **bandwagon** and buy a product because "everybody does it." Viewers need to pay attention to ads and sift the hype from the facts. Of course, they can always press the mute button on their remote control unit.*

The map shown in Figure 8.1 is very simple. It breaks down the topic *Five Common Fallacies* into its five supporting details, providing the key term for each one. For a more detailed map, you could attach two more boxes to each of the five detail boxes. In one you could write a definition of the term; in the other you could write an example of your own that is similar to one given in the paragraph. Concept maps can break down ideas as far as you need to in order to show how they relate.

In some material, an order of importance, or *hierarchy,* is stated or implied. When that is the case, your map must show that one concept is more important than another or that one stage precedes another.

Read the next paragraph. Then look at Figure 8.2 for two ways to map the information.

Abraham Maslow was a psychologist who believed that five basic needs motivate human behavior. In Maslow's view, low-level needs have to be at least partially satisfied before higher-level needs can be met. At the bottom of Maslow's hierarchy

Figure 8.2	Two Ways to Map Maslow's Hierarchy of Needs

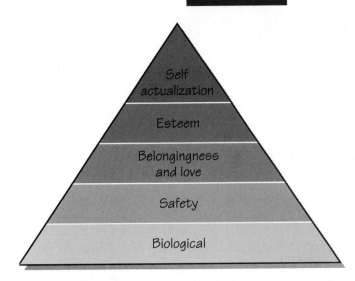

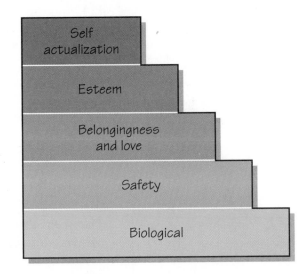

are **biological** needs for food, oxygen, water, and sleep. At the next level are **safety** needs: the need for shelter and clothing and the need to protect oneself from harm. Working to satisfy safety needs consumes the energy of many people. When safety needs are met, the need for **belongingness and love**—the desire for affection and the need to feel part of a group or society—asserts itself. At the next-to-highest level is the need for **esteem,** or recognition by others of one's self-worth and achievements. At the top of Maslow's hierarchy is **self-actualization,** the need to achieve one's fullest potential as a human being. Maslow believed that only a few people, such as Jesus or Gandhi, have ever achieved self-actualization, though everyone has the potential to do so.

Notice how the pyramid and the staircase shown in Figure 8.2 effectively illustrate the hierarchy of needs described by Maslow. The staircase and pyramid are common patterns that you can use to represent any hierarchical arrangement of ideas.

To study from an information map, look it over a few times. Read the information you have diagrammed. Then close your eyes and try to picture the diagram. If you were studying the staircase of Maslow's needs, for example, you would picture the staircase and visualize each need falling into place on the appropriate stair. During a test, you would visualize your map to recall the information.

EXERCISE **8.1**

FROM ONE OF YOUR TEXTBOOKS, select some material that is hierarchically arranged—that is, arranged in a certain order from lowest to highest or most important to least important. Map this information to clearly show the hierarchy. Use the pyramid or staircase pattern illustrated in Figure 8.2 or devise a pattern of your own. Then share your map with the rest of the class.

Comparison Charts

COMPARISON CHARTS ORGANIZE facts and other information into categories according to similarities and differences or group characteristics. A comparison chart enables you to take information out of context and reorganize it in a way that makes sense to you. Furthermore, a comparison chart arranges information visually, allowing you to *see* relationships among categories and to compare information that is sorted into each category. If your learning style is visual, you may enjoy making and using comparison charts as study guides. Read the following annotated paragraph and examine the comparison chart shown in Figure 8.3. The annotations show how one student thought through the information explained in the paragraph before making a comparison chart.

Main idea:
3 purposes for writing

1st: inform
2nd: entertain

3rd: persuade

Purpose determines language, goals, type of material

An author may have one of three major purposes for writing. Authors who want to inform the reader present facts in an objective way and cover all sides of a topic. Their language is usually formal, and their goal is to explain or instruct. Informational writing is characteristic of textbooks, periodicals, and scholarly journals. Authors whose purpose is to entertain are, primarily, storytellers. Their language may be formal or informal, but it is always descriptive. To amuse, delight, and engage the reader's imagination are goals of writers who want to entertain. They write short stories, novels, essays, and poems. Authors whose purpose is to persuade have taken a stand on an issue of importance to their readers. These authors may attempt to inflame their readers with emotional language. Their prose is a mix of fact and opinion, and they may slant evidence in their favor. Their goal is to change readers' minds; they speak out from books, from the editorial pages of newspapers, and from popular magazines. Authors' purposes may determine what they write, how they write, and for whom they write.

Figure 8.3   **Comparison Chart**

An Author's Three Purposes

	Inform	Entertain	Persuade
Language	Usually formal	Formal or informal; descriptive	May be emotional, slanted
Goals	To explain or instruct	To amuse, delight, engage imagination	To change reader's mind
Type of Material	Textbooks, periodicals, journals	Short stories, novels, poems, essays	Books, editorials, magazine articles

EXERCISE **8.2**

READ THE PASSAGE THAT FOLLOWS. Then organize the important information on the comparison chart, which is partially filled in. Give the chart a title that indicates what the paragraph is about.

Several types of social groups play important roles in our lives. Sociologists study two major types of social groups. ***Primary groups*** *are small, and people's relationships within these groups are intimate and personal. Examples of primary groups include families, teams, friends, and lovers. The function of these groups is to act as a buffer against the larger society. You can always come back to a primary group and find security and acceptance.* ***Secondary groups*** *may be either small or large. They are usually organized around a task or a goal, and relationships within them are usually impersonal. Examples of secondary groups include the military, businesses, colleges, and universities. The purpose of these groups is to help you reach a goal or accomplish some type of work. These groups remain fairly impersonal in order to get their work done, but it is possible to develop close relationships with members of your secondary group.*

Title: _____

Type	Size	Relationhips		
Primary groups				Families, teams
		Usually impersonal		

Figure 8.3 shows the relationship among three purposes for writing and compares their similarities and differences in three categories: the language, goals, and type of material best suited to each purpose. Read down the chart for purposes; read across for a comparison of similarities and differences.

A comparison chart lets you organize a lot of information into a relatively small and compact format that you can put in a notebook for frequent review. You may be able to draw comparison charts on 5" × 7" note cards, which are even easier to carry with you.

Time Lines

TIME LINES ARE effective organizers for material that is presented chronologically. They are especially useful for visualizing a historical development or a sequence of events. Review a time line by looking at it and reciting the events in order. Then close your eyes and try to visualize the events as positions on the line.

To make a time line, draw a vertical or horizontal line. Divide the line into sections. On one side of the line, write dates; on the other side, write events

Figure 8.4   **Time Line**

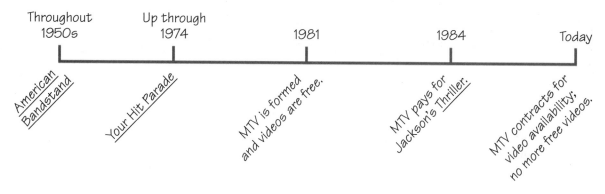

The Rise of Music Television

that correspond to the dates. Give your time line a title that indicates what it covers.

Read the following paragraph and follow the sequence of events. Then examine the time line shown in Figure 8.4.

> *Except for variety shows and a few programs such as* American Bandstand, *which in the 1950s became one of television's first hits, and* Your Hit Parade, *which aired from 1950–1974, television paid little attention to popular music. That changed in 1981 with the formation of the Music Television (MTV) cable network. . . . MTV quickly became a 24-hour-rock-video powerhouse that targets teens and young adults ages 12 to 24. A co-owned network, Video Hits One, programs to attract 25–34-year-olds.*
>
> *Originally intended to promote record sales, music videos became a television genre in their own right. Performers act out song lyrics, interpret them, or otherwise create imaginative visual images for songs. As promotional tools, videos came free of charge to stations and networks. But MTV changed the ground rules in 1984 by paying for exclusive rights to Michael Jackson's much-publicized* Thriller *video. MTV now contracts for exclusive early* windows *(periods of availability) for some videos. These strategies essentially demolished music videos as a source of free program material. . . .*
>
> From *Broadcasting in America*, 2nd ed., Sydney W. Head, Christopher H. Sterling, and Lemuel B. Schofield, Houghton Mifflin Co., 1996.

Process Diagrams

PROCESSES **ARE METHODS,** steps, and stages that describe how events occur. They are an essential part of most courses. In a biology class, you learn how diseases are transmitted or how food is processed in the human body. In a political science class, you learn how a bill becomes a law. In an economics class, you learn how periods of inflation and recession develop. In a social science or psychology class, you read about experiments that explain certain aspects of human behavior. A chart that visually represents a complicated process may make it easier for you to learn and remember each step or stage. The process diagram shown in Figure 8.5 on page 199 illustrates the natural movement of water from the ocean to freshwater sources and back to the ocean.

EXERCISE **8.3**

WORK WITH GROUP MEMBERS TO identify and read a process diagram. Follow the guidelines for successful collaboration that appear on the inside back cover. Search through your textbooks to find a good example of a process diagram. These diagrams are typical of science and social science textbooks but may also appear in other texts.

Process diagrams are easy to recognize. Look for drawings connected by arrows showing the direction of the process. Look for stages illustrated by connected boxes or circles, as in the diagram of the water cycle (Figure 8.5). When you have found a process diagram, examine it carefully and read the textbook explanation that accompanies it. Use the following questions to guide your discussion. Record the group's answers to the questions and the group's evaluation.

1. What process does the diagram illustrate?

_____

_____

_____

2. How many stages or steps are in the process, and what are they?

_____

_____

_____

3. Which seems easier to understand, the textbook explanation or the process diagram? Why?

_____

_____

_____

4. Does the answer to question 3 depend on your learning style? How?

_____

_____

_____

Group Evaluation:

How will you use what you learned about process diagrams? Did your group complete its tasks successfully? What improvements can you suggest? How will you find answers to your questions?

_____

_____

_____

Figure 8.5   **Process Diagram**

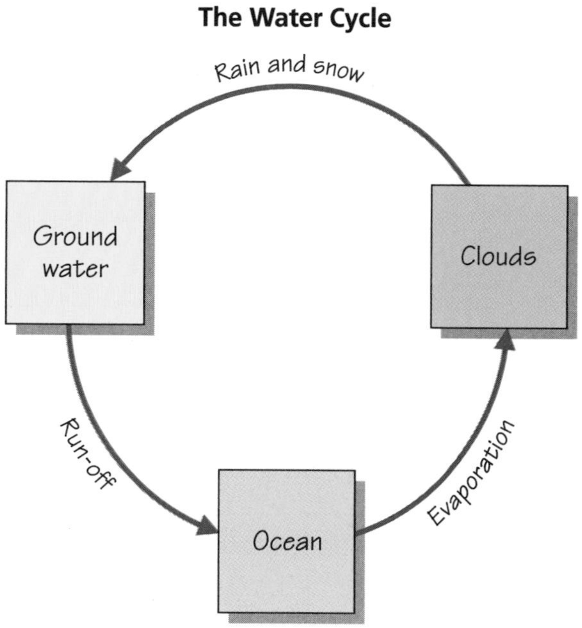

The Water Cycle

Informal outlines

LIKE MANY STUDENTS, you probably use some form of outlining to take notes during lectures, to organize your ideas before writing, or to plan a speech. You can also use outlining to organize information for study. An informal outline illustrating essential concepts and the details that explain them can be a convenient study guide.

Suppose that you are taking a psychology course. You have just finished reading a chapter on motivation and listening to a lecture in class on theories of motivation. During the lecture, your instructor listed some theories on the board and said, "This is important." You have a test in a few days, and you know what you should study: theories of motivation. Your study guide for Maslow's theory might look like the outline shown in Figure 8.6. The outline has four major details indicated by the numbers *1, 2, 3,* and *4.* Stars and indentations signal material that supports or explains each of the four major details.

You could write the outline on a 5" × 7" note card. You could make outlines on note cards for all of the theories and cover the same four points: the name of the originator, the gist of the theory, a weakness, and what makes the theory useful. How would you study from your guides? You could read and recite the information written on your cards. You could mentally try to fill in details. For example, can you explain each level of need in Maslow's hierarchy without looking back at the chapter? Suppose you get to esteem needs and draw a blank. Suppose you can't even remember Maslow's definition of *esteem.* The value of your study guide becomes clear: It tells you what information you need to review or reread.

An outline serves the same purpose as any other type of organizer. It shows how ideas relate to one another and to the topic, and it indicates the relative

Figure 8.6   **Study Guide for Maslow's Hierarchy of Needs**

Maslow's Hierarchy

1. Originator: Abraham Maslow

2. Theory: Five basic needs motivate human behavior
   and form a hierarchy from lowest to highest.
   Lower-level needs have to be met first.
   * Biological, physiological needs (lowest level)
   * Safety
   * Belongingness and love
   * Esteem
   * Self-actualization (highest level)

3. Weakness of theory: People don't always act
   according to the hierarchy.
   * A higher-level need might be satisfied
     before a lower-level need.

4. Researchers agree theory useful because it describes
   motivation in general.

importance of the ideas. Outlines use a listing and indentation system that makes clear which ideas support one another.

A study guide that is easy to make is an outline of a chapter's title and headings. For an example, see Figure 8.7 above. By making the guide, you not only reveal the writer's outline, but you also condense the chapter's most important ideas into one review sheet. Instead of re-reading a chapter before a test or flipping through all the pages to read the headings, simply read the outline on your

Figure 8.7   **Outline of a Chapter's Title and Headings**

Social Responsibility

    The Economic Dimension
        * The Economy
        * Competition
        * Technological Concerns

    The Legal Dimension
        * Laws Regulating Competition
        * Laws Protecting Consumers
        * Laws Protecting the Environment
        * Laws Promoting Equity and Safety

    The Ethical Dimension
        * Ethics As a Force in Social Responsibility
        * Organizational Direction for Ethics and Social
          Responsibility
        * Future Issues

    The Philanthropic Dimension
        * Quality-of-Life Issues
        * Philanthropic Issues

O.C. Ferrell and John Fraedrich, *Business Ethics*, Second Edition. Copyright ©1996 by Hougton Mifflin Company. Reprinted by permission.

review sheet. As you read a heading, try to recite the main idea and a few details covered in that section. If you can recall the important ideas, then you know the material. If you cannot remember some of the information under a certain heading, then you know exactly which section of the chapter you should study some more. If you like to study with a partner, take turns quizzing each other from your review sheets.

Branching Diagrams

BRANCHING **IS A** less formal, less structured technique than outlining or other techniques for creating study guides. In a branching diagram, ideas radiate outward from a central point instead of following a sequence. To branch out from a topic, draw a circle in the middle of your page. Inside the circle, write a key word or phrase that summarizes the author's main idea. Draw lines from the circle like the spokes of a wheel, but don't put them too close together. On these lines write the major details that support the main idea. Draw more lines coming off these lines and write in additional examples that support each of the details. Figure 8.8 shows a branching diagram of the five organizational techniques described in this chapter.

Like outlining, branching can also be used as an organizational method for writing, speaking, and taking notes. But unlike outlining, which creates a linear organizer, branching creates a visual organizer. To brainstorm a topic for writing, draw a circle in the center of your paper around your topic. Add branches to the circle as ideas occur to you. Unlike outlining, branching does not require that you list your ideas in order. You can branch all over your paper, leaving one branch when you think of an idea to connect to another branch. You can also use branching to diagram the major points of a speech. Transfer your diagram to a 5" × 7" note card for easy reference during your speech. Finally, branching is a good note-

Figure 8.8   **Branching Diagram**

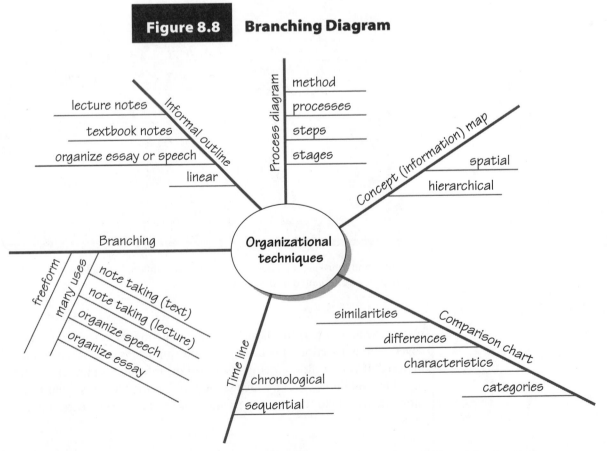

EXERCISE **8.4**

READ THE FOLLOWING PASSAGE ABOUT the five objectives of financial planning. Using a computer, make a study guide for the passage. As explained in this chapter's Computer Confidence, for example, you could make an informal outline or experiment with different fonts to make important ideas stand out. Share your study guide with the rest of the class and discuss any advantages or disadvantages of making study guides on a computer that you may have discovered during the process of making your guide.

For most people, effective financial planning takes into account five lifetime objectives. Making money is a goal that can be reached either through employment or investments. Managing money so that there is some left over for savings after spending is a goal people can reach by becoming effective consumers. Preparing and following a budget, using credit wisely, choosing good investments, buying economical insurance, establishing inexpensive bank accounts, and keeping accurate records of all transactions are all part of being an effective consumer.

Living well is a goal many people strive for, in part, by trying to achieve financial success. Personal achievement, a challenging career, good health, satisfying relationships, community service, and material comforts are among some of the factors most people equate with living well. The decisions a person makes about all these factors determine the level of income and savings needed to achieve the quality of life he or she desires.

Becoming financially secure is a goal best achieved through effective money management. People who are financially secure are free from debt and concerns about money. They have enough to buy the things they need plus occasional luxuries. They have savings, investments, and insurance to maintain their quality of life in the future.

Planning for the future is a primary reason for saving money and making investments. It is a goal of many people who want to save money for their children's education, to live well in retirement, and to leave an estate for their heirs. This objective, like the other four, is a lifetime one.

Making money, managing money, living well, becoming financially secure, and planning for the future are related goals in the sense that achieving one usually requires achieving the others.

---

taking method to use when listening to a speaker who does not explain ideas sequentially. Add a new branch whenever the speaker makes another point. If the speaker returns to a previous point that you have already branched, add another line to that branch.

To study from your branching diagrams, read them over several times. Make sure that you understand how the ideas relate. Then turn your diagram over and, on a clean sheet of paper, try to recreate your diagram. When you've finished, check your new diagram against the original, filling in any details you might have missed.

COMPUTER CONFIDENCE

Using a Computer to Make Study Guides

Once you become comfortable using your computer to organize notes, you can use it to create study guides as well. If you like concept or information maps, experiment with ways to arrange your notes on screen. Some software programs allow you to place boxes and circles around type. You can also use your tabs and margins to set off words or blocks of type in an ordered way. Then pencil in boxes or circles on the hard copy.

If you want a map that shows a hierarchy, your program may allow you to use various type sizes to represent levels. Start with the largest type for the most important concept and reduce the type size for each step, ending with the least important stage in the smallest type. You can also use type style functions to diagram differences. Use capitals, boldface, italics, underlines, double underlines, and plain text to make up your own hierarchy, selecting a different style for each idea on your map. Write a key to remember your choices. For example, ALL CAPS = most important idea; **boldface** = secondary idea; *italics* = supporting detail.

If you already use the computer to make informal outlines from class notes, you can begin constructing a study guide by inputting chapter titles and headings from your textbook in outline form. Then, using the "copy" and "move" functions on your computer, pick up portions of your class notes and insert them in appropriate places in the chapter outline.

Try using numbers for main ideas and asterisks (stars) for details. Or make up your own symbols to set off main and supporting ideas. You can also use different spacing, type styles, or type sizes to make distinctions. Some programs give you a choice of typeface or font so that you can even change the look of the letters. Have fun experimenting with different treatments for important ideas until you find one that helps you visualize your outline at test time.

CRITICAL THINKING

Form a group with two or three other people in your class. Plan and rehearse an oral report on an effective study strategy explained in this chapter or in another chapter. Choose a strategy that you have used successfully so that your report will have practical value. Define the strategy, explain how to use it, and provide examples. Be creative: illustrate your report with diagrams or other graphics or present your report as a skit.

EXERCISE 8.5

READ THIS EXCERPT FROM A psychology textbook; then underline and mark it to make the important ideas stand out. Using an organizer that best supports your learning style, make a study guide.

Freud's Structure of Personality. Have you ever had a burning urge to kiss or embrace someone you're attracted to, or to hit someone who has angered you, only to hear the haunting voice of your conscience? How do you resolve these dilemmas? Based on his clinical experiences, Freud believed that people are driven by inner conflicts (conscious vs. unconscious, free association vs. resistance, life vs. death)—and that compromise is a necessary solution. Freud thus divided the human personality into three interacting parts: the id, ego, and superego.

The **id** is the most primitive part of personality. Present at birth, it is a reservoir of instincts and biological drives that energize us. According to Freud, the id operates according to the **pleasure principle,** motivating us to seek immediate and total gratification of all desires. When a person is deprived of food, water, air, or sex, a state of tension builds until the need is satisfied. The id is thus a blind, pleasure-seeking part of us that aims for the reduction of all tension. If the impulsive, id-dominated infant could speak, it would scream: "I want it, and I want it now!"

The **superego** is a socially developed aspect of personality that motivates us to behave in ways that are moral, ideal, even perfect. Whereas the id pushes us to seek immediate gratification, the superego is a prude, a moralist, a part of us that shuns sex, aggression, and other innate sources of pleasure. Where does the superego come from? According to Freud, children learn society's values from their parents. Through repeated experiences with reward for good behavior and punishment for bad, children eventually develop internal standards of what's right and wrong. There are two components to the superego. One is the ego-ideal, an image of the ideals we should strive for. The other is conscience, a set of prohibitions that define how we should not behave. Once the superego is developed, people reward themselves internally for moral acts by feeling pride, and they punish themselves for immoral acts by suffering pangs of guilt.

The third aspect of personality is the **ego**, which mediates the conflict between the "wants" of the id and the "shoulds" of the superego. According to Freud, the ego is a pragmatic offshoot of the id, the part of personality that helps us achieve realistic forms of gratification. In contrast to the id (which strives for immediate gratification) and the superego (which seeks to inhibit the same impulses), the ego operates according to the **reality principle**—the goal being to reduce one's tensions, but only at the right time, in the right place, and in a socially appropriate manner. The ego is thus a master of compromise, the part of us that tries to satisfy our needs without offending our morals. The ego, said Freud, is the executive officer of the personality, the part that controls our behavior....

Saul Kassin, *Psychology.* Copyright ©1995 by Houghton Mifflin Company. Reprinted by permission.

thinking *ahead* ┅┅┅➤

What practical knowledge have you gained from this chapter that you can use to solve real-world problems? To find out, read the following scenario and complete the items after it.

Midterm exams are two weeks away, and Miranda is worried. The reading in her psychology class is difficult. So much information is packed into each chapter—psychologists and their theories, details about experiments, and other important facts—that she doesn't know what to study. Her lecture notes are incomplete. When she is interested in the topic, she pays attention, listens carefully, asks questions, and, as a result, she takes thorough, well-organized notes. But when she is not interested, or when personal problems occupy her mind, her notes are sketchy—if she takes notes at all. She remembers a discussion in her student success class about making graphic organizers to condense complicated information, making it easier to review. "Maybe I should use one of those," she thinks. Although Miranda is the first to admit that her organizational skills need improving, she is not a procrastinator when it comes to studying, and she wants to use her two weeks before the exam as productively as possible. She just doesn't know where to begin.

1. What is Miranda's problem?

_____

_____

_____

_____

2. What are some possible solutions Miranda might consider?

_____

_____

_____

_____

3. What do you think is the best strategy that Miranda could use to prepare for the exam?

_____

_____

_____

_____

4. Write a plan that would help Miranda use her study time productively.

_____

_____

_____

_____

_____

chapter review

To review the chapter, reflect on the following confidence-building attitudes, complete **Concepts to Understand,** and practice your new skills at every opportunity.

ATTITUDES TO DEVELOP

- commitment to a goal
- persistence of effort
- openness to new strategies
- refusal to give up

CONCEPTS TO UNDERSTAND

This chapter explains how to organize information and create several types of study guides. Outlines and time lines are _____ because they arrange information sequentially according to what comes first, next, and so on. These organizers appeal to your sense of order. Maps and other types of _____ organizers such as comparison charts and process and branching diagrams are useful for nonlinear thinkers because they arrange information in ways that are logical but not necessarily _____ . The organizers explained in this chapter share one thing in common: They help you see the _____ among ideas. All of these organizers are effective although some may work better than others, depending on your learning style and the kind of information you need to learn.

Making organizers is a good idea for several reasons. For one thing, the process of deciding what is important and how to organize it forces you to think about ideas and how they relate to each other. Also, arranging the information in a format that appeals to you makes it easier to remember.

To access additional review exercises, see http://college.hmco.com/success.

SKILLS TO PRACTICE

- deciding what is important
- deciding what to study
- organizing information

Your Reflections

Your Reflections

Reflect on what you have learned about the ways to organize information for study and how you can best apply that information. Use the following list of questions to stimulate your thinking; then write your reflections. Your response may include answers to one or more of the questions. Incorporate in your writing specific information from this chapter or from previous chapters as it's needed.

- Of the types of organizers explained in this chapter, which ones have you tried?

- Are you satisfied with the ways you have found to organize information for study? Why or why not?

- Which step or steps in the SQ3R system could be strengthened by the use of study guides?

- How do you plan to use this chapter's information in your courses?

- Of the attitudes and skills listed in the Chapter Review, which do you think will be most useful at work or in your career?

Controlling Your Concentration

WOULD YOU LIKE to improve your ability

to concentrate while reading, studying,

and taking notes in class? Do you have trouble fighting

distractions? Are you ready to take control?

TO CONCENTRATE MEANS *to pay attention by focusing your thinking on what you are doing.* Whether listening to a lecture, writing a paper or report, participating in a group discussion, or studying for an exam, you must be able to concentrate on the task at hand. Even when surfing the Web, you need to stay in control, avoid letting interesting links distract you, and remain focused on finding the information you want.

Concentration and memory are linked. In fact, they are essential aspects of your information-processing system, which also includes active reading and critical thinking—topics covered in later chapters. By becoming aware of the ways you process information and by choosing strategies that aid the process, you can take control of your learning.

Self-assessment and learning style are your keys to managing concentration. Through self-assessment you can find and eliminate your distractions. A familiarity with your learning style will help you make the choices that put you in control of where and how you study. Whether you are working independently or with others, being able to maintain concentration is an academic and career asset.

This chapter explains what you must do in order to take control of your concentration:

- Know what causes you to lose concentration.

- Identify your distractions and eliminate them.

- Find or create your best study environment.

- Study with a system that helps you concentrate.

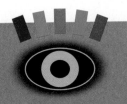

Awareness Check 15

WHAT CAUSES POOR CONCENTRATION?

Check the statements that apply to you. If you can think of another cause of poor concentration, write it in the space provided at the end of the list.

- ☐　　1. I am easily distracted when I study.

- ☐　　2. My mind wanders when I read.

- ☐　　3. I can't seem to find time to study.

- ☐　　4. I have a tendency to procrastinate and put off studying to do something else.

- ☐　　5. My mind goes blank on a test.

- ☐　　6. If I don't like the instructor, I lose interest and don't pay attention.

- ☐　　7. If the subject doesn't relate to my major or career choice, I have a hard time concentrating on it.

- ☐　　8. If an assignment takes too long or if it's difficult, I may not stick with it.

- ☐　　9. I don't have a career goal or a reason to study.

10. It's hard for me to listen and take notes at the same time.

11. I spend more time on the Internet than is necessary.

12. I also have trouble concentrating when _____

_____

_____

Now that you have identified reasons for your inability to concentrate, read the rest of the chapter. The next section suggests ways to eliminate distractions. Subsequent sections discuss ways to eliminate other causes of poor concentration. Be sure to read the sections referred to in other chapters if the cause is a significant problem for you.

Eliminate Distractions

FIRST, YOU NEED to identify *what* is distracting you so that you can eliminate its source. You may need to change your home study environment or your daily habits. The following discussion and Figure 9.1 will give you some guidance.

Distractions can have internal or external causes. *Internal distractions* originate within you. They include feelings of hunger, tiredness, and discomfort that

Figure 9.1	What Distracts You from Studying?

INTERNAL DISTRACTIONS	EXTERNAL DISTRACTIONS
☐ Hunger	☐ People talking to each other
☐ Tiredness	☐ Telephones ringing
☐ Illness	☐ Music or television playing
☐ Thinking about work or personal problems	☐ Noise or activity going on outside
☐ Worrying about grades, personal matters, etc.	☐ Lighting too bright or too dim
☐ Stress	☐ Temperature too high or too low
☐ Physical discomfort	☐ Lack of proper materials
☐ Not knowing how to do an assignment	☐ Party or other activity that you want to take part in
☐ Negative feelings about courses or instructors	☐ Family members asking you to do something
☐ Lack of interest or motivation	☐ Friends wanting to talk
☐ Other internal distraction? _____	☐ Other external distraction? _____
_____	_____
_____	_____

you can control. *External distractions* originate outside you. They include noise, temperature, and interruptions. You may not be able to eliminate all external distractions, but you can change the way you respond to them so that they don't keep you from concentrating. Figure 9.1 lists some common internal and external distractions. Put a check next to those that trouble you. If you are often distracted by something that is not listed in the figure, write it in under the appropriate column.

You can eliminate some internal distractions if you *anticipate your needs.* For example, study when you have eaten and are rested. Study in a comfortable place. Make sure you understand how to do an assignment before you begin. If you are not feeling well, postpone studying until you feel better. Worrying about grades, dwelling on job-related or personal problems, and having negative feelings about courses and instructors cause stress and distracting thoughts. When you have distracting or negative thoughts, stop studying for a moment and remind yourself of what you are trying to accomplish. Focus your attention on completing the task. If you lack interest in what you are studying, or if you don't have the motivation to do the work, studying with a partner might help. Choose someone who *is* interested and motivated. Studying will be more enjoyable, and the time will seem to pass quickly.

You can eliminate most external distractions by creating a study place where *you* may be able to control the lighting, temperature, noise level, and the availability of materials needed for study. Say *no* to friends who distract you from studying by tempting you with invitations to go out and have fun. If you save the fun as a reward for studying, you'll have a better time.

EXERCISE 9.1

THE PURPOSE OF THIS EXERCISE is for you and the members of your group to gain experience identifying internal and external distractions and ways to eliminate them. Follow the guidelines for successful collaboration that appear on the inside back cover. Your tasks are as follows: Read and discuss the following scenario about a student who has trouble concentrating. Use the questions as a guide. Then record the group's answers to the questions and the group's evaluation.

Yesterday afternoon I had some time between classes, so I went to the library, found a comfortable couch in the reading section, and began reading a chapter in my psychology book. Two students came in, sat on the couch next to me, and began talking about their dates from the night before. Their evenings sounded pretty funny. I didn't mean to eavesdrop, but I was sitting right there! Suddenly I realized I was shivering. Why had I forgotten to bring a sweater? I knew the library's temperature was kept at energy-efficient levels. Not only was I cold, but the light cast a glare on my book. I moved to a warm spot near the window where the sun was coming in and decided to take notes for the upcoming test. I looked all through my backpack for the pen I was sure I had packed. By the time I had borrowed a pen and sat down to take notes, it was time for my next class. I like psychology. Why was I unable to complete my reading assignment? I felt as though I was struggling with an unknown language.

1. **What is the first distraction the student encounters? Is it an internal or external distraction?**

_____

_____

2. **What should the student have done immediately?**

_____

_____

3. **What are the student's other distractions? Are they internal or external?**

_____

_____

4. **Why is the student unable to complete the reading assignment?**

_____

_____

5. **What behavioral changes would help the student eliminate distractions?**

_____

_____

Group Evaluation:

What have you learned about internal and external distractions? Do you think some distractions cannot be eliminated? Why or why not? Did your group complete its tasks successfully? What improvements can you suggest? What additional questions do you have about concentration, and how will you find answers to your questions?

_____

_____

Find Your Best Study Environment

Do you do most of your studying at home, in the library, or in some other place? Where you study is not as important as whether you are able to concentrate on studying when you are there. If you have a lot of distractions at home—small children who need attention, other family members who make demands on your time, or noise from the television, the stereo, or ringing telephones—you may find it more pleasant and productive to study on campus. But many students find they can't concentrate in the library or other places on campus, so they set aside a place to study at home.

If you prefer to do most of your studying at home, use your learning style to help you create a home study place that meets your needs. Manage your time so that you do most of your studying when your concentration is greatest. To adapt your study place to your learning style, try these suggestions:

- **Visual learners.** Make your place visually appealing. Display calendars, lists, and study aids where you can see and use them.

- **Auditory learners.** Keep a cassette recorder in your study place. Some instructors or departments tape lectures to supplement classroom activities, and they make these available through the library. If you are studying a foreign language, you probably attend a language lab. Find out if lab tapes may be checked out for use at home. You can also tape your notes, vocabulary words, and other practice material. Turn on the recorder and recite along with your tape.

- **Tactile learners.** If you have a personal computer, use a word-processing program to make your own study guides. Get a program that lets you create a calendar on which you can record important dates and assignments. Using a computer will also activate your visual sense.

You don't have to spend a lot of money to set up an efficient and convenient workplace in your house, apartment, or residence hall. Consider the following six factors when you plan your study environment: location, lighting, temperature, furniture, supplies, and motivational aids.

Location. You need a study place where you feel comfortable and where you are likely to have few distractions. Ideally, you should do all your studying in the same place, and you should not use your study place for anything but studying. For example, if you get sleepy while studying, don't nap at your desk. Leave your study area and return after you have rested. If you get hungry, don't eat at your desk. Take a break, have something to eat, and then return to finish studying. In this way, studying will become a habitual response triggered by your study place, and you will be able to maintain concentration.

If you have a spare room in your house, turn it into a home office, a workplace where you can shut the door and shut out distractions. If space is limited, turn a corner of your bedroom into a study area. If you share space with someone—in a residence hall, for example—arrange the furniture, if possible, so that your desks are on opposite sides of the room facing a wall. When you sit at your desk, you will have the illusion of privacy. Plan or negotiate your time so that each of you can study when you are most alert, in a room free of noise and distracting activity.

Lighting. Too much studying in too little light causes eyestrain. Keeping your eyes focused for too long on the pages of your textbook or on a computer screen, especially in poor light, can make you feel tired and tense. Study in a well-lighted place and look up from your work occasionally. Rest your eyes by looking off in the distance without focusing on anything or by closing them for a few seconds.

Overhead lighting that illuminates your whole study area without casting glare or creating shadows is best. If you do not have an overhead light, use a lamp that can handle a 250-watt bulb and position it close to your work so that you are not reading or writing in glare or shadows. Two lamps, one on each side of your desk, will achieve the same effect if you put a 150-watt bulb in each. There is no need to buy new lamps if you can't afford them. Make the best use of whatever lamps are available by placing them properly and by choosing the right bulbs.

Temperature. The right temperature for studying is the one at which you feel most comfortable. A room that is too hot will make you feel drowsy and sluggish. Cooler temperatures raise your energy level and keep you alert. Your body is a gauge that registers changes in climate and temperature. Extreme changes affect your ability to concentrate because they cause you to focus your attention on your body's discomfort. Optimum temperatures for most people are between 68 and 70 degrees Fahrenheit. In your study area, you may be able to control the temperature and keep it at the level at which you feel most energetic.

Temperatures in public buildings may vary greatly from room to room, and they are usually controlled automatically. If one of your classrooms stays uncomfortably cold, pack a sweater or light jacket in your book bag when you go to that class because it is unlikely that your instructor will be able to adjust the temperature. You are probably aware of the hot and cold spots on your campus, so if you prefer to study there, find a comfortable place.

Furniture. To save money, use furniture that you have on hand or pick up what you need at a used-furniture store or garage sale. You'll need a desk or sturdy table big enough to hold a computer (if you have one), with space left over for reading a book, writing a paper, or studying from notes. If you can afford to buy a new desk, get one with drawers for storing paper, pens, and other supplies. If you have a computer, you might want to invest in a desk or table made especially to hold a computer, printer, disks, manuals, and other supplies.

Don't underestimate the importance of a comfortable chair that provides adequate support for your back and is neither too low nor too high for the table or desk you are using. Studies have shown that many employees who work at computers all day suffer from chronic pain in their necks, arms, and backs. Such discomfort is the result of sitting in one position for long periods of time in a chair that doesn't provide enough support. Your arms or neck may become sore if your elbows and wrists are not supported as you type or if your computer screen is not at eye level. If you cannot buy or do not own a chair that provides enough back support, experiment with placing a pillow behind your lower back and adjusting it for comfort. Figure 9.2 illustrates an ergonomically correct seating posture: one that provides proper back support and distance from keyboard and computer screen.

Whenever you have been sitting at your desk for a while and are beginning to feel tired or uncomfortable, try this exercise. Look up from your writing or away from your computer screen. Look to the right or left without focusing your eyes on anything in particular. Lower your shoulders and let your arms hang limp at your sides. Shake your hands. Push back from your desk and stretch your legs. If you still feel tired or stiff, take a short walk before returning to work.

Supplies. Keep your supplies handy and replenished. Most students use pens, pencils, lined and unlined paper, paper clips, a stapler and staples, note cards, and markers or highlighters in several colors. Whatever you need, including textbooks, make sure your supplies are available so that you don't have to interrupt your studying to look for them.

Using a cardboard file box is a convenient and inexpensive way to organize your papers, returned tests, and materials from previous courses that you want to keep for future reference. You can buy a file box at your campus bookstore or office supply store.

Motivational Aids. Personalize your study environment. Be creative. Make it *your* place. Keep a calendar that lists exam dates, due dates for papers, and other important information, and display it on a bulletin board or tack it to the wall above your desk. Check off the days as you progress through the semester or

Figure 9.2 Sitting comfortably

The science of ergonomics studies the conditions under which people work most comfortably and efficiently. The design of some office furniture is based on information about the way the human body is structured and best supported.

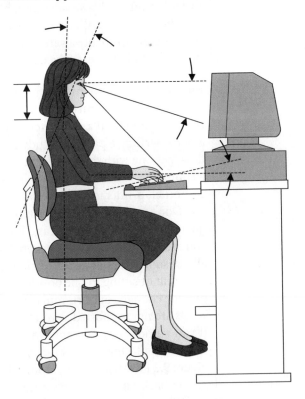

quarter. Keep a record of your grades. This will help you see whether your studying is paying off, and it will signal when you need to make an extra effort. Tack up papers and tests on which you earned good grades. When you are feeling discouraged, look at the evidence of your success.

If studying away from home or the residence hall is a better option for you, your college library may be a good choice. It usually has quiet areas with desks or small tables that are away from traffic and noise. Explore your library to find a corner that meets your lighting and temperature requirements. Also, visit the library at different times of the day to find a time when it is most distraction-free.

Make studying in your place a habit so that it becomes your trigger for concentrated effort. Research has shown that studying at the same time every day reinforces the habit. Although your present schedule may not permit a set study time, this is a goal you can work toward.

An added advantage of finding or creating your best study environment is that you can transfer what you have learned in the process to your workplace environment. The same conditions will apply: location, lighting, temperature, furniture, supplies within reach, and motivational aids. You might not have control of all these conditions, but you may be able to make some changes in the environment that help you increase your productivity.

EXERCISE 9.2

YOUR BODY'S REACTIONS AND YOUR preferred learning environment are aspects of your learning style that affect both concentration and your choice of a study place. To review these aspects of learning style, complete the following items.

1. **Based on the items you checked in Figure 9.1, page 211, are your distractions mostly internal or external?**

_____

2. **What seems to be your greatest distraction, and why?**

_____

_____

_____

_____

3. **What relationship do you see between your locus of control and the distractions you checked in Figure 9.1? Remember that** *locus of control,* **as explained in Chapter 2, means "source of motivation." The more internal your locus of control is, the more self-motivated you are. The more external your locus of control is, the more you need others to motivate you.**

_____

_____

_____

_____

_____

_____

4. **What is your preferred learning environment? Do you prefer working alone or with others, and why?**

_____

_____

_____

_____

5. **Taking into consideration your learning environment preference and your body's reactions to hunger, tiredness, temperature, and lighting, describe your ideal study place and explain what you will do to achieve it.**

_____

_____

_____

_____

_____

Think about this statement: *Concentration may be linked to motivation.* Do you think the statement is true? Write a short paper in which you explain your answer.

As you think about what to write, remember what you have learned about *locus of control*—people are motivated in one of two ways, either externally or internally. Do you think that locus of control has anything to do with concentration? For example, is an externally motivated person more subject to internal and external distractions than an internally motivated person? Who is more likely to accept responsibility for his or her level of concentration, an externally or an internally motivated person? What about your own locus of control and the kinds of distractions that affect you? Locus of control is explained in detail in Chapter 2.

Use a Study System

Another way to eliminate distractions and maintain concentration is to study with a focused, consistent approach such as SQ3R or a system of your own. For additional strategies, try these six suggestions:

- **Break large assignments, such as research papers, into smaller tasks.** Schedule those tasks over several days or weeks, depending on when the completed assignment is due.

- **Study difficult subjects first.** Tackle your toughest or most unpleasant assignments when you are alert and can give them your full attention. Study easier subjects later. Even if you are tired, you can complete the work successfully if it is not too difficult for you.

- **Separate similar subjects.** Suppose you are taking a history course, a math course, and an accounting course. Study history between math and accounting so that you won't confuse the two courses that require you to use computational skills.

- **Take breaks.** Do not try to study for several hours straight. You'll become distracted, tired, and cranky. Take a short break every hour. Stand up, move around, or relax away from your desk. Look out the window to rest your eyes and to relieve tension.

- **Reward yourself.** When you complete a difficult or unpleasant task, have a nutritious snack, listen to some music, or call a friend. Then get back to work.

- **Study from your own textbooks.** Do not share books with a friend. If you can afford to, resist buying textbooks in which passages have been un-

To prevent eyestrain during long study sessions, rest your eyes by periodically looking up from your notes or your reading.

© Karim Shamsi/Basha/The Image Works

derlined or highlighted. Although new or nearly new books cost more, they're worth it because unmarked books require you to think for yourself, making decisions about what should or should not be underlined or highlighted. Moreover, you can't be sure that the markings of a previous owner accurately identify the most important ideas. Such markings may be more distracting than helpful.

Most people cannot concentrate for more than an hour without becoming distracted. Take short breaks away from your desk or study area to refresh your mind and body.

Eliminate Other Causes of Poor Concentration

PERHAPS YOU HAVE eliminated distractions, but your concentration remains poor because of test anxiety, ineffective note-taking skills, or a tendency to procrastinate. Listed next are nine common causes of poor concentration and ways to eliminate them.

Mind Wanders While Reading

If your mind wanders when you read, you may be losing concentration because the material is unfamiliar, technical, or too difficult. You can't remember what you don't understand. It is also true that you can't concentrate on what you don't comprehend. To comprehend more, become actively involved in the process of reading by following these suggestions:

- **Have a purpose for reading.** Know what you are expected to learn. For the author's expectations, look for a list of objectives at the beginning of a chapter. If no objectives are listed, look for a statement of purpose in the introductory paragraph or section. For the instructor's expectations, listen for purpose statements in lectures or discussions. Sometimes an instructor will introduce a chapter or an assignment by explaining why it is important or how it meets a course objective.

- **Turn headings and subheadings into guide questions and look for the answers as you read.** Remember that headings and subheadings are clues to an author's most important ideas.

- **Read for main ideas and the details that support them.** Underline key words or phrases that will help you recall these important ideas.

- **Make marginal notes.** Write definitions, examples, or summaries of important findings—whatever you need to remember.

- **Look up any unfamiliar words or terms.** Check your textbook glossary first. If there is no glossary, then use your dictionary as necessary.

- **Use the RMO (read, mark, organize) strategy.** Read a section, mark it, read the next section, and so on. When you are finished, make graphic organizers (charts, concept maps, diagrams) of any important information you will need to review.

EXERCISE **9.3**

SET A GOAL FOR COMPLETING assignments. Choose a block of time, during the day or in the evening, during which you will study or complete assignments for the following day's classes. Decide on the order in which you will complete your tasks and estimate the amount of time you will need to finish each one. Then list them on the following lines. Check off each assignment as you complete it, noting the actual time it took. This exercise will help you determine whether you are allowing enough time to complete your work.

Task	Estimated Time	Actual Time
1. _____	_____	_____
2. _____	_____	_____
3. _____	_____	_____
4. _____	_____	_____
5. _____	_____	_____
6. _____	_____	_____
7. _____	_____	_____

Can't Find Time to Study

If your concentration is poor because you can't seem to find time to study, then you are not managing your time effectively. You may be trying to do too many things at once. Try taking fewer courses next term, adjusting your hours at work, convincing family members or roommates to share more of the housekeeping responsibilities, or participating in fewer extracurricular activities. If studying is a low-priority item on your list of things to do, review your goals and reasons for coming to college. You can improve your concentration by focusing your attention on a positive goal. If you have trouble managing time, use a semester or quarter calendar for planning, make and follow weekly schedules, and write daily lists as reminders.

Tendency to Procrastinate

If you often put off studying to do other things, then you are procrastinating. You are probably concentrating on something other than studying, and that distraction is interfering with your ability to concentrate on your tasks at hand. If you need help beating procrastination, Chapter 5 makes several suggestions.

Mind Goes Blank on Tests

If your mind goes blank during a test, you may have test anxiety, which causes you to lose concentration and interferes with your ability to recall the information you have studied. Adequate preparation for tests will reduce mild anxiety. Severe anxiety may have causes that good preparation alone will not overcome; therefore, you must discover the causes and eliminate them. If test anxiety interferes with your ability to concentrate, try relaxation techniques and the other suggestions explained in Chapter 12.

Negative Attitudes About Instructors

During your college career you will encounter a number of instructors who are lively, entertaining lecturers. But unfortunately, some of the most knowledgeable people are not excellent speakers. Accept your instructors' limitations and don't let negative attitudes about them keep you from doing well in your courses. Instead, focus your attention on your assignments and make connections between the new information you are learning and what you already know. Remind yourself that doing well in your courses will help you reach your goals, and keep your goals in mind as you go about the daily business of attending classes and studying.

Controlling your feelings about instructors also has applications in the workplace. Negative feelings about employers, supervisors, or co-workers may distract you. Learn to control these feelings by focusing your attention on your goals and the task at hand.

CONFIDENCE Builder

A Desktop Relaxation Technique

When you are taking a test and your mind goes blank because you are nervous, this simple technique will calm you down so that you can finish the test.

1. Relax your shoulders and sit comfortably with both feet on the floor.

2. Place your elbows on the desktop, lower your head, close your eyes, and gently cup the palms of your hands over your eyes. Your fingers should be curled over the top of your head, and you should see no light coming in around your hands.

3. In this position, slowly count to ten while you breathe deeply.

4. Empty your mind of all negative thoughts by concentrating on feeling calm and relaxed.

5. When you are feeling calm, lower your hands and open your eyes.

6. You should feel relaxed enough to continue taking the test.

This technique works because you can't feel relaxed and anxious at the same time. As you concentrate on becoming calm, you forget about your test anxiety. When you return to the test calmly, the information you had blanked out because of nervousness will come back to you. You need not be self-conscious because other students will not know what you are doing. They may think you are just resting your eyes.

To pursue this topic further, do an online search using these key words as a starting point: *relaxation techniques, relaxation response, stress relief.*

EXERCISE 9.4

ATTITUDE AND BEHAVIOR AFFECT CONCENTRATION. Your attitude and behavior in a class are related to the degree of responsibility you take for your performance in a course. Select as a target a course in which you would like to do better. Complete the analysis that follows; then decide what you can do to become a more internally controlled student.

1. **What is the name of the course in which you would like to improve your grades?** _____
_____

2. **Is there anything about the course that you don't like or that you think is difficult?** _____
_____
_____

3. **What are your distractions in this class?** _____
_____
_____

4. Are the distractions internal or external? _____

_____

_____

5. What is your attitude toward this class? Answer *yes* or *no* to the following statements.

	Yes	No
I enjoy coming to this class.	☐	☐
I like the instructor's teaching style.	☐	☐
I feel confident in this class.	☐	☐
I am not afraid to ask questions in this class.	☐	☐
I am learning something in this course.	☐	☐
I see a relationship between this course and my goals.	☐	☐
I am interested in the subject taught in this course.	☐	☐

6. Make a plan to improve your concentration in this course by selecting a behavior or attitude that you will try to change. Describe what you will do. _____

_____

_____

_____

_____

_____

_____

_____

_____

Try out your plan long enough to receive two or more test or assignment grades. If you are satisfied with the results, continue with your plan. If not, examine this analysis again to see if there is something else you can do to improve your performance in this course.

EXERCISE **9.5**

AS NOTED AT THE BEGINNING of this chapter, surfing the Web can be a distraction if you don't remain focused on your topic. On the other hand, if you do remain focused, online researching can help you find information quickly, leaving you more time for study. Discuss with class members other ways in which using a computer can both help and hinder studying. Come up with a list of guidelines for avoiding distractions and remaining focused while researching, writing, or doing other learning activities online.

Subject Doesn't Relate to Job, Major, or Career Goal

If you can't put your mind to a subject that doesn't seem to relate to your job, major, or career goal, then you are missing one of the great opportunities of a college education: to broaden your mind and discover new interests. Also, consider that most people change careers two or more times during their lives. If you take only courses that relate to your chosen career, you will be handicapped if you ever change jobs.

Moreover, whatever career you have chosen for now may require skills of which you are currently unaware. Courses that seem unrelated may teach you skills that you *can* use in the workplace or in other life experiences.

Long and Difficult Assignments

If you feel like giving up when you encounter a very long or hard assignment, you probably have a low tolerance for unpleasant tasks. You can change your attitude toward unpleasant tasks so that you can concentrate and get them done. First, remind yourself that the sooner you start, the sooner you will finish. Next, remind yourself that your attitude toward studying may be causing you to lose concentration and may be keeping you from doing your work as well as you can. Third, make long or difficult assignments easier to handle by breaking them into smaller segments that you can complete in one sitting. Then reward yourself for doing the work.

Lack of Goals or Reason to Study

If you don't have a goal or if you can't find a reason to study, perhaps you don't know yet why you're in college or what you want out of life. You may be a young student attending college at your parents' request. Or you may be undecided about a major. Before you make serious career plans, you may want to explore possibilities for a term or two, taking required courses and electives until you get a feel for college life and being on your own.

Eventually, however, you must decide what you want to do and get on with it. A visit to your college's career center or to your academic advisor might be helpful. Without a goal or a clear purpose for studying, it is difficult to concentrate. Once you know what you want to do, then you can set the long-term and short-term goals that will help you achieve your dreams.

Can't Listen and Take Notes

Listening to a lecture while taking notes is a new experience for many students, and it may seem impossible at first. Usually when you try to concentrate, you are focusing on one of many things competing for your attention. If you are successful, you can block out irrelevant sensory impressions as you concentrate on that one important thing. But in a classroom lecture, you must attend to two things: listening and taking notes. In a sense, this is no different from eating an apple while reading a book, watching a TV program while carrying on a conversation, or driving a car while looking for an address. Your attention shifts rapidly back and forth between the two activities on which you are concentrating.

It may take time and practice to become an effective note taker. Keeping your attention focused on the speaker is a basic step toward understanding what is important in a lecture.

Taking notes during a lecture actually improves your concentration because you must make an extra effort to follow the speaker's ideas and get them down on paper in a condensed form. If you can't listen and take notes at the same time, then your note-taking skills probably need improvement. Try these suggestions:

- Sit near the front of the room.

- Focus attention on the speaker.

- Watch for gestures or facial expressions that signal important ideas.

- Watch your body language. Maintain the posture of concentration by sitting up straight, making eye contact with the speaker, and looking interested. These simple actions promote concentration by forcing you to involve yourself in what is going on. They have a positive effect on the speaker as well.

- Listen for key expressions such as "Now, this is something you need to remember."

- Copy in your notes whatever the speaker writes on the chalkboard or projection screen.

- Skip several lines between main ideas, leaving room to write in details and examples.

See pages 85–92 of Chapter 4 for a more detailed discussion of how to take notes.

Now help yourself by reviewing the strategies summarized in Figure 9.3 to combat the causes of poor concentration.

Figure 9.3	**Strategies to Improve Concentration**

CAUSE OF POOR CONCENTRATION	STRATEGIES
1. I am easily distracted.	**Eliminate your distractions:** • Create a good study place; do all your studying there. • Get enough sleep. • Study when rested. • Eat well so that you won't be hungry. • Study with a partner to increase motivation.
2. My mind wanders when I read.	**Become an active reader:** • Have a purpose for reading. • Turn headings into questions. • Underline main ideas. • Summarize key ideas in margins. • Look up unfamiliar words.
3. I can't find time to study.	**Learn to manage your time:** • Make a study schedule. • Use a calendar and daily lists. • Take fewer courses. • Adjust work hours. • Ask family members to help out with chores.
4. I procrastinate.	**Follow a six-step plan:** • Schedule time for long assignments. • Break long assignments into smaller parts. • Assemble your materials. • Think positively about your ability to complete assignments. • Get help if you need it. • Reward yourself for completing work.
5. My mind goes blank on tests.	**Reduce test anxiety:** • Prepare adequately for tests. • Learn how to practice a relaxation technique.

6. I don't like my instructor.

Develop an internal locus of control:

- Accept your instructor's limitations.

- Accept your responsibility to raise your own interest level.

- Accept the course as a step you must take to reach your goals.

7. The course doesn't relate to my job, major, or career goal.

Look to the future:

- Welcome new learning opportunities.

- Set realistic and flexible goals.

8. The assignment is too hard.

Make assignments easier:

- Be sure you know what to do.

- Break long assignments into smaller parts.

- Allow plenty of time.

- Ask your instructor for help.

9. I don't have a goal.

Decide what you want to do:

- Get a feel for college life.

- Visit the career center or see an advisor.

- Choose a major; make career plans.

10. I can't listen and take notes at the same time.

Learn how to take notes:

- Sit up front.

- Watch the speaker's gestures and expressions.

- Listen for key words.

- Copy information from the chalkboard or screen.

- Skip lines between main ideas.

thinking *ahead* ----->

What practical knowledge have you gained from this chapter that you can use to solve real-world problems? To find out, read the following scenario and complete the items after it.

Jamal has a job in social services. Much of his workday is spent meeting with clients. He also spends considerable time at his desk filling out forms and keeping records. To meet government regulations and deadlines, Jamal must apply a high degree of concentration to such work. Jamal loves working with people and helping them get the services they need. But he does not enjoy the paperwork. Sometimes his concentration wavers, so he has to take extra time to make corrections later.

Jamal shares a large office with several co-workers. His desk is behind a cubicle. Although he is not distracted by noise, his working environment leaves something to be desired. The lighting is poor, the office is often cold, and he has an old, uncomfortable desk chair. At the end of the day, he is tired and irritable. The cubicle is not very attractive; consequently, it does not inspire him. Fortunately, supplies are no problem. He has everything he needs well within his reach. Jamal thinks that if his office space weren't so dreary and uncomfortable, he could work more efficiently. Jamal's supervisor has said that employees are free to arrange their office space in any way they want—they can even bring in their own furniture. Jamal wonders whether he should take the time to create a more pleasant work environment.

1. What is Jamal's problem?

_____

_____

_____

2. What aspects of Jamal's work area seem to be satisfactory?

_____

_____

_____

3. What aspects need improving?

_____

_____

_____

4. Based on what you have learned about creating a good study environment, what suggestions can you offer Jamal?

_____

_____

_____

chapter **re**view

To review the chapter, reflect on the following confidence-building attitudes, complete Concepts to Understand, and practice your new skills at every opportunity.

ATTITUDES TO DEVELOP

- self-discipline
- flexibility
- positive thinking about instructors
- openness to new ideas and different opinions

CONCEPTS TO UNDERSTAND

You can improve your concentration by identifying and eliminating distractions. _____ distractions are physical feelings that you can take control of since they originate within you. _____ distractions may be beyond your control, but you can learn to control your reactions to them. To minimize _____ and _____ distractions, take care of your _____ needs such as hunger and tiredness before beginning a task, maintain a _____ attitude towards studying, and work to solve problems that you know cause you worry and stress.

You can improve your concentration by having a good place to study. The ideal home or residence hall study environment is as distraction-free as you can make it. Choose a quiet location with adequate _____. Select comfortable furniture suited to your needs. Keep your books and _____ readily available so that you don't have to interrupt your studying to find them.

Prominently display _____ _____, such as a calendar, weekly and semester or quarter plans, or assignments on which you have received good grades. If studying away from home or your residence hall works best for you, find a study place that has as many of the characteristics of a good _____ _____ as possible.

How you study can also affect your concentration. Use your time efficiently. Break large tasks into smaller ones. Study _____ subjects at different times. Take frequent _____. Reward yourself for work accomplished. Purchase new textbooks to use so that you are not influenced by what another student thought should be underlined or highlighted.

To access additional review exercises, see http://college.hmco.com/success.

SKILLS TO PRACTICE

- controlling your concentration
- eliminating distractions
- using a study system

Your Reflections

Your Reflections

Reflect on what you have learned about controlling your concentration and how you can best apply that information. Use the following list of questions to stimulate your thinking; then write your reflections. Your response may include answers to one or more of the questions. Incorporate in your writing specific information from this chapter or from previous chapters as it's needed.

- Which distractions have you been able to overcome?

- Which distractions are still causing you to lose concentration?

- Which of the causes of poor concentration listed in Figure 9.3 apply to you?

- How do you plan to use this chapter's information to improve your concentration?

- Which of the attitudes and skills listed in the Chapter Review do you think will be most useful for you at work or in your career?

Improving Learning and Memory

WHAT IS MEMORY, and how does it work?

Why do you forget? Did you know that

you can improve your memory and learn ways to

combat forgetting?

YOUR MEMORY IS an information-processing system. All learning takes place through this system. By concentrating, you can control or manage the system. By making changes in the way you learn, you can regulate the flow of information through the system, combat forgetting, and build a powerful memory.

Becoming aware of and taking control of the way you process information can lead to lifelong learning. A college degree does not represent knowledge gained or skills learned once and for all. On the contrary, a degree merely represents where you stand academically at a given time. In your career, as in life, you will be faced with tasks, problems, and decisions that require you to apply your knowledge in new ways and to develop new skills. One of the best things you can do for yourself while you're in college is to *learn* how to learn. Critical thinking and study skills are your keys.

This chapter will help you understand the stages and functions of memory so that you can improve the way you learn. As you read the chapter, keep in mind these simple truths about memory:

- It is normal to forget.

- You can probably remember more and retain more for a longer period of time than you think you can.

- A few memory aids that many students have found useful may work for you.

- The best memory techniques may be those that you create or adapt for yourself and that correspond to your learning style.

How Memory Works

WHEN YOU WERE a child, your teacher explained the multiplication tables and wrote them on the chalkboard. While you were listening to the teacher and looking at the board, you were *receiving* information about the tables through your senses of sight and sound. Then, to help you learn them, your teacher asked you to write them out on paper, and that activity engaged your sense of touch. You also recited the tables aloud. Those practices in the classroom helped you to *retain* the tables. Finally, the teacher told you to practice your tables at home because you would be tested on them. You would have to *recall* them. If your practice and memory techniques have served you well, then you have retained the tables and can recall them even now.

Memory is a three-stage process by which your mind receives information and either discards it or stores it for later use. Memory involves *reception* of information, *retention* of information that has been received, and *recollection* of information that has been retained. (Researchers also refer to these activities as *encoding, storage,* and *retrieval.*) Figure 10.1 suggests a convenient way to remember the stages.

Reception

Your mind receives, takes in, or processes information through your five senses. It is important for you to understand the information you receive because you can't retain or recall material that you don't understand.

Relating new information to something familiar can aid understanding and reception because it either adds to or changes what you already know. As you con-

Figure 10.1   **The Three Rs of Memory**

Reception

Retention

Recollection

nect new information with prior knowledge, you begin thinking critically about it. The information now has a *context* and is easier to remember. Suppose you have been assigned a chapter on stress in your psychology text. Before reading, assess your prior knowledge. Ask yourself what stress means to you. Imagine yourself in stressful situations, and recall what you have done to overcome stress. If you have not successfully managed stress in the past, the chapter may suggest a new method to try. Read to find out whether the author's ideas about stress confirm what you already know or give you new information.

Here are some more tips to improve your reception:

- **Become more attentive and observant.** If you stay alert in class and keep your attention focused, you will be a better receiver.

- **Engage as many of your senses as possible when receiving information.** During a lecture, *look* at the speaker. *Listen* attentively to what he or she says. *Take notes* to help you remember. If you do these things, you will be making full use of your visual, auditory, and tactile senses.

- **Ask questions, as needed, to aid understanding.** Remember: *You can't recall what you don't understand.* Make sure that you understand the information you receive.

- **Before you read a textbook chapter,** *survey* it to get an overview of its content and to establish a purpose for reading. This step is especially helpful when the chapter covers a topic that is new to you. Surveying is the first step in the SQ3R study system: *survey, question, read, recite,* and *review.*

Retention

Your mind stores and retains, for varying lengths of time, the information it receives. Some information—your name, your birthplace, your birthday—you remember for life. Such information is part of you, although you may not remember when you first learned it. You retain other information—the multiplication tables, how to ride a bicycle—through use or practice. Was it difficult for you to learn to drive a car? You probably had trouble at first, but eventually you were able to get into a car and drive without mentally reviewing each step. When you reached that point, you had *internalized* the process of driving. You do not easily forget information you have internalized. Like your name, it has become part of you.

Anything you really want to learn is going to stay with you because you are motivated to remember it. The key to retaining academic information is to *make a conscious effort to remember.* Here are some ways to make retention an active and effective process:

- **Become an active reader.** Have a purpose for reading. Know what you are supposed to learn from an assignment. Assess your prior knowledge about the author's topic before reading. During reading, maintain concentration and ignore distractions. Read one section at a time. Then go back and underline or mark the most important ideas. Review immediately after reading.

- **Review frequently.** The more often you review information that you hope to learn and remember, the longer it will stay in your memory.

- **Recite to improve retention.** When you repeat information to yourself that you want to remember, you are activating your auditory sense and opening another pathway into your brain. To aid retention, recite information from your note cards and study guides.

If you make reception an *active* process by looking at the speaker, listening attentively, and taking notes, then you are more likely to understand the information you receive and to be able to remember it later.

© Gary Conner/PhotoEdit

- **Do all work assigned.** Assignments provide practice in using new information or procedures. Frequent practice helps you internalize information.

- **Find a reason to remember.** Motivating yourself to learn because you want better grades is a start, but try to get beyond grades. Think about what you are learning and how it relates to your goals and your hopes.

Recollection

Problems with Recollection.   Your mind enables you to recall information you have retained. Sometimes recollection is difficult. When you are taking a test, you might know one of the answers but be unable to remember it. Later, after the test is over, you remember the elusive answer. Or perhaps you have gotten confused because two similar kinds of information were competing for your attention. That was the problem plaguing a student named Otis.

Otis decided to take trigonometry and statistics in the same semester. Because his grades had been consistently high in math courses, he didn't anticipate any difficulty. Unfortunately, his first grades in both courses were not as good as he had expected: an F on his trig test and a D on his statistics test.

With an instructor's help, Otis realized that he had been confusing the information from one course with information from the other because the two courses both dealt with numbers and mathematical procedures. Since one class met after the other, he had no time to absorb information from one before going to the other.

Otis realized that he should have taken the courses at different times or on different days. He also realized that he should study the subjects at different times or at least take breaks between study sessions.

Otis knew it would be hard to maintain his current average without withdrawing from one of the courses. He decided to remain in statistics, and because of the time he then had available for study, he passed the course with a B.

CRITICAL THINKING

Do this application on your own or with a group. Re-read and discuss Otis's dilemma as explained above. Otis decided to withdraw from his trig class so he could concentrate on raising his grade in statistics. Some might think this was not such a good idea. They might feel that Otis had wasted his time and money. Also, if trig is required for his program, he will have to take the course again, which will cost more money. Do you think these are valid criticisms? Why or why not? Suppose withdrawing from the course is not an option. What else could Otis do to solve his problem? Talk it over; then write down your suggestions to share with the rest of the class.

Improving Recollection. Otis had problems with recollection because he was confusing one course's information with the other's. If you have this problem, or if you need to improve your recollection for other reasons, try one or more of these suggestions:

- **Before a test, organize the information you want to study** in a way that is meaningful to you. Make summaries or set up categories in which you group similar items. Chapter 11 suggests ways to organize information as you prepare for a test.

- **Use your preferred sensory mode.** If you learn best visually, make diagrams, charts, or information maps of material you want to remember. Picture these in your mind when you are studying and when you are responding to test questions. See Chapter 8 for detailed information on mapping and other visual organizational techniques. If auditory modes work best for you, try reciting aloud information you want to remember. Or you could study with a partner and quiz each other orally. If you are a tactile learner, try combining recitation with a physical activity such as walking or jogging. In this way, you are engaging both your auditory and tactile senses.

- **Give yourself practice tests.** Try to anticipate test questions and write some of your own. Answer them; then check your answers against your textbook and your notes.

- **Go over old tests.** Review material that gave you trouble in the past. Your mistakes are clues to information that you haven't retained.

EXERCISE **10.1**

IMAGINE THAT YOU WILL BE tested on the part of this chapter that you have read so far. You need to practice organizing the information in a way that will help you study for the test. Fill in the following outline by answering the questions with information from this chapter.

1. **What are four simple truths about memory?**

   a. _____

   b. _____

   c. _____

   d. _____

2. **What are the three Rs of memory?**

   a. _____

   b. _____

   c. _____

3. What are some tips for improving memory?

_____

_____

a. **How can you improve reception?**

(1) _____

(2) _____

(3) _____

(4) _____

b. **How can you improve retention?**

(1) _____

(2) _____

(3) _____

(4) _____

(5) _____

c. **How can you improve recollection?**

(1) _____

(2) _____

(3) _____

(4) _____

Why You Forget

DO YOU EVER wish you could read something once and remember it? Unfortunately, the mind doesn't work that way. One reading of textbook material is seldom enough. Much of the information printed in textbooks will be new to you, and you may need several readings to understand and absorb it. Also, you forget most of what you read soon after reading it unless you make a conscious effort to remember it. Finally, if you want to retain information, you must periodically review what you have read.

Forgetting is not only normal; it's also necessary. If you never forgot anything, your mind would be so crammed with useless information that you wouldn't be able to think. Do you remember what your phone number was in every place you have lived? You probably don't. Information that you cease to use soon passes out of your memory unless it has special significance. _Your mind remembers only what you need and discards the rest._ In fact, when you learn something new, forgetting starts within an hour. After several days, you remember very little of the new information unless you take action to prevent forgetting.

The stages of memory—reception, retention, and recollection—work because of three functions. Your *sensory memory, short-term memory,* and *long-term memory* determine what you remember and for how long. You have some control over each of these functions. Together, the stages and functions of memory make it possible for you to process information. Figure 10.2 illustrates the process.

Sensory Memory

Your five senses—sight, hearing, taste, smell, and touch—are the media through which you experience the world. Everything that is happening around you is conveyed to you by your senses. Your mind takes in all this information and, through a process called *selective attention,* sorts the important from the insignificant.

You've felt this process at work whenever you've been so caught up in watching a television program that you didn't hear someone speak to you. Your mind screened out the interfering sound of the person's voice. Had you lost interest in the show, you would have found yourself suddenly aware of other things going on around you, and your attention would have shifted to those things.

In class, when you are listening to a lecture, your task is to concentrate on the speaker's words and take notes on the important ideas. Although everything the speaker says registers on your sensory memory, you may have to work at maintaining concentration and ignoring external stimuli such as a conversation between two students who are sitting next to you.

Everything registers on your sensory memory—but only for a few seconds. By concentrating on a certain idea, image, or piece of information, you transfer it to your short-term memory, where you can retain it for a while longer.

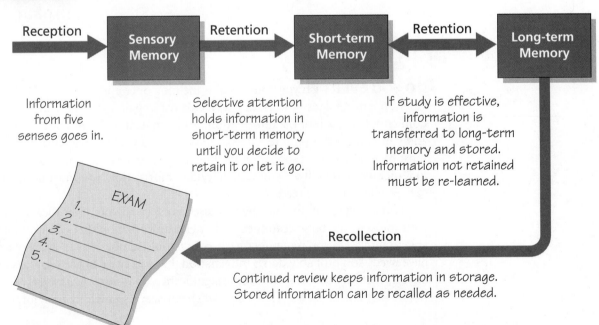

Figure 10.2 **How You Process Information**

Reception → Sensory Memory → Retention → Short-term Memory ← Retention → Long-term Memory

Information from five senses goes in.

Selective attention holds information in short-term memory until you decide to retain it or let it go.

If study is effective, information is transferred to long-term memory and stored. Information not retained must be re-learned.

Recollection

Continued review keeps information in storage. Stored information can be recalled as needed.

Short-Term Memory

You can hold information in your short-term memory for a little under a minute. For example, you meet someone at a party. He tells you his name, and you strike up a conversation. A few minutes later you see a friend you want to introduce to the person whom you just met, but you can't remember his name. Or you're in a phone booth, and you look up a telephone number. You close the directory and start to dial; you reach in your pocket for some change, and you realize you've forgotten the number. You probably have had such experiences, but you can do something about them. You will remember names, phone numbers, and other bits of information longer if you recite them. Reciting activates your short-term memory by engaging another of your senses. Every time you look up a phone number, repeat it to yourself; you may soon be able to dial it from memory.

Research has shown that short-term memory has a limited capacity. You can hold only about five to nine numbers at a time in your short-term memory. Seven is average for most people. Most phone numbers have seven digits; most zip codes have five digits. You might have difficulty remembering your nine-digit driver's license number or credit card number unless you make a point of transferring it into your long-term memory. You won't remember the important ideas from lectures or textbook chapters either—unless you review them enough to transfer them into long-term memory. Using a study system aids the transfer of information from short-term memory to long-term memory.

EXERCISE **10.2**

HOW GOOD IS YOUR SHORT-TERM memory? Imagine that you are at a party full of strangers. By the end of the evening, you have met many people and have learned a great deal about them. How much can you remember? Study the facts about these people for three or four minutes. Then cover up the facts and try to answer the questions.

Name:	Matt	Claudia	Bill
Age:	34	29	23
Eye color:	Brown	Blue	Brown
Favorite book:	*War and Peace*	*The Wind in the Willows*	*The Terminal Man*
Favorite place:	Disney World	The Grand Canyon	The Wind River
Favorite film:	*The Quiet Man*	*Casablanca*	*The Matrix*
Favorite activity:	Traveling	Hiking	web surfing
Favorite color:	Purple	Red	Sky Blue

1. Whose favorite activity is hiking? _____

2. How old is Matt? _____

(Continued)

3. Who has blue eyes? _____

4. Who loves to travel? _____

5. Who would love to hike in the Grand Canyon? _____

6. Who is the youngest? _____

Now uncover the facts and check your answers. How accurate was your short-term memory? If you got fewer than three answers right, you probably did not use a memory aid such as recitation or grouping of similar items. For example, did you notice that Claudia's favorite activity, hiking, could be done at her favorite place, the Grand Canyon? Bill's favorite book, film, and activity are all related, too.

Long-Term Memory

Your long-term memory is more or less permanent and can hold a vast amount of information—everything from names, dates, facts, and images to learned skills and personal experiences. Stored information falls into three categories. *Verbal information* comes from books and other printed sources. Verbal information that is oral, such as music or a lecture, is transmitted through your auditory sense. To improve retention of verbal information, become an active reader and listener. *Visual information* includes everything you see—paintings and other artwork, photographs, dance, the world around you. To improve retention of visual information, become more observant, attentive, and involved in what you are learning. *Physical and motor information* includes things you learn by doing: writing, drawing, participating in sports, and operating machines, for example. To improve retention of physical and motor information, you must practice new skills or activities until they become automatic.

Do you see a relationship between the categories of stored information and learning style? Which kind of information is easiest for you to remember? Which is the hardest? For example, some visual learners may find it easier to remember visual information than physical or motor information. Imagine a person who is learning to drive a vehicle with a standard transmission. Whereas a strongly tactile/kinesthetic learner would be able to feel or sense where the gears are, a strongly visual learner would do better with a diagram that illustrates the positions of the gears. You can see in this example that the diagram enables the visual learner to adapt to a physical learning task. Similarly, you must find effective ways to learn any kind of information, no matter what your learning style is.

In conclusion, getting and keeping information in your long-term memory requires your active involvement, a desire to remember, and regular practice. Actions such as using study systems, reciting and reviewing, and making study guides all aid retention.

Try Awareness Check 16 to see more examples of the information stored in your long-term memory.

WHAT'S IN YOUR LONG-TERM MEMORY?

Write your answers on the lines provided.

1.   Write your zip code here. _____

2.   Describe the contents of your medicine cabinet. _____

_____

_____

_____

3.   Describe how to start a dishwasher. _____

_____

_____

4.   Multiply 5 times 9. _____

5.   Write the capital of your home state. _____

6.   Think of someone you know well. What color is this person's hair?

_____

7.   Describe in detail a piece of furniture in your home or in your room. _____

_____

_____

_____

8.   Describe how to pedal a ten-speed up a steep hill. _____

_____

_____

_____

9.   Write the names of any three United States presidents.

_____

_____

_____

10. How many ounces are in a pound? _____

Items 1, 4, 5, 9, and 10 call for verbal information. Items 2, 6, and 7 call for visual information. Items 3 and 8 call for physical or motor information.

Increase Your Memory Power

THE STRATEGIES THAT follow have worked for many students. Perhaps you already use some of them, or maybe you'll discover a new technique to try.

- **Decide to remember.** Resist passivity. Become an active learner by making a conscious, deliberate decision to remember. Follow through on this decision. This is the most important step you can take. Unless you *decide* to remember, none of the other techniques will work.

- **Try relaxed review.** Don't wait until the last minute before a test to do your reviewing. Review regularly and do it in a relaxed way. When you are tense, you cannot concentrate. Try the chair-seat relaxation technique described next and shown in Figure 10.3.

1. **Start off in a positive frame of mind. Believe that you can and will remember.**

2. **Sit in a straight-backed chair with your feet together, flat on the floor.**

3. **Close your eyes; grasp the chair seat with both hands.**

4. **Pull up on the chair seat as hard as you can.**

5. **While you are pulling up with your hands, press your feet firmly to the floor.**

6. **Hold that position and count slowly to ten. Feel how tense all the muscles of your body are becoming.**

7. **Now relax completely, letting your arms hang loosely at your sides. Settle down into the chair and feel how calm you've become.**

8. **With your eyes still closed, visualize yourself being successful. Experience how success feels.**

9. **Slowly open your eyes and, in this calm state, begin to review your study material.**

10. **If you feel yourself becoming tense again, repeat steps 1–9.**

This relaxation technique is a variation of anxiety-reduction techniques used by professionals in fields such as psychology, medicine, education, and sports.

- **Combine review with a physical activity.** Each sense that you use while reviewing provides another pathway for information to reach your brain. Recite, either silently or aloud, while riding a bicycle, while doing aerobics or calisthenics (floor exercises like sit-ups and jumping jacks), and while walking and running. Feel good about yourself for keeping fit *and* for exercising your mind. This technique works well for anyone but is especially good for student athletes.

- **Use mnemonics.** *Mnemonics* are tricks, games, or rhymes that aid memory. You learned some as a child—for example, "In 1492, Columbus sailed the ocean blue." Also, you may have learned the rhyme that begins with "Thirty days hath September" to help you remember the number of days in each month. Here is one that you probably haven't heard: "Tyranny nixed in

| Figure 10.3 | **The Chair-Seat Relaxation Method** |

Steps 1 and 2   **Steps 3–6**   **Steps 7 and 8**   **Step 9**

'76." This rhyme recalls the year the Declaration of Independence was signed.

- **Use acronyms.** An *acronym* is a word formed by the first letters of other words. COPE, a problem-solving method, and GRAB, a time-management technique, are just two examples of acronyms used in *The Confident Student.* You probably know many others such as ASAP, a business acronym that means *as soon as possible,* and HUD, a government acronym that stands for the Department of Housing and Urban Development. An acronym may help you remember the steps in a process. Choose a key word that will help you remember each step. Then, using the first letter of each key word, create your acronym.

- **Associate to remember.** *Association* is the process of connecting new information that you want to remember to something that you already know. An association is often personal. For example, a student who wanted to remember the particles of the atom—proton, electron, and neutron—associated the names of the particles with the names of her brothers—Paul, Eric, and Norman. Her brothers' names and the particle names begin with the same letters, and they form the acronym *PEN.*

  To help yourself remember the three stages of memory, you could associate the mind with a computer and associate memory's three stages (reception, retention, and recollection) with three computer processes (input, storage, and output). If your instructor asks you to describe the three stages of memory, think of how a computer works, and you should be able to recall the three stages.

- **Visualize.** Form an image, or picture, in your mind of something that you want to remember. Visualization is an especially good way to link names with places or parts with locations. In geography, visualize places on a map. In physical science, draw an idealized continent that could stand for any continent and fill in climate zones. When reviewing this information or recalling it during a test, picture the continent and visualize the zones. In anatomy, label the bones on a drawing of a human skeleton. When reviewing or recalling, close your eyes and see the skeleton with your labels.

- **Use an organizational technique.** Organize information in a meaningful pattern that shows how each item relates to the others. List steps in a process. Outline complex material. Make charts, diagrams, and information maps that show the relationship of parts to a whole or one part to another. Figure 10.4 is a comparison chart showing the memory functions and stages discussed in this chapter. The chart condenses the information into one page that you can use for quick reference. Read the chart across the rows *and* down the columns. As you can see, the stages and functions are related: Your sensory, short-term, and long-term memory functions process information throughout the three stages.

- **Sleep on it.** Reviewing before sleep helps you retain information. Because you are relaxed, your concentration is focused. The information stays in your mind while you are sleeping, and interference from conflicting sounds, images, or ideas is minimal. When you wake, try to recall what you reviewed the night before. Chances are good that you will remember.

- **Remember key words.** Sometimes you have to remember a series of connected ideas and explanations, such as the chair-seat relaxation technique described early in this chapter. To recall items stated in phrases or

---

Figure 10.4   Your Memory Box

FUNCTIONS OF MEMORY	STAGES OF MEMORY		
	RECEPTION: GETTING INFORMATION	RETENTION: STORING INFORMATION	RECOLLECTION: RECALLING INFORMATION
Sensory Memory	Registers perceptions	Quickly lost without selective attention	Automatic from second to second
Short-Term Memory	Focuses on facts and details	Quickly lost unless recited or reviewed	Possible for short time only until information is lost
Long-Term Memory	Forms general ideas, images, and meanings	Integrates information transferred from short-term memory for storage	Possible for long periods of time or for a lifetime

sentences, select one or more key words in each item that sum up the phrase or sentence. Recalling key words will help you recall the whole item.

- **Memorize.** Some educators have reservations about memorization. They say memorization is not learning because it is usually done out of context. Students may not be able to recall items memorized in a certain order if the instructor puts them in a different order on a test. Critics also say that memorization is an inefficient technique and that memorized items are difficult to recall. Yet memorization does work. What is 9 times 9? You probably know the answer.

  Memorization can be a useful technique for recalling certain kinds of information, especially if it is combined with another memory strategy and is not the only technique you know how to use. Of course, you cannot expect to remember anything that you do not understand. First, make sure you comprehend any new information well enough to link it to knowledge you have already acquired. Memorization works best on information such as the spelling and definition of words, math and chemical formulas, poetry, and facts that belong in a certain order, such as historical events, life cycles, or food chains.

  To use memorization effectively for recalling the life cycle of a parasitic organism, for example, try this: Combine memorization with the use of key words to remind you of each stage in the cycle. Learn the stages in order but also be able to recall *any* stage in the cycle and what stages come before and after it. Figure 10.5 shows the stages in the life cycle of a malaria-causing parasite and key words you could use to recall them.

Figure 10.5   Life Cycle of *Plasmodium Vivax*

STAGES IN THE LIFE CYCLE	KEY WORDS
1. Female Anopheles mosquito bites someone who has malaria.	Mosquito, bites
2. Mosquito sucks up gametes of the parasite with the victim's blood.	Gametes
3. Gametes form a zygote in the mosquito's digestive tract.	Zygote
4. Oocysts develop from the zygote.	Oocysts
5. Oocysts divide into spindle-shaped cells called *sporozoites,* which migrate to the mosquito's salivary glands.	Sporozoites, salivary glands
6. Mosquito bites a new person and infects him or her with the sporozoites.	Mosquito, infects
7. Sporozoites enter person's liver cells and divide.	Sporozoites, liver
8. Merozoites, formed from the sporozoites, enter red blood cells and divide.	Merozoites, blood cells
9. Merozoites break out of blood cells about every 48 hours and produce fever.	Merozoites, fever
10. Parasites produce gametes through asexual reproduction, and cycle begins again if the parasites are ingested by a mosquito.	Parasites

EXERCISE **10.3**

THIS EXERCISE ASKS YOU TO work with group members to practice selecting appropriate memory strategies. Follow the guidelines for successful collaboration that appear on the inside back cover. Your tasks are as follows: From the following list, choose a learning activity that you think may be difficult for some students. Then review the memory strategies explained in this chapter. Using the questions as a guide, discuss which strategy would best help students complete the activity. Then record the group's answers to the questions and the group's evaluation.

- **Reading a chapter from a biology textbook**
- **Listening to a lecture**
- **Taking notes from a lecture**
- **Learning the bones of the human body**
- **Creating a spreadsheet**
- **Matching the names of artists with examples of their work**

1. **Which learning activity did your group choose, and why do you think it may be difficult for some students?** _____

_____

_____

2. **Does the activity require students to process verbal, visual, or physical/motor information?**

_____

_____

3. **Which memory strategy would improve students' *reception* of the information? How?**

_____

_____

_____

4. **Which memory strategy would improve students' *retention* of the information? How?**

_____

_____

_____

5. **Which memory strategy would improve students' *recollection* of the information? How?**

_____

_____

_____

Group Evaluation:

What have you learned about memory strategies? Which ones do you currently use, and which ones will you try? Did your group complete its tasks successfully? What improvements can you make? What additional questions do you have about memory, and how will you find the answers to your questions?

_____

_____

_____

_____

CONFIDENCE
Builder

Do Something Weird to Jog Your Memory

Many students have a favorite memory trick or strategy. Do you have one? Your best memory tricks are those you invent. Here are some suggestions to build on.

In the old days, people tied a string around one of their fingers as a reminder. Today, some people set their electronic organizers or beepers to remind them of something they need to do at a specific time. As in the past, many people today have learned that doing *anything* out of the ordinary can serve as a memory aid. Experiment with these three ideas. Either adapt them to suit your personal style or invent your own memory aid.

The Car Key Technique Do you forget to take your umbrella or books to class? As you're walking out the door, do you forget to pick up a stack of letters you need to mail? Try putting your car keys on or beside anything you want to take with you. Since you can't drive anywhere without your car keys, you will also be reminded of the books, letters, or other things you need to take along.

The Fence-Post System If your learning style is visual, this memory technique may appeal to you. Imagine that you have several items you need to remember. They might be things you want to take on a trip, a few purchases you need to make at the supermarket, or some materials you need to take to class tomorrow. First, visualize a row of fence posts. Then picture each item on a different fence post. Fix in your mind the order of the items. When this image is clear, picture again the empty fence posts. Then try to make each item appear, one at a time, on its appropriate post. Repeat these steps as many times as needed to recall all the items.

The Odd Object Method One student puts a large, empty cardboard box in front of the door when he wants to remember to make a phone call or do something important. Each time he starts toward the door, he wonders why the box is there; then he remembers what he has to do. Another student has a pewter dinosaur she received as a birthday gift that she places beside her purse to remind her of something she needs to do. When she starts to pick up her purse, the dinosaur jogs her memory. Any odd object placed somewhere you don't expect it can serve as a memory cue. To pursue this topic further, do an online search using these key words as a starting point: *memory systems, memory techniques, improving memory.*

SOMETIME SOON YOU WILL FACE midterm or final exams. Understanding your learning style and using the appropriate memory strategies suggested in this chapter will help you prepare effectively. Answer the following questions about strategies you plan to try.

1.   **Underline your preferred learning style: visual, auditory, tactile. How have you determined that this is your preferred learning style?**

_____

_____

2. **List three memory strategies from this chapter that seem best suited to your learning style. Write one sentence about each strategy to explain why you believe it is appropriate for you.**

a. _____

_____

_____

b. _____

_____

_____

c. _____

_____

_____

3. **List two memory strategies that do not fit your learning style but that you are willing to try. Write a sentence about each to explain why you would like to try it.**

a. _____

_____

_____

b. _____

_____

_____

4. **What relationship do you see between the type of information to be learned (verbal, visual, or physical/motor) and your learning style preference (visual, auditory, or tactile/kinesthetic)?**

_____

_____

_____

_____

_____

thinking *ahead*   ▪ ▪ ▪ ▪ ➔

What practical knowledge have you gained from this chapter that you can use to solve real-world problems? To find out, read the following scenario and complete the items after it.

Tracy has landed a summer job at an architect's firm. She is excited about working there because she is majoring in architecture, and this job will give her some first-hand experience. Her duties include various secretarial services such as running errands, copying and delivering blueprints, and any other tasks her bosses assign her. This job gives Tracy the opportunity to meet everyone in the firm and acquaints her with the duties and responsibilities of everyone from the chief architect to the maintenance crew. Because Tracy has so many different jobs to do for so many people, she has difficulty remembering who is who and who needs what. Tracy would like to try some of the memory techniques she studied last quarter in her student success class—if only she could remember them!

1. What is Tracy's problem?

_____

_____

_____

_____

2. What seems to be causing the problem?

_____

_____

_____

_____

3. What can Tracy do?

_____

_____

_____

_____

4. What memory techniques have you tried that might work for Tracy?

_____

_____

_____

_____

chapter review

ATTITUDES TO DEVELOP
- the desire to become an active learner
- the willingness to take control of your learning
- a commitment to lifelong learning

CONCEPTS TO UNDERSTAND

The three Rs of memory are _____, _____, and _____. During every waking moment, you are receiving information about the world around you through your five senses. This information is stored, or retained, for varying lengths of time so that you can recall it as you need it. All the information that you receive from the environment stays briefly in your _____ memory. Through selective attention, important information is separated from the insignificant and is stored briefly in _____ memory, enabling you, for example, to hold a phone number in your mind long enough to dial it. If you are reading a textbook passage or listening to a lecture, the information that you receive from these sources must be stored in _____ memory and reviewed frequently to aid retention.

Stored information falls into three categories: _____, _____, and _____ information. Some memories, such as how to drive a car, stay with you all your life. Forgetting occurs because of the brevity of _____ memory and _____ memory. To combat forgetting, you must transfer information into your _____ memory. Transference is a process you can influence by employing various memory techniques, the most important of which is deciding to remember. Information is more likely to stay with you if you relate it to your existing knowledge.

As you try the memory suggestions in this chapter and in other sources, keep in mind that they may or may not work for you. In the end, your best memory strategy will be one that corresponds to your learning style. If your preferred learning style is _____, try visualization. If you prefer the _____ learning mode, recite. If the _____ mode works best for you, combine reviewing with a physical activity. Also try to vary your style. Though you may prefer one mode of learning, it is not the only mode you can learn to use.

To access additional review exercises, see http://college.hmco.com/success.

SKILLS TO PRACTICE
- using proven memory techniques and study systems
- creating your own memory aids and study systems

Your Reflections

Your Reflections

Reflect on what you have learned about information processing and memory and how you can best apply that information. Use the following list of questions to stimulate your thinking; then write your reflections. Your response may include answers to one or more of the questions. Incorporate in your writing specific information from this chapter or from previous chapters as it's needed.

- How are concentration and memory linked?

- What kinds of information are easy for you to learn? What kinds are difficult?

- What are some learning strategies that have worked for you?

- What new strategies have you learned from this chapter? How do you plan to use them?

- Of the attitudes and skills listed in the Chapter Review, which do you think will be most useful at work or in your career?

Preparing for Tests

ARE YOU ALWAYS well prepared for

tests? Do you know what, when, and

how to study? Do you use specific strategies for taking

different kinds of tests such as multiple-choice

tests and essay exams?

IF YOU ASK college students what their most persistent academic worry is, many will say "Grades." Like most college students, you may be looking for ways to improve your grades and may even wish there were a secret formula or short-cut to success. Although there are no shortcuts, there *is* a key to good grades, and it's no secret: preparation.

Time management, planning, and the use of appropriate study skills are your keys to preparing for tests. Individual responsibility and self-management keep you motivated and on task. Being responsible means accepting that grades are the direct result of your effort. Being a good self-manager means having the self-discipline to put study first.

As you can see, preparing for tests requires the interaction of several skills and attitudes that not only lead to good grades but also have an added benefit. Planning, managing your time, being responsible, and choosing appropriate strategies are marketable workplace competencies you can carry into the future.

Do you need to improve the way you prepare for tests? Find out by taking Awareness Check 17. The strategies explained in this chapter can help you prepare for tests with confidence:

- Decide what, when, and how to study.

- Have a test-taking routine and use it consistently.

- Know how to prepare for any kind of test.

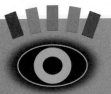

Awareness Check 17

HOW DO YOU STUDY FOR TESTS?

Yes	No	*Answer yes or no to the following questions.*
☐	☐	1. Do you allow sufficient time to prepare for tests?
☐	☐	2. Do you usually know what to study?
☐	☐	3. Do you use a study system such as SQ3R?
☐	☐	4. Are you usually satisfied with your test grades?
☐	☐	5. Do you know what kinds of errors you make?
☐	☐	6. Do you often become distracted during tests?
☐	☐	7. Do you enter a testing situation feeling mentally and physically prepared?
☐	☐	8. Do you have a test-taking routine that you follow?
☐	☐	9. Do you know how to take multiple-choice, true-false, and fill-in-the-blank tests?
☐	☐	10. Do you know how to plan and write an essay for an exam?

If you answered no to any of these questions, you will benefit from this chapter, which shows you how to prepare for tests and what to do in a testing situation to improve your performance.

How to Prepare for Tests: Three Steps

IF YOU WALK into a test knowing that you are well prepared, you will feel confident that you can succeed. If you do not prepare sufficiently, you will probably feel a lack of confidence and perhaps even some anxiety that you will not earn a good grade. To ensure that you will be prepared for every test, follow these three essential steps:

1. Make a study schedule.

2. Decide what to study.

3. Use your study system.

These steps are the answers to three common questions students ask about studying for tests: When should I study? What should I study? How should I study?

Make a Study Schedule

The purpose of making a study schedule is to establish fixed times for review so that review becomes a habit. Allow time in your schedule for daily, weekly, and exam reviews.

Daily Reviews. Take five to ten minutes per day to review each course. Begin by reviewing your notes and assignments for the previous class. Immediately or as soon as possible after class, review new material and try to relate it to what you have learned in the course so far. In doing this, you will make connections among topics and gain a broad perspective on the course.

Weekly Reviews. In addition to the time you spend doing assignments, spend about an hour a week reviewing each subject. Review lecture notes, textbook

Relaxing and talking with others for a few moments is a good way to break from an exam review.

© Jim Whitmer

notes, and your study guides and try to anticipate test questions. A weekly review is an in-depth look at what you have covered in a course during one week. Relate the week's work to the previous week's work and determine how the new material fits into the course.

Exam Reviews. About one week before a test, conduct a major review. Exam reviews will take longer than weekly reviews because they may cover several weeks' material. To prepare for exams, review lecture notes, textbook notes, study guides, note cards, instructors' handouts, and previous tests, papers, or graded assignments. Your daily and weekly reviews will make the material seem familiar so that you may see a pattern in the topics you are studying and may think of possible test questions.

Your study schedule should allow five to ten minutes a day per course for daily reviews, an hour per course for weekly reviews, and two hours or more for a specific exam review. Enter times for review on your schedule and make a commitment to follow it.

Exam reviews are the hardest because they take the longest and cover the most material. Try these tips for improving concentration when you have to study for two or more hours:

- Review at the time of day when you are most alert.

- Study for your hardest exam first.

- About once every hour, take a break. Get up and walk around; do something unrelated to studying.

- Reward yourself for getting the job done. Plan to go out with friends or do something that's fun when you have finished your review.

Decide What to Study

Test questions can come from a variety of sources. To study for a major test, review lecture notes, textbook chapters, textbook notes and study guides, previous tests, papers, homework, and instructors' handouts. Don't waste time reviewing information you already know; study material you have not fully grasped. Study the most difficult material first. If you study the easiest topics first, then by the time you get to the hard ones, you will probably be tired and unable to give them your best effort. Study the most complex or technical concepts when you are most alert; be willing to look up definitions and re-read sentences until you grasp their meaning. Later, when you are tired, take a short break and then study less challenging material. Your understanding of the subject will lead to improved confidence and productivity.

Lecture Notes. Lectures often supplement information presented in textbooks. They are usually organized around a major topic in the course outline. If your instructor gives weekly lectures, the lecture topics probably build upon weekly assigned chapters and the week's topic listed in your syllabus.

Textbook Chapters. Review your underlining and marginal notes. If you have underlined or annotated the most important ideas, your review will be both efficient and thorough.

Textbook Notes and Study Guides. Review any additional notes, maps, outlines, note cards, or other study materials you have made. Since your own

© Brian Halmer/PhotoEdit

Outdoor exercise is a great reward for completing your review. It can help to relieve pre-exam stress and ensure a good night's rest as well.

notes and guides are summaries of textbook material written in your own words, they will be the easiest for you to remember.

Graded Tests, Papers, Homework, and Other Assignments. Your previous tests are useful for two reasons. First, you can determine from these tests the kinds of questions your instructor asks. Second, you can learn from your mistakes. Questions that you missed enable you to spot weak points in your studying—information that you forgot, ignored, or didn't understand. Instructors' comments on papers and other graded assignments may also point out strengths and weaknesses and provide clues about what you should study.

Instructors' Handouts. Anything your instructor hands out is bound to be important. Instructors frequently summarize information on handouts. Don't overlook these important study aids when you review for a major test.

You may benefit from studying with another student. Comparing your notes with someone else's can help both of you. What one of you misses the other may have in his or her notes. Also, students vary in their understanding of lectures and textbooks chapters. A topic that gave you trouble may have been easy for a friend. Talking it over gives you another perspective on the subject.

Use Your Study System

Once you have decided *what* to study, *how* you study will determine the effectiveness of your review. Don't study in a hit-or-miss fashion and don't re-read chapters. Instead, use a system. By now you may have tried the suggestions in Chapter 7 for using SQ3R or for adapting a system to your learning style. If your system is working, use it. If you would like to try a different strategy, follow these steps to prepare for a major test in one of your courses:

EXERCISE **11.1**

MAKE OUT A NEW WEEK'S schedule. Include time for daily reviews and for one weekly review. After you have completed this schedule, update your semester or quarter calendar. Schedule times for major exam reviews one week before each test date. Go to http://college.hmco.com/success to download extra copies as needed.

	Sunday	Monday	Tuesday	Wednesday	Thursday	Friday	Saturday
6:00 – 7:00							
7:00 – 8:00							
8:00 – 9:00							
9:00 – 10:00							
10:00 – 11:00							
11:00 – 12:00							
12:00 – 1:00							
1:00 – 2:00							
2:00 – 3:00							
3:00 – 4:00							
4:00 – 5:00							
5:00 – 6:00							
6:00 – 7:00							
7:00 – 8:00							
8:00 – 9:00							
9:00 – 10:00							
10:00 – 11:00							
11:00 – 12:00							
12:00 – 1:00							

1. One week before the test, schedule two or more hours of time to review all chapters and topics that the test will cover. Do not attempt to study for two hours straight without taking a break because you will lose interest and concentration. Instead, plan your study time to review specific material in several short sessions, taking a break in between.

2. Organize your materials. Sort lecture notes, textbook notes, study guides, handouts, and previously graded tests and assignments by chapter or topic; then make a list of the important topics, kinds of problems, or other specific information you think will be on a test.

3. If you must review a lot of facts, terms, formulas, steps in a process, or similar material, put the information on 3" × 5" note cards to carry in your pocket or purse. Recite from these cards, silently or aloud, at every opportunity. Look at the sample note cards in Figure 11.1 for examples of the kind of information to include and how much to write. Keep your cards simple; write just enough to serve as a memory cue.

Figure 11.1   **Note Cards for Review**

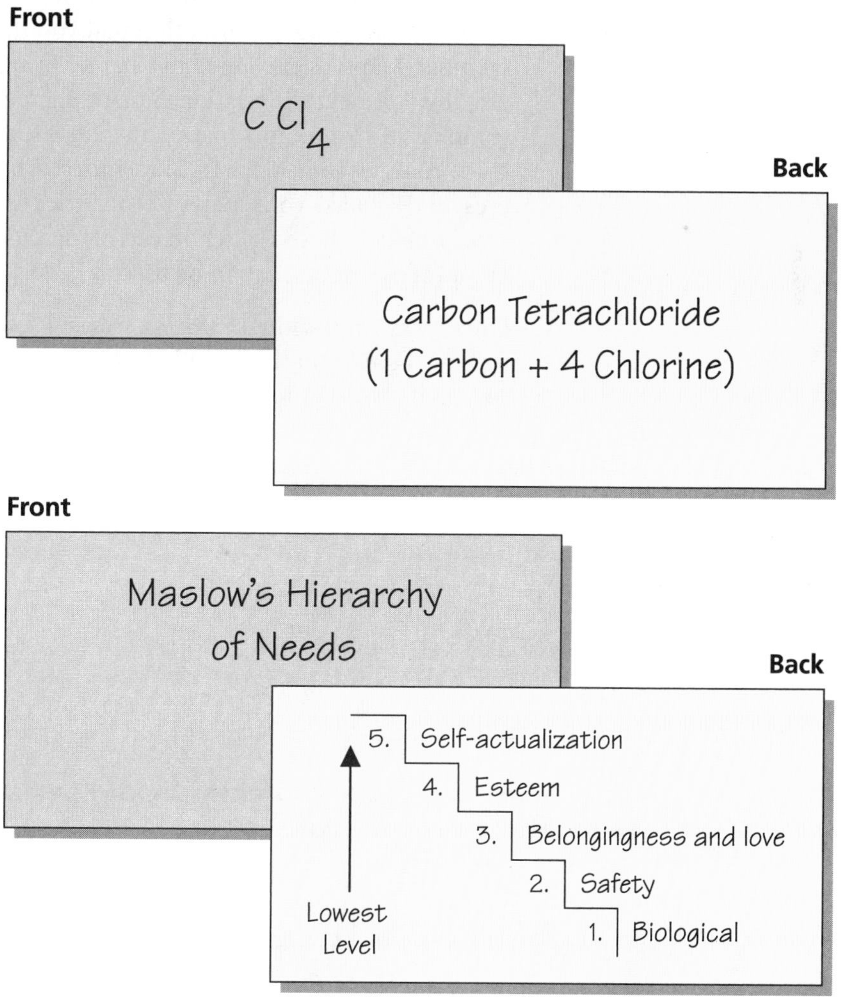

Front

$C Cl_4$

Back

Carbon Tetrachloride
(1 Carbon + 4 Chlorine)

Front

Maslow's Hierarchy
of Needs

Back

5. Self-actualization

4. Esteem

3. Belongingness and love

2. Safety

1. Biological

Lowest
Level

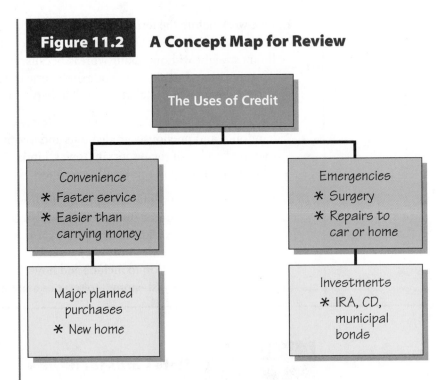

Figure 11.2   **A Concept Map for Review**

The Uses of Credit

Convenience
* Faster service
* Easier than carrying money

Emergencies
* Surgery
* Repairs to car or home

Major planned purchases
* New home

Investments
* IRA, CD, municipal bonds

4. Map or diagram any information that you think will be difficult to remember. Maps, as explained in Chapter 8, are charts and diagrams that visually represent the relationship among ideas. Maps are convenient; they summarize a lot of information in a little space. When studying for a test, try to re-draw your maps from memory. When taking a test, close your eyes and visualize your maps. Reconstruct them in your mind and try to "see" what you have written in each square or circle. Figure 11.2 is an example of a concept map to be used as a study guide.

5. Once a day until you take the test, review your maps and other materials. Review them again the night before the test, just before you go to sleep. Research shows that studying before sleeping improves retention. Then review once more the day of the test.

EXERCISE **11.2**

DISCOVER YOUR OWN BEST WAY to prepare for a test by answering the following questions about test preparation and your learning style.

1. **Based on your answers to Awareness Check 17, what are your strengths and weaknesses in preparing for tests?**

_____

_____

_____

2. **What relationship do you see between your body's reactions and the way you prepare for tests? For example, when is your best time to study, and how do you accommodate your body's reactions to hunger, tiredness, stress, and so on when preparing for tests?**

_____

_____

_____

3. **What is your preferred learning style (visual, auditory, tactile/kinesthetic), and how does it affect the way you prepare for tests?**

_____

_____

_____

4. **Are you self-motivated or other-motivated, and how does your locus of control (source of motivation) affect your ability to study for tests?**

_____

_____

_____

5. **What changes can you make in the way you prepare for tests that will help you take advantage of your learning style preference?**

_____

_____

_____

_____

Choose a partner or form a small group of students who are taking the same course, whether it's psychology, biology, algebra, economics, your student success course, or another. Discuss what your class has covered recently and when your next test will be. Then write at least five test questions that you think your instructor is likely to ask. Your questions can be true-false, multiple-choice, fill-ins, or essay. Write the answers to your questions and then determine what the most effective way to study for this test would be. Share your results with the rest of the class.

Develop a Test-taking Routine

YOU CAN IMPROVE your grades on tests by developing a routine to follow that helps you stay calm, avoid distractions, and demonstrate your knowledge. Your test-taking routine should include most or all of the following steps.

Arrive on Time

If hearing other students discuss the test makes you nervous and distracted, don't arrive early. Arrive on time and try to sit near the front of the room, where you are less likely to be distracted. If you feel a little nervous, close your eyes, take a few deep breaths, and think positive thoughts. If anxiety either before or during tests is a problem for you, see Chapter 12 for an explanation of how to reduce test anxiety.

Jot Down Memory Cues

If you are likely to forget facts, formulas, dates, names, terms, or other items, write them in the margin or on the back of the test as soon as you get it. For example, math students tend to get nervous when they are working on a difficult problem or can't remember the next step in a mathematical operation. This anxiety can cause them to forget other concepts and applications. The facts, formulas, and other items that you jot down on your test are memory cues. Knowing that the cues are there will boost your confidence. You won't be worried about forgetting the information, and you will be able to concentrate on taking the test.

Survey the Test

As soon as you receive your test and after you have jotted down your memory cues, survey the test to determine how many questions there are, how many points each is worth, and what kinds of questions you must answer: true-false, multiple-choice, fill-in, or essay. If it's not clear from the test how many points each question is worth, ask your instructor. A quick survey of the test will let you know what you must accomplish within the time limit so that you can plan your test-taking time.

Plan and Use All Your Time

Plan to spend the most time answering the questions that are worth the most points. If twenty-five multiple-choice questions are worth one point each, and two essay questions are worth twenty-five points each, and you have fifty minutes to complete the test, answer as many of the multiple-choice questions as you can in ten minutes. That will leave you forty minutes to complete the two essay questions. Spend fifteen minutes answering the first question; then stop and go on to the next one, even if you have not finished. Spend fifteen minutes on the second question. You will now have ten minutes left. Use the ten minutes as needed. You can return to the multiple-choice questions if you have completed the essays, or you can work more on your essays if you finished the multiple-choice questions earlier. Save a few minutes to proofread the whole test and answer any multiple-choice questions that you may have skipped.

Although there are many ways to plan your time, the one suggested here will help you gain some points for each part of the test, even if you are unable to finish all of the questions. If you plan your time and stick to your plan, you will not have to rush. Use all of your time, even if you don't need it. The extra care you take may help you spot mistakes or think of a better way to state an answer.

Read Directions

It may seem obvious that you should read test directions before beginning, but a surprising number of students skip directions. Perhaps they think that reading directions wastes time or that they already know what to do. To avoid needless mistakes, always read directions and ask the instructor to explain anything that you do not understand.

Do Easy Questions First

When you survey the test, you will probably spot questions that will be easy for you to answer. Do those first since you have a good chance of getting the answers right. In addition, doing the easy questions first will raise your confidence in your ability to answer the rest of the questions.

Skip and Return to Difficult Questions

Don't spend too much time on a difficult question. Skip it and return to it later. If something you read or recall as you answer the other questions triggers your memory, you can go back to the one you didn't answer and then resume the test where you left off.

Guess (If There Is No Penalty)

If there is a penalty for wrong answers, the test directions will probably say so. If you are in doubt, ask the instructor. If there is no penalty, guess. Don't leave questions blank; even if you don't think you know the answer, write something anyway. You may pick up a few points. If you guess the answer to a multiple-choice question that has four choices, your chances are one in four that you will get the right answer. If you don't answer, your chances are zero.

Control Your Feelings and Attention

Remain in control of your feelings and attention throughout the test. To avoid becoming distracted, focus your attention on the test. Keep your eyes on the test and don't look up or around. If you don't know what other students are doing, you're not likely to be disturbed by them. You won't notice what page someone else is on or whether someone finishes early.

Maintain a positive attitude. If you sense negative thoughts creeping in, don't let them undermine your work. Counteract them with positive ones. Say to yourself, "I have studied, and I am doing fine." If you become anxious, close your eyes, breathe deeply, and relax. When you feel calm, return to the test and give it your full attention. See Chapter 12 for more suggestions on how to reduce test anxiety.

Check Your Work

Always save time to proofread your test for careless errors and for questions you skipped or forgot to answer. Change answers only if you're absolutely sure your first answer was wrong. First choices are usually correct, so if you have doubts about one of your answers, don't change it.

Learn from Your Mistakes

The next time your instructor returns a graded test, determine what kinds of mistakes you made. Look for a pattern. If you are like many students, you probably make the same mistakes over and over again. If you can prevent these errors, you will improve your test scores.

Master Objective Tests

IF YOU ARE well prepared for a test, you should be able to answer the questions whether they are true-false, multiple-choice, fill-in-the-blank, or essay. But when confronted with questions you cannot answer, try to gain points by making informed guesses.

True-False Tests

Since a true-false question has only two possible answers, you have a 50 percent chance of choosing the right answer if you guess. Use two strategies for guessing the answer to a true-false question when you are sure that you don't know the answer:

1. **Assume a statement is false if it contains absolute words.**

2. **Assume a statement is false if any part of it is false.**

Mark a statement *false* if it contains absolute words such as *always, never, invariably, none, no one, all,* and *everyone.* Absolute words tend to make statements false because they do not allow for exceptions. For example, you should mark the statement "It never gets cold in Florida" *false* because the word *never* means "never in the history of the world." It is highly unlikely that there is a place on Earth where it has never gotten cold even once. Is the next statement true or false? "A statement that contains an absolute word is always false." The statement is false. Remember, absolute words *usually* make statements false, but not always.

Mark a statement *false* if any part of it is false. If part of a statement is untrue, then the whole statement is untrue. For example, the statement "*Hamlet, Macbeth,* and *The Dream Merchant* are three of Shakespeare's most famous tragedies" is false. Although Shakespeare did write *Hamlet* and *Macbeth,* he did not write *The Dream Merchant.* If you don't know whether a statement is true or false, but you're certain that part of it is untrue, mark it *false.*

Multiple-Choice Tests

The part of a multiple-choice item that asks the question is called the *stem.* The answer choices are called *options.* The incorrect options are called *distractors* because they distract your attention away from the correct option. Usually there are

EXERCISE **11.3**

USE THE GUESSING STRATEGIES YOU just learned to mark the following statements *T* for *true* and *F* for *false*. Work with a partner or complete the exercise on your own.

	T	F
1. **The heart contains a left and right ventricle.**	☐	☐
2. **You can look up the meaning of a word in a glossary, index, or dictionary.**	☐	☐
3. **All fears are acquired at an early age.**	☐	☐
4. **Making note cards is the only way to study vocabulary.**	☐	☐
5. **Whenever there is a fatal accident on the highway, drinking is invariably involved.**	☐	☐
6. **It is doubtful whether there is human life on other planets.**	☐	☐
7. **College graduates will always be able to find good jobs.**	☐	☐
8. **Most violent crime today is drug related.**	☐	☐
9. **Carl Jung has been called "the father of modern psychology."**	☐	☐
10. **The numbers *1, 3, 5,* and *9* are prime numbers.**	☐	☐

four options, though there might be three or five. Your job is to identify the one correct option. You can do this in several ways.

- If you know the material, first answer the question mentally and then read all the options and choose the correct one.

- If you know the material but cannot answer the question mentally, read the options, eliminate those you know are incorrect, and choose the answer from those remaining. The more options you eliminate, the more likely your choice will be correct.

- If you do not know the material, or if you cannot figure out the answer, guess.

Options that contain the phrases "all of the above" or "none of the above" are frequently the correct choices. If two options are similar—for example, "Northern Hemisphere" and "Southern Hemisphere"—one of the options is probably the correct answer. Finally, if one option is more complete or contains more information than the others, it may be the correct one.

An option that contains an absolute word such as *all, always,* or *never* is probably a distractor, an incorrect answer. An option that contains an unfamiliar word may also be a distractor. Many students assume that an unfamiliar term is probably the correct answer, but it is more often a wrong answer. When you are guessing, you are more likely to choose the right answer if you choose an option that is familiar to you. Finally, if the list of options is a list of numbers, middle numbers tend to be correct answers, and the highest and lowest numbers in the list tend to be distractors. These strategies are not foolproof, but they may be useful as a last resort if you must guess the answer to a question.

One final word of caution: A well-written multiple-choice test makes guesswork difficult. Thorough preparation is still your best strategy for taking any kind of test.

EXERCISE **11.4**

THIS EXERCISE ASKS YOU AND the members of your group to practice the guessing strategies that are appropriate to use when you do not know the answer to a multiple-choice item. Follow the guidelines for successful collaboration that appear on the inside back cover. Your tasks are as follows: First, each person should answer questions 1–10. Next, discuss your answers and come to a consensus about the best answer choice for each question. Be able to explain why you think your answer is correct and the strategy you used to arrive at it. Review the guessing strategies explained in this chapter as needed. Finally summarize your answers and explanations on a separate piece of paper to be handed in along with the group evaluation.

1. **A marriage may have a better chance of succeeding if the wife and husband have which characteristic in common?**

   a. **a similar level of education**

   b. **similar social and economic backgrounds**

   c. **shared interests and goals**

   d. **all of the above**

2. **Most of the assignments college students are asked to do require them to use**

   a. **left-brain capacities.**

   b. **right-brain capacities.**

   c. **learning styles.**

   d. **visualization.**

3. **Which of the following are examples of fallacious reasoning?**

   a. **glittering generalities**

   b. **plain folks**

   c. **bandwagon**

   d. **glittering generalities, plain folks, and bandwagon**

4. **A balanced diet should include**

   a. **milk, cheese, and fruit.**

   b. **bread, cereal, and whole grains.**

   c. **milk, fruit, vegetables, meat, and whole grains.**

   d. **vegetables, fruit, and meat.**

5. **Most of the world's population is situated**

   a. **in the Pacific islands.**

   b. **in the Northern Hemisphere.**

   c. **in the Southern Hemisphere.**

   d. **near the equator.**

6. **Approximately what percentage of immigrants to the United States between 1971 and 1984 came from Asia?**

   a. **60 percent**

   b. **30 percent**

   c. **40 percent**

   d. **15 percent**

7. **Which of the following words is a synonym for *intractable*?**

    a. **synergistic**

    b. **acerbic**

    c. **exacerbating**

    d. **stubborn**

8. **Television commercials**

    a. **always attempt to deceive viewers.**

    b. **are sometimes interesting to viewers.**

    c. **are never in the public interest.**

    d. **influence only people who listen to them.**

9. **The first quiz programs were televised**

    a. **in the 1970s.**

    b. **in the 1950s.**

    c. **in the 1940s.**

    d. **before 1920.**

10. **A smile**

    a. **may mean different things in different societies.**

    b. **always signifies happiness.**

    c. **occurs among the people of only some societies.**

    d. **never occurs involuntarily.**

Group Evaluation:

What advantage do guessing strategies offer? What is the best way to avoid having to guess? Did your group complete its tasks successfully? What improvements can you suggest? What additional questions do you have about taking multiple-choice tests, and how will you find answers to your questions?

Fill-in-the-Blank Tests

A fill-in test may require you to recall an answer from memory or choose an answer from a list of options. Choosing an answer from a list is easier than recalling an answer from memory. In either case, the information given in the incomplete statement may provide clues that will help you decide what to write in the blanks. Three strategies can help you fill in the blanks correctly.

First, decide what kind of answer the statement requires. Read the statement carefully and decide whether you are supposed to supply a name, a date, a place, or some other kind of information. Knowing what the question asks will help you recall or select the right answer.

Second, the way in which a statement is written may help you decide how to complete it. Your answer should complete the statement logically and grammatically. For example, if you are asked to choose options from a list to fill in the blanks, and the statement you are working on requires a verb to complete it, scan the list for verbs and choose one of them.

Third, key words in statements may help you determine what topic the question covers. Knowing the topic will help you recall information needed to complete the statement. For example, if a question asks you to briefly describe Piaget's third stage of development, the key words *Piaget* and *third stage of development* let you know that the topic is Piaget's stages. If you can't recall the third stage, reconstructing the other stages in your mind may jog your memory.

EXERCISE **11.5**

THE FOLLOWING FILL-IN-THE-BLANK test covers the preceding section, Master Objective Tests. Review the section; then complete the test for practice without looking back at the book. When you have finished, look back to check your answers. Any questions that you missed indicate material that you need to review.

1. **Three common types of objective tests are** _____, _____, **and** _____.

2. **Words such as** *always, never,* **and** *only* **are called** _____.

3. **These words generally indicate a wrong answer because** _____

   _____.

4. **A statement is false if any part of it is** _____.

5. **The question part of a multiple-choice item is called the** _____.

6. _____ **are the possible answers to a multiple-choice question.**

7. **Incorrect answer choices to a multiple-choice question are called** _____.

8. **Three strategies to use when taking fill-in-the-blank tests are** _____, _____,

   and _____.

Know How to Answer Essay Questions

YOU CAN EXPECT to see two kinds of essay questions—those that require a short answer and those that require a longer, more developed answer. You can often tell how much you are expected to write by the number of points a question is worth or the amount of space left between questions. Sometimes the directions will be specific: "Answer any two of the five questions that follow and devote no more than a page to each." If you are not sure how much you should write or how detailed your instructor expects your answer to be, ask. In general, follow these guidelines for composing answers to essay questions of the short-answer type:

- Read the question carefully and make sure you understand what the question asks.

- Watch for instruction words. Short-answer questions often ask you to supply definitions, examples, or other specific pieces of information.

- Concentrate on answering the question briefly and precisely.

- Stay on the topic and avoid stating your opinion or making judgments unless the question asks you to do so.

- Restate the question in your answer. Doing this makes it easier for your instructor to read and follow your explanation.

If you do not know the answer to a question, go on to another part of the test and return to it later. Information you read in another question may jog your memory. In any case, don't leave a question unanswered. Try to write something. Essay questions are often worth several points, and you have nothing to lose by attempting to answer. Read the following sample test question and its answer:

Question: Define *memory* and illustrate your definition with examples.

Answer: Memory is a mental process that occurs in three stages: reception, retention, and recollection. In the reception stage you take in information through your senses. Most of this is information you will forget unless you store it during the retention stage in your short-term or long-term memory. Short-term memory is fleeting. It enables you to remember a phone number you have looked up long enough to dial it, or the name of someone you met at a party long enough to introduce him or her to someone else. Long-term memory can be permanent. For example, you never forget your birthday. In the recollection stage you retrieve information you have stored much as you would retrieve a file from a computer's directory.

This answer responds to both instruction words in the question: *define* and *illustrate*. The student defines memory as a three-stage process, names and explains each stage, and gives examples of each. Figure 11.3 contains a list of instruction words that are frequently used in essay questions and their meanings.

Figure 11.3	Instruction Words Used in Essay Questions
INSTRUCTION WORDS	**MEANINGS**
Compare	Explain similarities and differences.
Contrast	Explain differences only.
Criticize or evaluate	Make a judgment about strengths and weaknesses, worth or merit, or positive or negative aspects.
Define	Give a precise and accurate meaning.
Describe	Give a mental impression, a detailed account.
Discuss or explain	Give reasons, facts, or details that show you understand.
Enumerate or list	State points one by one and briefly explain.
Illustrate	Explain by using examples.
Interpret	Explain in your own words and discuss significance.
Justify or prove	Construct an argument for or against and support with evidence.
Outline	Describe in general and cover main points.
Relate	Show a connection among ideas.
Summarize	Condense main ideas; state them briefly.
Trace	Describe a series of steps, stages, or events.

Some easy questions require a longer answer that may cover several points. You will stand a better chance of getting a good grade if your answer is detailed but not rambling, if you stick to facts and information and avoid opinions and judgments, if your answer follows a logical plan of development, and if you state your ideas clearly in error-free sentences. In general, apply the same skills you use for writing essays in your composition class to composing answers to essay questions. Be sure to look for instruction words in each question that will tell you what kind of answer to write.

The following general guidelines will help you compose good answers to longer essay test questions:

- Read the question carefully. Watch for instruction words and make sure you understand what the question asks you to do. Ask the instructor for an explanation if necessary.

- Think about what you will write. Plan your answer and allow yourself enough time to write thoughtfully.

- Jot down a scratch outline of the important ideas you will cover so that you don't forget them.

- Incorporate the question into your first sentence and briefly state your answer to the question.

- In the rest of your essay, provide enough details to explain your answer and to demonstrate your knowledge of the material.

- Save time at the end of the exam to proofread your essay and correct errors.

The following essay question and list show how to plan an effective answer. The instruction word and topics are in italics.

Question	How can a student learn to improve *time management?* Discuss the effective use of a *semester schedule,* a *weekly schedule,* and a *daily list.*
Paragraph 1:	Briefly introduce and restate the question, and briefly state your answer.
Paragraph 2:	Discuss semester schedule.
Paragraph 3:	Discuss weekly schedule.
Paragraph 4:	Discuss daily list.
Paragraph 5:	Summarize what you have said.

Time management is the topic, and it is broken down into three types of schedules. The instruction word *discuss* tells you to supply reasons, facts, or details to explain the schedules.

When your test paper is returned to you, read over your answers to the essay questions. Notice how many points you gained, how many you lost, and the reasons for each. Check for these three common mistakes: First, did you read the directions carefully? If not, your answer may be off the topic. Second, did you cover all parts of the question to receive full credit? Third, did you include enough details? If not, you may have lost points. Read your instructor's comments to determine what you need to do to improve your grade on the next test. If you scored poorly on the essay portion of the test, and you do not understand why, make an appointment with your instructor to discuss your grade. Be sure to ask your instructor what you can do to improve.

EXERCISE **11.6**

SEARCH THE INTERNET FOR MORE suggestions on ways to prepare for and take tests. As a starting point, try these search words: *test-wiseness, study skills, test-taking techniques.* If you have trouble, go to http://college.hmco.com/success to begin your search. Also, visit your college's web site to see what is available. In addition, choose another college or university and check out its web site for information on preparing for tests. Share what you find with the rest of the class.

CONFIDENCE Builder

How to Raise Scores on Standardized Tests

You can't study for a standardized test, but try these ways to prepare yourself for success.

Check your campus or local bookstore to see if you can purchase a study guide for the test you need to take. Find out if your college offers a prep course or review session that will help you get ready for the test. In addition, try these suggestions:

- Know how many sections there are on the test and what each section covers. Find out whether you will be required to write one or more essays.

- Find out whether the test will be timed, how long it will last, and how much time you will have to complete each section. If the test will last longer than two hours, take a snack that you can eat during a break for a quick energy boost.

- If you must write an essay as part of the test, practice writing in a timed situation. Choose a topic, set a timer or alarm clock, and write your essay. If you practice writing within a time limit, you are less likely to become anxious when taking a timed test.

- Find out if you will be allowed to use a dictionary, calculator, or other aids during the test.

- Find out whether the test is administered online or with examination booklets. Then purchase any special materials you will need.

- Get a good night's sleep, eat a nourishing breakfast, and arrive at the testing site on time, rested, and in a positive frame of mind.

- To increase your chances of scoring well, apply the test-taking strategies you have learned from this chapter. Use guessing strategies if there is no penalty for guessing, and you do not know the answer.

- During breaks between sections of the test, stand up and move around to increase your circulation. This little bit of exercise will make you feel more alert when you return to the test.

- Whether working online or on an answer sheet, use any remaining time to proofread and correct your answers.

Don't worry if you are unable to complete a section of the test. On some standardized tests, hardly anyone finishes. Also, you can miss many of the items and still make a passing score. Finally, even if you score below a cutoff on a standardized test, you may be allowed to retake the part of the test on which you scored low.

To pursue this topic further, do an online search using these key words as a starting point: *testing, standardized tests, preparing for tests.* To find out about a particular test and any prep courses or materials that may be available, use the name of the test such as *GRE, LSAT,* and so on as a search word.

thinking *ahead* - - - - ➔

What practical knowledge have you gained from this chapter that you can use to solve real-world problems? To find out, read the following scenario and complete the items after it.

Dan has almost completed his program in respiratory therapy. Soon he will graduate and begin his long-awaited career. However, he has one more hurdle to jump: his qualifying exams. He knows that these exams include a standardized test, and he is nervous because he usually doesn't do well on that type of test. Other than that, he is feeling confident because he has earned high grades in his courses and is certain that he knows the material. Also, he is willing to do whatever is necessary to prepare for the exams.

1. What is Dan's problem?

_____

_____

_____

2. With respect to his upcoming exams, what are Dan's strengths and weaknesses?

_____

_____

_____

_____

_____

3. What general suggestions can you offer Dan to help him prepare for his exams?

_____

_____

_____

_____

_____

4. What specific strategies would help him prepare for the standardized portion of the exams and relieve some of his anxiety?

_____

_____

_____

_____

_____

chapter **re**view

To review the chapter, reflect on the following confidence-building attitudes, complete Concepts to Understand, and practice your new skills at every opportunity.

ATTITUDES TO DEVELOP

- responsibility
- self-management
- positive thinking

CONCEPTS TO UNDERSTAND

Sufficient preparation for tests involves three steps: First, make a _____ _____ that allows time for daily, weekly, and exam reviews for each course. Next, decide what topics or specific information to study by reviewing your lecture notes, textbook notes and study guides, previous tests, papers, homework, other graded assignments, and instructors' handouts. To make efficient use of your study time, use the _____ study system or one you have adapted.

To improve your grades on tests, develop a test-taking routine that includes these steps: arrive on time, jot down _____ _____, survey the test, plan and use all of your time, read the directions, do _____ questions first, skip and return to _____ questions, guess if there is no penalty, control your feelings and attention, check your work, and learn from your mistakes.

Your test-taking routine should also include strategies for taking true-false, multiple-choice, fill-in-the-blank, and essay exams as well as strategies for taking standardized tests.

To access additional review exercises, see http://college.hmco.com/success.

SKILLS TO PRACTICE

- making and following schedules
- preparing for tests
- using study systems

Your Reflections

Your Reflections

Reflect on what you have learned about preparing for tests and how you can best apply that information. Use the following list of questions to stimulate your thinking; then write your reflections. Your response may include answers to one or more of the questions. Incorporate in your writing specific information from this chapter or from previous chapters as it's needed.

- What are your grades in your courses so far, and are you satisfied with them? Why or why not?

- To what extent has each of the following affected your grades on tests: anxiety, amount and kind of preparation, attitude, and health?

- Which of the factors affecting your grades can you control? How?

- How good are you at taking tests? What routine do you use, and does it need improvement?

- Of the attitudes and skills listed in the Chapter Review, which do you think will be most useful at work or in your career?

12

Reducing Test Anxiety

DO YOU FREEZE up on tests, become

anxious, and have trouble recalling the

information needed to answer a question, even though

you studied the material? What is test anxiety,

and what causes it? What can you do to

reduce test anxiety?

TESTING IS STRESSFUL. Poor test scores may lower a grade average. In some courses, a final exam may determine whether you pass or fail. Scholarships, admittance to graduate school or a profession, entry to some job markets or careers, and even a promotion within a company may, in part, depend on test scores. It is no wonder that you may feel some anxiety when faced with a test. In fact, it would be unusual if you didn't.

Test anxiety is stress that is related to a testing situation, and it may affect students in different ways. Bonnie's test anxiety causes her to have various physical and mental reactions. Before she takes a test, her palms sweat, her head aches, or her stomach may be upset. During the test she tries to calm herself, but her anxiety increases. She reads a question, and her mind goes blank, even though she may have known the answer before the test began. Her inner voice says, "I'm going to fail." Bonnie's reactions are triggered by any test, whether she is prepared for it or not. However, Jerome has reactions like Bonnie's only when he is not well prepared. Although he should be able to answer all the questions for which he has studied, he may miss some of them because his anxiety blocks his recall. As soon as the test is over, he remembers what he should have written.

Jerome's test anxiety results from lack of preparation. Effective study skills and a test-taking routine, as explained in Chapter 11, are his keys to anxiety relief. However, Bonnie's anxiety may be the result of causes that are not so easily or quickly resolved. Self-assessment is Bonnie's key to what causes her anxiety. Eliminating the causes will bring relief.

The good thing about test anxiety is that it is a *learned response;* therefore, it can be unlearned. This chapter explains what you can do to reduce test anxiety:

- Determine what causes your test anxiety.

- Eliminate the causes.

- Choose a strategy that works for you.

Eliminate the Causes of Test Anxiety

WHAT CAUSES TEST anxiety? Besides lack of preparation—the main cause—test anxiety may result from one or more of three other common causes:

- Being afraid that you won't live up to the expectations of important people in your life, worrying that you will lose the affection of people you care about if you don't succeed

- Believing grades are a measure of self-worth

- Feeling helpless, believing that you have no control over your performance or grades.

Expectations

Many students' *perceptions* of what their parents or important others expect may be inaccurate. If you worry that you may alienate people you care about unless you do well in college, you may become fearful and anxious that you will disappoint them or make them angry. If you believe that you can't live up to the expectations of others, tests may make you especially anxious. Suppose your parents or

Awareness Check 18

DO YOU HAVE TEST ANXIETY?

Never	Sometimes	Usually	*Check the response that seems most characteristic of you.*
☐	☐	☐	1. I have trouble sleeping the night before a test.
☐	☐	☐	2. During a test, my palms sweat.
☐	☐	☐	3. Before a test, I get a headache.
☐	☐	☐	4. During a test, I become nauseated.
☐	☐	☐	5. Because of panic, I sometimes cut class on a test day.
☐	☐	☐	6. I have pains in my neck, back, or legs during a test.
☐	☐	☐	7. My heart pounds just before or during a test.
☐	☐	☐	8. I feel nervous and jittery when I am taking a test.
☐	☐	☐	9. During a test, I have trouble remembering.
☐	☐	☐	10. I lose my appetite before a test.
☐	☐	☐	11. I make careless errors on tests.
☐	☐	☐	12. My mind goes blank during tests.
☐	☐	☐	13. I worry when other students are finished before I am.
☐	☐	☐	14. I feel pushed for time when I am taking a test.
☐	☐	☐	15. I worry that I may be doing poorly on a test but that everyone else is doing all right.
☐	☐	☐	16. When I am taking a test, I think about my past failures.
☐	☐	☐	17. During a test, I feel as if I had studied all the wrong things.
☐	☐	☐	18. I can't think clearly during tests.
☐	☐	☐	19. I have a hard time understanding and remembering directions when I am taking a test.
☐	☐	☐	20. After a test, I remember answers to questions I either left blank or answered incorrectly.

Items 1–10 on the Awareness Check refer to physical symptoms of test anxiety, and items 11–20 refer to mental symptoms. If you checked "sometimes" or "usually" ten or more times, you may have some test anxiety. To be sure, you might want to talk to your advisor about how you feel before, during, and after taking tests.

important others become angry if you earn any grade lower than an A or B. You need to talk this over with them to determine the source of their anger. Perhaps they feel that a grade lower than an A or B means that you aren't trying hard enough or that you aren't committed to getting an education. But there may be other reasons why you are not performing as expected in a course. You may have been unprepared for the level of the course, or illness or other hardships may have affected your level of performance. It is unreasonable to expect a student to achieve someone else's ideal grade, but it is not unreasonable to expect a student to do his or her best. If a C represents a student's best effort, then it is a good grade. Try to separate yourself from others' expectations of you. Focus instead on what *you* expect from yourself and work hard to achieve it.

Grades and Self-Esteem

Much test anxiety results from placing too great an emphasis on grades. A low grade for some students translates into "I don't measure up." The result is a loss of self-esteem. One way to reduce test anxiety is to emphasize *performance* instead of grades. Rather than letting grades control your feelings, take control of your performance.

Turn each testing situation into an opportunity for self-assessment. Use tests to track your performance in a course. Keep a record of the number and type of items you missed, your level of anxiety during the test, your level of preparation, and what you now need to review. Over a period of time, you may see a pattern in your study and testing behavior. For example, if you consistently miss the same type of question or if your level of anxiety goes up when you haven't prepared sufficiently, then you will know what and how much to study for the next test.

When you emphasize performance over grades, a test becomes a personal challenge, a chance for you to apply your knowledge and skill to new problems and tasks, an opportunity for you to discover your strengths and weaknesses. Improved performance is the goal. Grades are not a measure of self-worth. They are just a way to keep score. To track your performance on tests, make a chart like the one illustrated in Figure 12.1 or devise one of your own. The chart is filled in as an example. To download a blank copy of the chart for your own use, go to http://college.hmco.com/success.

| Figure 12.1 | **A Chart for Tracking Performance on Tests** |

Test/ Course	Items Missed	Type of Item	Anxiety Level	Preparation Level	To Do
Chemistry chapter quiz	# 3	Avogadro's Law	high	low (1 hr.)	1. Review laws.
	# 6, # 7	ratio of effusion ratio of gasses			2. Do more practice problems.
	# 10	partial pressures and mole fractions			

Feelings of Helplessness

Are you self-motivated (internal locus of control) or other-motivated (external locus of control)? Other-motivated students often do not see a connection between studying and grades. They blame their poor grades on the perceived unfairness of the instructor or the difficulty of the test instead of blaming their own lack of preparation. As a result, they feel helpless and out of control and experience test anxiety. The more self-motivated you are, the more likely you are to see a connection between your preparation and your grades. When you are well prepared for a test, you are in control of your emotions and of your reactions to the testing situation. As a result, you enter the classroom feeling calm and confident, ready to do your best.

By identifying the cause of your test anxiety, you can do what is necessary to eliminate it. Figure 12.2 lists common causes of test anxiety and how to eliminate them.

Figure 12.2	Test Anxiety: Causes and Eliminators
CAUSES	**ELIMINATORS**
1. **Trying to meet others' expectations**	Decide whether living up to these expectations is something you want to do for yourself. Set your own goals and live up to your own expectations.
2. **Letting grades determine your self-worth**	Emphasize performance over grades. Take control by tracking performance to overcome weaknesses.
3. **Inadequate preparation and guilt**	So you weren't prepared this time. Keep your goal in sight and resolve to do better.
4. **Feeling helpless, with no control over what happens**	The way to take control is to develop an internal locus of control. Improve your study habits. Prepare for your next test and observe the connection between the amount and quality of your studying and the grade you receive.

Learn to Relax

A PROVEN WAY to reduce the physical and mental discomfort caused by test anxiety is to learn how to relax. You can't be relaxed and anxious at the same time. When you feel nervous before or during a test, you need to be able to relax so that you become calm enough to focus your attention on the task of taking the test.

Figure 12.3 **Sixteen Muscle Groups**

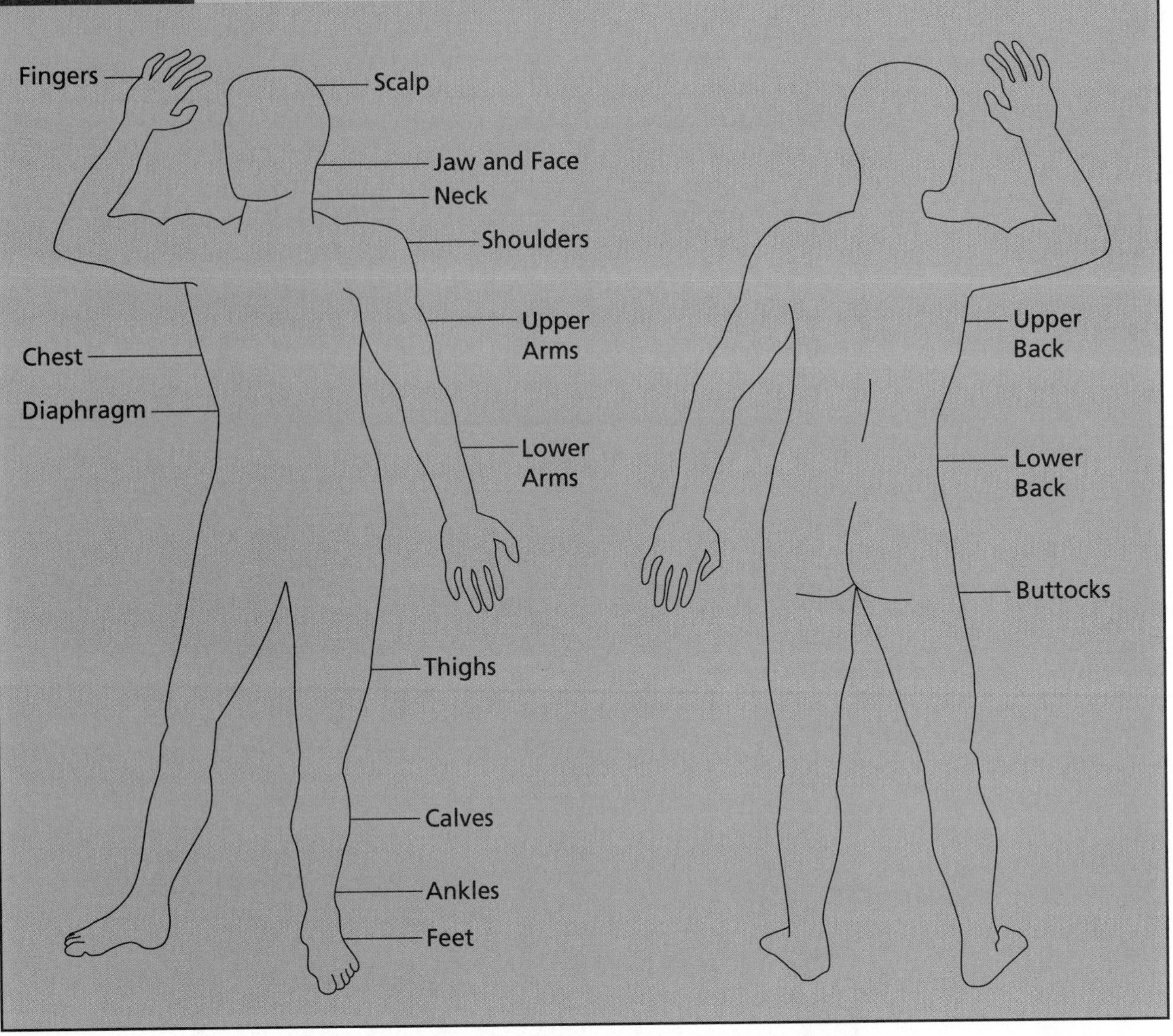

Fingers — Scalp
— Jaw and Face
— Neck
— Shoulders
Upper
Arms
Chest —
Diaphragm —
Lower
Arms
Upper
Back
Lower
Back
Buttocks
Thighs
Calves
Ankles
Feet

Muscle relaxation exercises can help you control the physical symptoms of test anxiety. Become aware of the sixteen muscle groups of your body (see Figure 12.3) and practice a technique that will help you relax each group. When you are relaxed, you can program yourself for success.

Some people don't even know when they are tense. As you locate each of the sixteen muscle groups in Figure 12.3, try to sense whether you are holding any tension in your own muscles at each location. Try this exercise: Close your eyes and search for the tension in your body. Are you clenching your teeth? If so, open your mouth slightly and relax your jaw. Are your shoulders hunched? Lower your shoulders and feel an immediate sense of relief. Now breathe deeply. Uncross your legs if they are crossed and press your feet flat on the floor. Do not tense your leg muscles. Settle comfortably into your chair and enjoy how good you feel when your muscles are relaxed. Imagine taking a test when you are this calm.

To feel the difference between tension and relaxation even more, try this exercise: Clench your hand into a fist. Squeeze as tightly as you can until you feel your fingers pressing uncomfortably into your palm. Hold that position for a few seconds. Feel your pulse pounding in your fingertips. Very slowly, open your hand. Uncurl your fingers and let go of the tension. When you are experiencing test anxiety, your mind is like your clenched fist. When you relax, your mind is like your hand opening and letting go of the tension.

Here is another relaxation exercise you can do the evening or morning before a test. Either sit or lie down comfortably; close your eyes and breathe deeply for a few seconds. Beginning with your feet, focus on each muscle group, one at a time; tense and then relax the muscles so there is a sharp difference between tensing and letting go. While you are relaxed, visualize a pleasant scene. For example, imagine yourself lying on a beach in the warm sun. Hear the waves washing up on the shore. Enjoy this scene for a few seconds; then let it fade. Concentrate on relaxing your body even more. Breathe slowly and deeply for a few more minutes; then open your eyes.

To relax yourself in a classroom situation, try these two simple but effective exercises. No one will know you are doing them. You will look as if you are concentrating or taking a moment to relax.

1. Take a deep breath and relax your shoulders. Put your hands in your lap and clench your fists to feel the tension. Slowly open your hands and let them drop down at your sides, letting go of the tension.

2. With your elbows on the desk, bow your head over your open book or test paper while resting your forehead on top of your hands. Either close your eyes or leave them open but unfocused. Breathe slowly and deeply until you feel calm.

Face Your Fears

STUDENTS WHO HAVE severe test anxiety are anxious and fearful not only while taking a test but also while they are studying for tests. As Bonnie said, "I can be taking notes in a class and doing all right until the instructor says that we are going to have a test the following week; then I freeze up." If you are this anxious, you may be spending more time worrying about tests than preparing for them.

To face your fear, accept the fact that you have a problem. Facing the fear puts *you* in charge so that you can eliminate the cause of your anxiety. Any positive step you take toward overcoming your anxiety is another way of facing your fear. Define your fear and determine its origin. For example, a fear of failure may have its origin in past experiences. If you have a history of failure in a certain subject, you may fear that you will fail again. But if you can discover and eliminate the cause of those past failures so that you are less likely to repeat them, then you may overcome the fear.

Test anxiety is like any bad habit. The longer you practice it without any attempt to control it, the more ingrained it becomes. When you learn to relax, you are replacing an old, destructive habit with a new, productive one. Eventually, relaxation may become as natural to you as anxiety is now.

Your best defense against test anxiety is preparation for tests.

Fight Distractions

ANOTHER WAY TO relieve test anxiety is to become task-oriented. Give all your attention to the test. While sitting at your desk before a test and while papers are being passed out, silently review what you have studied. When you get the test, read each question carefully so that you know what you are required to do. Look only at the test. If you need to relax a few minutes or think over an answer, close your eyes so that you will not notice what is going on around you. Test-anxious students tend to become distracted by other students. Their anxiety increases as other students begin handing in their papers. If you do not look at other students, you are less likely to start worrying about how you are doing in comparison to them.

Avoid self-preoccupation. For example, if you start focusing on your physical discomfort or on the likelihood that you will fail, then these thoughts will distract your attention from the test. Fight distracting thoughts and focus your attention on the test in front of you. Re-read the question you are working on. Mentally review everything you studied that is related to that question. Underline or circle key words in questions to increase your concentration. Read questions slowly; move your lips to involve your tactile and auditory senses. If oral distractions such as gum smacking, whispering, or paper shuffling bother you, try distancing yourself from them either physically or mentally. Choose a seat away from those who tend to create these distractions. If that is not possible, distance yourself mentally by focusing your attention on the task. Silently re-read the question or the words of your answer as you write. Your own inner dialogue may drown out the distractions.

Talk Positively to Yourself

ALTHOUGH YOU MAY sometimes think that your mind is blank, it really is not. A mental dialogue plays like a radio in your mind, no matter what else is going on. While you are listening to a lecture, you are also thinking ahead to what you will do when class is over, or recalling something that happened earlier, or thinking about a problem that has been on your mind. When you have a conversation with someone, while you are listening, you are also thinking about what you will say next. Your inner voice is talking to you, and it is extremely persistent.

Take a few minutes right now to listen to that inner voice. Try this simple exercise: Sit or lie down comfortably; close your eyes and breathe deeply. Concentrate on making your mind go blank. You will probably find it very hard to think about nothing because your inner voice will keep interrupting. What are your thoughts? Are they positive or negative? Do you praise or belittle yourself? Students who have test anxiety are frequently troubled by negative thoughts such as these:

"I'm going to fail this test."

"I hate this class."

"This course is doing nothing for me."

"The instructor doesn't care whether I pass or fail."

"Everybody in this class is doing better than I am."

Examine each negative thought and see how it hurts you. If you think and believe, "I am going to fail this test," then you probably will because you will become more anxious and less able to focus your attention on the test. If you say to yourself, "I hate this class" or "This course is doing nothing for me," you are wasting

You can relieve test anxiety by focusing all your attention on the test. Try to avoid thinking about what other students are doing and try to fight internal distractions such as minor physical discomfort or negative thoughts.

© Gary Conner/PhotoEdit

time indulging thoughts that keep you from concentrating on recalling information you need to answer questions. Saying to yourself, "This instructor doesn't care whether I pass or fail" or "Everybody in this class is doing better than I am" causes you to focus attention on other people instead of on the test. To combat negative thoughts, become task-oriented. Block out all but positive thoughts specifically related to the task of taking and passing the test. Negative thinking can become a habit. To break the habit and program yourself for success, do three things:

1. Become aware of all the negative messages you may be sending yourself.

2. Replace negative thoughts with positive ones such as these:

   "I'll pass this test."

   "I'm learning something in this class."

   "The instructor wants me to succeed."

   "This course is a step toward my goals."

   "I am well prepared, and I will do my best."

3. Change your inner voice into one that is calm and confident.

You may have to apply conscious effort for a long time before you learn to control your inner voice. Chances are good that your negative thoughts about

---

EXERCISE **12.1**

PRACTICE POSITIVE THINKING. Listen to your inner voice. In the first column, list any negative thoughts. Then, in the second column, rewrite them as positive self-directions. For example, the negative thought "I'm going to fail this test" becomes the positive direction "I'm well prepared for this test, so I will earn a good grade."

Negative Thoughts

1. _____

   _____

2. _____

   _____

3. _____

   _____

4. _____

   _____

5. _____

   _____

Positive Thoughts

1. _____

   _____

2. _____

   _____

3. _____

   _____

4. _____

   _____

5. _____

   _____

yourself go back to your early childhood; they are probably so automatic that you hardly even notice them when you are involved in an activity such as taking a test. But learning to silence those thoughts and to replace them with positive, supportive ones will have a positive effect on other areas of your life besides test taking. You may find yourself having more fun in your classes and in activities such as sports, hobbies, and work if you aren't so critical of your performance. Studying will become easier, too, and your chances for success in college will improve. Thinking positively about yourself can even change the expression on your face. If you look and feel confident, people will have a higher opinion of you.

Once you have learned to focus all of your attention on taking a test, to speak positively to yourself, and to feel confident that you will be able to demonstrate your knowledge, test taking may become an enjoyable intellectual challenge for you.

CONFIDENCE Builder

A Meditation Exercise

To meditate is to think deeply and continuously about something during a time you have set aside for that purpose. When you combine meditation with muscle relaxation, the result is a deep level of mental and physical calm which may be accompanied by a heightened level of awareness. During meditation, many people become very receptive to self-directions for making positive changes in their lives. The following meditation exercise will help you practice the kind of positive thinking that can lead to success. Follow these steps to complete the exercise:

1. Select a time of day or night when you are alone and won't be disturbed.

2. Find a quiet, comfortable place such as your bedroom; go in and shut the door.

3. Lie flat on the floor, on your back.

4. If you need one, put a pillow under your head.

5. Place your arms down at your sides with your palms open and the backs of your hands resting on the floor.

6. Breathe slowly and deeply through your nostrils; exhale through your mouth.

7. If you feel any tension in any part of your body, release it.

8. Concentrate on becoming calm and relaxed. Empty your mind of all other thoughts.

9. When you feel completely calm, speak positively to yourself with your inner voice. Say the words that you alone know will make you feel confident and capable of doing your best.

10. Open your eyes. Remain lying down for a few minutes to enjoy feeling confident and calm. Then stand up and resume your day's or night's activities.

To pursue this topic further, do an online search using these key words as a starting point: *meditation* and *relaxation techniques.*

Some people find relief from stress through meditation.

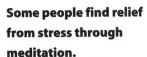

EXERCISE 12.2

CLAUDIA IS OVERWHELMED WITH TEST anxiety when she thinks about her biology midterm. Read about her attempt to overcome this problem; then answer the questions.

Even though the exam is more than three weeks away, Claudia is already waking up at night panicked by the thought of her biology midterm. She knows that she is always well prepared for class. She does all the reading. Why does she feel so anxious about the exam? In desperation, she decides to try a visualization technique that her psychology professor explained to her. Here is what she does.

Each day for about twenty minutes, she sits alone in her room. Closing her eyes, she begins to breathe deeply and then, through a process of tensing and relaxing each muscle individually, she relaxes her entire body. When she feels totally relaxed, she imagines herself sinking into the overstuffed pillows of a lovely old chair in a beautiful garden. Feeling the warmth of the sun on her face, she breathes in the fragrances that surround her. She enjoys this imaginary scene for a few long seconds, then lets the scene slowly fade and replaces it with another scene. She is sitting in her biology class, about to begin taking her exam. She feels totally relaxed and prepared for the test. Calmly, she opens the test booklet and begins to write. Again, she imagines how prepared she is, how good she feels at that moment. She knows she can pass the exam. She feels confidence flow through her body. After lingering for a few moments on this image, Claudia imagines one last scene. Her professor is handing back the test booklets. Confidently accepting hers, Claudia opens the cover and reads the handwritten note at the top of the page: "Great work. You should be proud of your success on this exam." Claudia concentrates on her intense feelings of success and then allows the scene to fade. She breathes deeply a few more moments, then slowly opens her eyes.

1. **How does Claudia begin her visualization technique?** _____

_____

2. **Why does she imagine a beautiful garden?** _____

_____

3. **What other scenes might she imagine?** _____

_____

4. **Why do you think she visualizes the garden scene before visualizing the classroom scene?** ___

_____

5. **What is the final image that Claudia visualizes?** _____

_____

6. **Why is it important for Claudia to visualize this final scene?** _____

_____

_____

7. **How might this visualization exercise help reduce Claudia's test anxiety?** _____

_____

_____

8. **Based on your learning style, what changes would you make to Claudia's visualization if you were to try this technique yourself?** _____

_____

_____

_____

Find Your Best Solution

TEST ANXIETY IS an individual problem. Anxiety differs in degree and kind from student to student. It is important to remember two things. First, a little anxiety won't hurt you and may even be the incentive you need to do your best. Second, even if you have a great deal of anxiety that causes you considerable discomfort, you are not a hopeless case. Furthermore, you have a lot of company. For many students, test anxiety has become a way of life, but it doesn't have to remain so.

The coping strategies discussed in this chapter have worked for many students. Here are six more tips for reducing test anxiety:

- Improve the way you prepare for tests by allowing sufficient time for study, by using a study system, and by reviewing frequently. Most test anxiety is the result of irrational fears. The only real cause for fear is insufficient preparation for a test, which almost always *does* result in a poor grade. If you know you are not prepared, then you must expect to have some anxiety. Calm yourself by using one of the relaxation techniques explained in this chapter; then do your best on the questions you are able to answer.

• Your body will tell you when you are becoming anxious during a test. Learn to recognize the signals that may be signs of stress: increased pulse rate, excessive perspiration, shallow breathing, sweaty palms, upset stomach, and headache.

• Dress comfortably for tests. Wear loose-fitting clothes and comfortable shoes. Dress in layers so that you can put something on or take something off if the temperature in the room is too cold or too hot.

• Arrive at the testing site on time. Don't be too early. If you have time on your hands before the test, waiting may make you nervous. Also, you may get into conversations with other students who will shake your confidence by reminding you of material you haven't studied.

• Develop a test-day tradition. Viana wears a pair of "good luck" jeans on test days. For reasons only she knows, these jeans have pleasant associations and make her feel successful. Another student, Nguyen, plays the *1812 Overture* to get himself ready for a test. Maybe you have a lucky pen or some other talisman that can serve as a confidence builder.

• See test anxiety for what it is—a learned response that you can unlearn, a habit that you can break.

C R I T I C A L   T H I N K I N G

What have you learned about test anxiety and your experiences with it? Relate the anxiety you may feel in a testing situation to the stress or anxiety you may feel in other situations. For example, does having to give a speech make you nervous? Does a trip to the dentist provoke anxiety? Do you feel stress when something goes wrong at work or when your child is sick or has a problem at school? What are the similarities and differences between these real-life stressors and test anxiety? Write about the ways you have found to cope with stress in your daily life. Which of these strategies might also help you to reduce test anxiety?

EXERCISE **12.3**

APPLY WHAT YOU HAVE LEARNED about test anxiety by completing this exercise with group members. Follow the guidelines for successful collaboration that appear on the inside back cover. The four steps of the COPE problem-solving method, as explained in Chapter 3, are *challenge, option, plan,* and *evaluation.* Discuss how a student could use COPE to solve a test-anxiety problem. Then work through COPE's steps to illustrate your solution. You can make up a hypothetical student with a problem, or you can use a real test-anxiety problem contributed by one of your group members. When you arrive at consensus, record your answers on the lines provided. Then evaluate your work.

1. *Challenge:* State the problem, its causes, and the result you want.

_____

_____

_____

2. *Options:* List possible options to reduce anxiety.

_____

_____

_____

3. *Plan:* Choose an option, write your plan, and set a time limit for reaching your goal.

_____

_____

_____

4. *Evaluation:* How will you evaluate your plan? How will you know whether it has worked? What will you do if it hasn't?

_____

_____

_____

Group Evaluation:

Evaluate your discussion. Did everyone contribute? Did you accomplish your task successfully? What additional questions do you have about test anxiety, and how will you find answers to your questions?

_____

_____

_____

EXERCISE **12.4**

VISIT THE INTERNET TO FIND out more about test anxiety, its causes, and ways to eliminate it. Search the Web for any information you can find on test anxiety, including any test
anxiety surveys students can take. Then discuss your findings with the rest of the class.
Some search words to try as starting points are *test anxiety, test anxiety reduction, stress
relief,* and *anxiety reduction techniques.*

thinking *ahead* -----▶

**What practical knowledge have you gained from this chapter that you can use to solve real-
world problems? To find out, read the following scenario and complete the items after it.**

*Jade is a recent college graduate with a degree in nursing. She is working the night shift at a large metropolitan hospi-
tal. Sometimes the stress gets to her. Trying to juggle patients' needs and answer physicians' requests keeps her so busy
that she hardly has time to take a break. If only she could relax—just a few calm minutes between crises would help.*

1. What is Jade's problem?

_____

_____

_____

2. What is causing the problem?

_____

_____

_____

3. What is one solution that you would recommend?

_____

_____

_____

**4. If Jade tries your suggestion, how will she know whether it is working? Moreover, if it doesn't
work, then what can she do?**

_____

_____

_____

chapter **re**view

To review the chapter, reflect on the following confidence-building attitudes, complete Concepts to Understand, and practice your new skills at every opportunity.

ATTITUDES TO DEVELOP

- positive thinking
- the willingness to take control
- the desire to self-motivate and self-manage

CONCEPTS TO UNDERSTAND

Test anxiety is _____ that is related to a testing situation. It may be caused by your inability to cope with the _____ of important people in your life, by a belief that grades are a reflection of your self-worth, or by feelings of _____ resulting from past failures. If you have test anxiety, you may suffer from _____ symptoms such as headaches and nausea and _____ symptoms such as a lack of confidence and negative thoughts and feelings. Because test anxiety is a _____ response, it can be unlearned.

Being prepared for tests and feeling confident about your abilities may reduce some of your anxiety. Or you may need to develop coping strategies such as learning to relax, facing and dealing with your fears, fighting internal and external _____, and programming yourself for success by replacing _____ thoughts with _____ ones. If your anxiety is extremely severe, you might want to talk about your problem with your instructor or advisor.

To access additional review exercises, see http://college.hmco.com/success.

SKILLS TO PRACTICE

- preparing for tests
- recognizing when you are tense or anxious
- using relaxation techniques
- fighting distractions
- controlling your inner dialogue

Your Reflections

Your Reflections

Reflect on what you have learned about test anxiety and how you can best apply that information. Use the following list of questions to stimulate your thinking; then write your reflections. Your response may include answers to one or more of the questions. Incorporate in your writing specific information from this chapter or from previous chapters as it's needed.

- Do you have physical or mental reactions to tests that are similar to Bonnie's and Jerome's as described at the beginning of the chapter? What are your reactions?

- Do you perform better on some kinds of tests than on others? Which ones, and why?

- What is the relationship between test anxiety and preparing for tests?

- What have you learned from this chapter that you can apply to reduce your test anxiety or other types of stress?

- Of the attitudes and skills listed in the Chapter Review, which do you think will be most helpful at work or in your career?

CHAPTER 13

Becoming an Active Reader

ARE YOU AN active reader? Do you use reading and marking systems? Did you know that by using active reading strategies, you can improve your comprehension, your memory, and your grades?

READING IS A lifelong skill and a key to success in college and career. As a college student, you must read, understand, and remember information not only from textbooks, but also from journals, periodicals, and other sources. In any career, good reading skills will help you understand correspondence (including email), manuals, graphics, and written specifications. In your personal life, too, active reading habits and good reading skills can help you make sense of nutrition labels, contracts, newspaper articles, and information printed on web sites.

Reading is also a necessary part of any study system. You can gain essential information from your textbooks by employing these three strategies to improve the way you read.

- Take control of your reading process by becoming an active reader.

- Read for main ideas, details, and their implications.

- Use a marking system to focus your attention and identify information to recite and review.

To find out whether you are an active reader, complete Awareness Check 19.

Awareness Check 19

ARE YOU AN ACTIVE READER?

To determine how actively you read, check the following statements that apply to you.

☐ 1. I usually read straight through a textbook chapter from beginning to end without stopping.

☐ 2. I stop frequently to re-read difficult parts or to check my comprehension by asking myself questions about what I have read.

☐ 3. If I don't understand something I have read, I wait to hear the instructor's explanation in class.

☐ 4. When I hit a rough spot, I make a note to remind myself to ask about it in class.

☐ 5. I usually have trouble deciding what is important in a chapter; often I'm not sure what the main idea is.

☐ 6. I can usually find the author's main idea, and I rarely have trouble determining what is important.

☐ 7. I often have a hard time relating textbook information to my life or to the course as a whole.

☐ 8. I can often see a connection between something I've read in a chapter and my life or the course.

☐ 9. I rarely underline, mark, highlight, or write notes in my textbooks.

☐ 10. I usually mark, underline, highlight, or write notes in my textbooks.

11. I have difficulty deciding what to mark or underline.

12. I can usually tell what to mark or underline.

13. I have to be interested in what I am reading to get anything out of it.

14. Even if a subject covered in a textbook doesn't interest me, I can still determine what I should learn and remember from it.

15. I think I should be able to read something once and remember the information covered in it.

16. I know that I may have to read something several times before the information sinks in.

17. When I read documents on the Internet, I can't tell which ones are reliable sources and which ones are not.

18. I am able to evaluate the reliability of Internet documents and sources.

If you checked mostly even-numbered statements, you are probably already an active reader. If you checked mostly odd-numbered statements, you may be a passive reader who would benefit from developing active reading strategies.

Reading Actively

READERS FALL INTO two categories: active readers and passive readers. *Active readers* control their interest level and concentration. They read with a purpose: They know what information to look for and why. Active readers constantly question what they read. They relate the author's ideas to their own experience and prior knowledge. On the other hand, *passive readers* are not in control of their reading. They lose interest easily and give in to distractions. They read the same way that they watch television programs and movies, expecting others to engage them and keep their attention. A common passive reading experience is to "wake up" in the middle of a paragraph, wondering what it is all about. Active readers control the process of reading; passive readers are unaware that reading *is* a process they can control.

The key to active reading is to *interact* with the text, to engage your mind with the author's. Taking notes, marking the text, questioning, thinking about the author's ideas, even talking them over with a friend—these are all ways to interact with the text. Passive readers do none of these things. They open the book to the assigned chapter and read from the first word to the last without really thinking about the author's ideas. As a result, they can't decide what is important, don't know what to review, and soon forget what they have read. Consequently, passive readers often feel "lost" in class. The chart in Figure 13.1 compares active and passive readers.

Becoming an active reader takes self-motivation, a commitment to try proven strategies, the desire to succeed, and the persistence to make it happen. To read actively, follow these suggestions:

Figure 13.1 **Active and Passive Readers**

ACTIVE READERS:	PASSIVE READERS:
• have a positive attitude toward reading	• have a negative attitude toward reading
• read for ideas	• read only words
• ask questions to guide their reading and thinking	• read without thinking or questioning
• manage their reading process	• unaware that reading is a process they can manage
• schedule time for reading	• read only if they have time
• have a purpose for reading	• read because "it is assigned"
• know how to keep their interest and motivation high	• expect the author to interest and motivate them
• control their concentration	• are easily distracted
• use study systems and memory strategies	• resist using study systems and memory strategies
• underline and annotate textbooks	• do not use marking systems
• make graphic organizers to use as study guides	• think making graphic organizers is too much work
• relate what they read to prior knowledge and experience	• see no connection between college reading and life or work
• review by reading notes and other materials	• review by re-reading entire chapters
• seek help as needed	• resist asking for help
• know what is going on in class due to active reading	• often feel lost in class due to passive reading

- **Set a realistic reading goal.** Don't try to read sixty pages all at once. Break up the assignment into two or three sessions—for whatever amount of time you think you can maintain optimum concentration. If you feel your concentration slipping before your time is up, stop, take a break, and then refocus your attention.

- **Read with a purpose.** Know what you are expected to get out of the assignment. Perhaps you will be tested on the material or asked to summarize the information, or perhaps you have several questions in mind that you expect the assignment to answer. Having specific information to look for may help you keep your attention focused on your reading and should give you a reason to talk yourself out of any boredom or lack of interest.

- **Read with a pen or highlighter** so you can mark parts of the chapter that answer your questions, suggest possible test questions, explain concepts, or expand on topics covered in class lectures. If you are reading from a library book or other source that you cannot mark, take notes on note cards or in a notebook, making sure to label them with the source's title, page number, web site address (or URL), or any other identifying information you may need later. For more information on marking textbooks, see pages 311–314 of this chapter.

- **Review and recite from your notes or markings.** Reviewing helps reinforce your learning so that it stays in your memory. Reciting from notes or textbook markings provides another pathway into your memory: the auditory sense. Reciting is especially helpful for those who have an auditory learning preference, but anyone can benefit from it.

The more active you become in taking control of your reading process, the less likely you will be to lapse into passive reading habits. As an active reader, you are *doing something* throughout the process, whether it is marking the text, stopping to think about what you have read, re-reading difficult passages, asking questions and looking for answers, or reciting from your notes and markings. These activities aid in the transfer of information from your short-term memory to your long-term memory. For more on how the memory process works and is enhanced by the way in which you study, see Chapter 10.

You can become aware of the times when you are either comprehending well or poorly. To read actively and consciously, you must be able to follow the development of ideas as they occur in a chapter or other source. One way you can do this is by reading for the main idea, details, and their implications.

EXERCISE **13.1**

WRITE AN EVALUATION OF YOURSELF as an active or passive reader. Describe your study system for reading a textbook chapter or other assigned reading material. Be specific. What type of learning style is dominant in the way you read? For example, would you rather read on your own, forming your own opinions, or would you prefer to read, then discuss the assignment with others? If possible, describe the study system you used for an assigned reading in one of your classes and any difficulties you had. Also, take into consideration your results of Awareness Check 19 as you complete this exercise.

Find the Main Idea, Details, and Implications

IDEAS DEVELOP FROM words to sentences, to paragraphs, to larger units of meaning such as multiparagraph essays, articles, and textbook chapters. The sentences in a paragraph are related: They all support one main idea. The paragraphs in a longer passage are similarly related: They all support the one central idea of the entire passage. This is why the main idea of a multiparagraph passage such as a textbook chapter or newspaper article is often called the *central idea* to distinguish it from the main idea of each paragraph.

In a textbook chapter, the title and introductory paragraphs usually provide strong clues to the chapter's central idea. In fact, the central idea of a longer passage is often stated near the beginning. Therefore, you can use the title and introduction to create a context for reading. For example, the title of this chapter, *Becoming an Active Reader,* and the introductory paragraphs make clear that the central idea is that several strategies can help you become an active reader. Both the title and the introductory paragraphs should raise two questions in your mind: "What is an active reader?" and "What are the strategies?" Using these as guide questions, you can read the chapter to find the answers. Each paragraph within a chapter provides important information that is essential to your understanding of the entire chapter's central idea.

To improve your reading, begin by learning how to find a paragraph's main idea. A paragraph can be anywhere from one to several sentences long, and it may contain three types of sentences:

1. The **topic sentence** is a direct statement of the author's main idea.

2. The **support sentences** contain major or minor details that develop, or explain, the main idea.

3. The **concluding sentence** may restate the main idea, introduce a new but related idea, make an inference, end the paragraph with another detail, or provide a transition to the next paragraph.

For examples of these three kinds of sentences, read the next paragraph and the explanation that follows it.

Topic sentence: Main Idea

Support sentences: Details

Concluding sentence

*Adjusting to college can be difficult for students because of the pressures they face from family, instructors, and friends. Family members, for example, may expect a student to add studying and attending classes to his or her other responsibilities. They may resent being asked to take on more chores or spending time alone while the student studies. A student who faces this kind of pressure from family may have difficulty reaching desired goals. Another pressure students face is from instructors. From the student's point of view, each instructor acts as if the student has no other courses to take. Add to this the need to get to every class on time, to attend class regularly, and to keep up with all assignments. Friends can also make a student's adjustment difficult. For one thing, they may pressure a student to put off studying to engage in leisure-time activities. Friends who are not attending college feel threatened and, without meaning to, may do or say things that can make a student wonder if college is worth it. **To overcome these pressures, a college student must have a strong desire to succeed.***

The first sentence of this paragraph is the **topic sentence,** which states the author's main idea: Pressures from family, instructors, and friends can make students' adjustment to college difficult. The last sentence of the paragraph is the **concluding sentence.** In between are the **support sentences,** which give examples of three kinds of pressures and explain how these pressures can make it difficult for a student to adjust to college. The concluding sentence then introduces a new but related idea: Students can overcome these pressures.

Find the Main Idea

In a paragraph, an author may express the main idea in one of two ways: (1) by stating it directly in a topic sentence, as in the example paragraph about pressures students face, or (2) by implying it through the choice of details and use of key words.

Now read another paragraph about students' pressures:

Some parents insist that a student carry a full-time load and maintain an A or B average while also working part-time and sharing household tasks. A student who has too many things to do may not be able to do any one of them very well. Another pressure students face is from instructors' expectations. Instructors expect students to arrive on time, to attend class regularly, and to keep up with all assignments. They also expect students to participate in class, ask questions, and do extra work or get help outside of class if they are having trouble meeting course objectives. Friends, too, can make a student's adjustment difficult. For one thing, they may pressure a student to put off studying in order to party or to engage in some other leisure-time activity. Friends who choose not to attend college may try to make a student feel guilty for leaving them behind. To overcome these pressures, a college student must have a strong desire to succeed.

This paragraph has no topic sentence, but several clues can help you infer the author's main idea. From the third sentence, which begins, "Another pressure," you can infer that the first two sentences explain one kind of pressure and that now you are reading about another kind. The sixth sentence, which begins, "Friends, too," introduces a third pressure students face. In the last sentence, the phrase "these pressures" is the strongest clue that the paragraph is about the effects of the three kinds of pressure.

When a paragraph has no topic sentence, the author's main idea is implied by the details in the supporting sentences. Once you identify the idea or topic that all the details support, you should be able to state the author's main idea in your own words.

To find the author's main idea, read a paragraph carefully and then follow these steps:

1. Look for the **topic sentence.** It can be anywhere in the paragraph, but it is often the first sentence. The topic sentence is the most general sentence in the paragraph. It combines the author's topic and opinion, and it summarizes *all* the information presented in the support sentences. The topic sentence expresses the author's main idea.

2. If the main idea is not stated in a topic sentence, identify the **topic** by inferring it from the details. Ask yourself, "What one idea do all the sentences

You may get more out of your reading by discussing the author's ideas with members of a study group.

in the paragraph support?" Look for signal words—such as *for one thing, another,* and *for example*—that introduce major details.

3. Determine the author's **opinion** about the topic. In general, what does the author say to expand your knowledge about the topic? Does the author *explain how* to do something? Does the author *compare two things?* Does the author *explain why* something exists or *give reasons* as to why something happens in a certain way? Does the author *argue for or against* one point of view? By identifying the author's opinion, you may be able to infer the main idea.

Finding the Details

By itself, the main idea is only a statement of fact or opinion that means little without evidence to support it. An author's evidence may include three types of details.

- Facts

- Reasons

- Examples

Facts. A fact is an observation, quotation, statistic, date, number, report of an event, or expert testimony that can be verified. For example, if a movie critic says there are twelve shootings within the first seven minutes of a new action film, you can verify this information by seeing the movie and counting the shootings that occur within the first seven minutes.

The authors of the following paragraph support the main idea with facts:

Most children receive the news of their parents' divorce as a shock, followed by depression, denial, anger, and low self-esteem. Fantasies of parental reconcilia-

© Ron Sherman

EXERCISE **13.2**

FIND THE MAIN IDEA IN each paragraph. If the main idea is stated, underline it. If the main idea is implied, write a sentence that expresses it.

---

1. *Increases in the number of college-level jobs depend generally on the overall rate of economic and employment growth in the United States but more specifically on employment growth in occupations that typically require college graduates. Additional college-level jobs open up in occupations when skill requirements or business practices change, resulting in employers hiring college graduates to fill positions formerly held by less educated workers, a phenomenon known as educational upgrading. A significant number of openings for college graduates will also arise as workers holding existing college-level jobs leave the labor force and need to be replaced....*

From "1994–2005: Lots of College-Level Jobs—But Not for All Graduates," Kristina J. Shelley, *Occupational Outlook Quarterly,* Summer 1996, Vol. 40, No. 2, Office of Employment Projections, Bureau of Labor Statistics, U. S. Department of Labor.

---

2. *You may frequently hear the terms* drug abuse *and* drug addiction *in certain college classes. Although all forms of drug addiction are classified as drug abuse, not all drug abuse is considered addictive. Drug abuse may be only an occasional indiscretion with a chemical substance, whereas addiction suggests a regular, dependent pattern of substance abuse. The individual who likes to get intoxicated for the weekend game may simply be abusing alcohol, but the person who makes drinking a dominant part of each day's activities is addicted to alcohol.*

From *Toward a Self-Managed Life Style,* 3rd ed., Robert L. Williams and James D. Long, Houghton Mifflin Co., 1988.

---

3. *Some carcinogens in the environment are present in such low concentrations that their effects can scarcely be noted. But one carcinogenic agent has an effect so strong that it cannot be ignored: cigarette smoking. Lung cancers, nearly 90 percent of which are caused by smoking, are now the leading cause of death from cancer among men and women in the United States. A decision to avoid smoking virtually ensures that an individual will not suffer from this disease.*

From *Biology,* Joseph S. Levine and Kenneth R. Miller, D. C. Heath and Company, 1991.

tion are almost universal. The adjustment period for children varies according to their age and emotional maturity, but usually children resume normal development within a year or two. Judith Wallerstein and Joan Kelly (1980) found that five years after a divorce 34 percent of children were resilient and happy, 29 percent were doing reasonably well, and 37 percent were depressed, looking back toward life before the divorce with longing. These researchers have noted age differences in their studies of children of divorce. Very young children and older adolescents seem to handle the situation best; adjustment appears most difficult for children ages seven to eleven.

From *Toward a Self-Managed Life Style*, 3rd ed., Robert L. Williams and James D. Long, Houghton Mifflin Co., 1988.

The authors' main idea, stated in the third sentence, is that the time it takes for children to adjust to their parents' divorce varies with the age and maturity of the children. The authors' supporting evidence is their summary of the findings of the researchers Wallerstein and Kelly. Using the appropriate database, you could verify the authors' details by going to the original sources where those authors reported their findings.

Reasons. Authors use reasons to support a main idea when their purpose is to explain *why* something happens, *why* something is important, *why* one thing is better than another, or *why* they feel or think as they do. Think of reasons as the *causes* that are responsible for producing certain effects, results, or outcomes. For example, a sportswriter may use reasons to explain why a basketball team lost an important game that it was favored to win. Or a political commentator might write an article explaining reasons for a presidential candidate's popularity among a certain group of voters.

In the following paragraph, reasons support the author's main idea:

One of the most important goals that a college student can aim for is an expanded vocabulary. One reason this goal is so important is that an expanded vocabulary can improve students' writing. With sufficient words and definitions at their command, students will have less difficulty writing what they mean. Also, increased reading improves vocabulary, which leads to greater comprehension. A third reason for improving vocabulary is the confidence students feel when they use words accurately. Students are less afraid to speak out in class discussions or to give reports and speeches when they know they are not going to mispronounce or misuse words. Increasing the vocabulary is a worthwhile goal for students who also want to improve their speaking, reading, and writing.

The main idea of this paragraph is that an expanded vocabulary is an important goal that students should try to reach. The main idea is stated in a topic sentence, which is the first sentence of the paragraph. The author supports the main idea with reasons that explain why students should increase their vocabularies.

1. An expanded vocabulary improves writing.

2. An increased vocabulary improves reading.

3. An improved vocabulary results in confidence.

The *signal phrases* "one reason" and "third reason" help you locate the major details. The second reason follows the signal word *also*.

Examples. Examples are situations, instances, or even people that authors use to illustrate, support, or clarify a main idea. Authors may use one extended example or several short ones. Or they may support a main idea with an example, then use facts or reasons as additional evidence. Some use examples as minor details to explain and clarify major details.

Notice how the authors of the next paragraph use examples:

Many legends were based on bizarre possibilities of matings between individuals of different species. The wife of Minos, according to Greek mythology, mated with a bull and produced the Minotaur. Folk heroes of Russia and Scandinavia were traditionally the sons of women who had been captured by bears, from which these men derived their great strength and so enriched the national stock. The camel and the leopard also mated from time to time, according to the early naturalists, who were otherwise unable—and it is hard to blame them—to explain an animal as improbable as the giraffe (the common giraffe still bears the scientific name of Giraffa camelopardalis). Thus folklore reflected early and imperfect glimpses into the nature of hereditary relationships.

From Helena Curtis and N. Sue Barnes, *Biology*, 5th ed., Worth Publishers, Inc., 1989.

In the first sentence of this paragraph, the authors state the idea that many legends are based on strange matings between members of different species. Examples of three legends support this main idea:

1. The Minotaur was a legendary being born of Minos's wife, who mated with a bull.

2. Russian and Scandinavian folk heroes were believed to have great strength because they were the sons of women who had mated with bears.

3. Because the giraffe was such an odd-looking creature, a legend developed that giraffes were the offspring of camels and leopards.

These examples, or major details, are easy to understand. The authors also add a minor detail that makes the giraffe example even more interesting: The animal's scientific name reflects earlier scientists' beliefs about its heredity.

EXERCISE **13.3**

READ EACH PASSAGE AND DETERMINE whether the details are mainly facts, reasons, or examples. Then check the appropriate box.

1.   No two people spend their money in exactly the same way because personal values influence financial decisions. Our values shape our standard of what we want our lives to be. Values are fundamental beliefs of what is important, desirable, and worthwhile that serve as the basis for goals. Each of us is different from others in the ways we value education, spiritual life, health, employment, credit use, family life, and many other factors. Values change little over a lifetime. Personal financial goals grow out of our values because we consider some things more important or desirable than others. Thus our personal values dictate our financial plans.

From Thomas E. Garman and Raymond E. Forgue, *Personal Finance,* Fourth Edition. Copyright © 1994 by Houghton Mifflin Company. Used with permission.

☐ **Facts**   ☐ **Reasons**   ☐ **Examples**

(Continued)

2.   *Memo to All Employees*
     From J. Todd, Manager

It is with deep regret that I inform you of the passing of one whose life has been an example to all of us. Spot was the mainstay of Curtis Nursery and Landscaping. The first to arrive and the last to leave, he greeted everyone warmly. He was a friend to all and discriminated against none. Who among us has not sought Spot's company when in need of a little cheering up? Spot has never been one to miss a day at work. This morning, we knew something was wrong when he was not waiting for us in the back of the truck. Instead, we found him in his favorite place under the house, where he had died peacefully during the night. A gentleman among dalmations, he will be missed.

☐ **Facts**   ☐ **Reasons**   ☐ **Examples**

3.   Although projections indicate there will be more openings over the 1994–2005 period than there were during the 1983–94 period, even more entrants are expected, making for somewhat increased competition in the job market for future college graduates....Between 1994 and 2005, job openings will average 1,040,000 annually, while college graduates joining the labor force are expected to average 1,340,000 each year. During the earlier 11-year period, openings averaged 970,000, while entrants averaged 1,180,000. Since the number of college graduate jobseekers will grow more quickly than the number of college-level jobs, the proportion of college graduate entrants expected to end up in noncollege jobs or unemployed will grow from 19 percent to over 22 percent.

From "1994–2005: Lots of College-Level Jobs—But Not for All Graduates," Kristina J. Shelley, *Occupational Outlook Quarterly*, Summer 1996, Vol. 40, No. 2, Office of Employment Projections, Bureau of Labor Statistics, U. S. Department of Labor.

☐ **Facts**   ☐ **Reasons**   ☐ **Examples**

Seeing Implications

To see an implications means to infer an idea that is implied, not stated. When the author's main idea is unstated, you must infer it from the details that are given. You might see many implications in an author's main idea and details, but most can be classified into one of two categories. *Personal implications* are those you can see by relating information you have read to what you know and have experienced. *Inferential implications* are educated guesses or conclusions you can draw about what an author means based on stated details. The ability to see implications enables you to use the information you gain from your reading to understand or learn something else.

Personal Implications. You probably see some personal implications in every day's events because your experience tells you what to expect or what seems likely. Suppose you are absent from several classes, and the next time you attend, the classroom is empty. You wait ten minutes, and still no one shows up. You conclude that class must not be meeting for some reason that was announced during your absence.

When you log on to your favorite web site, you know the information will be accurate and up-to-date because every time you have visited the site in the past, the information you have gained has proven to be reliable.

The manager of the company where you are employed needs someone to work overtime. You assume she will ask you because she knows you need the extra money and because you have helped out before.

Earlier in this chapter you found the main idea and details in a paragraph about the pressures students face from instructors, family, and friends. Now read a paragraph about another common source of pressure:

> *Stress is one pressure you bring on yourself when you go to class unprepared or when you don't manage your time effectively. Poor preparation results in inattention and that "lost" feeling. When you haven't read the assignment, you can't enter into the class discussion. If you haven't studied for a test, you are not likely to do well. In either situation, knowing your performance is not at its best creates stress. Being unprepared is almost always the result of poor time management. If you are like many students, you have more to do than you can possibly get done unless you schedule your time. Time management also involves setting priorities. You have to decide which is more important, seeing that new movie with a friend tonight or getting those algebra problems done for tomorrow's class. If you consistently put off doing things you need to do so that you can do what you want to do, the stress will eventually catch up with you. Make a decision now to improve your time management and to become better prepared for class, and you will have taken the first step toward reducing some of your stress.*

One student who read this paragraph said, "Boy, that's me; I can always find something else to do besides algebra." This student related a detail from the paragraph to his own experience: "It's not that I don't want to do the work or that I don't realize I'm undermining my chances for success in the course. It's just that algebra is so hard. I know I'm going to get frustrated, so I dread getting started. As a result, I wait until the last minute, and that stresses me out." Relating the idea that you can bring stress on yourself to what she had read about locus of control (source of internal or external motivation), another student said, "Since this kind of stress is the result of your own behavior, you can get rid of it by changing your behavior. In a way, this is easier to deal with than the stress that comes from the pressures you get from family, instructors, and friends. Those pressures are outside you, so they're harder to control."

Inferential Implications.   What you read in your college textbooks will be more meaningful for you if you relate it to your experience with and your knowledge of the author's subject. Just as you can see personal implications in what you read, you can make *inferences,* or base informed guesses, on stated information. A valid inference is one that can be supported by an author's main idea and details.

Read the following paragraph:

> *Styles in cars, dress, furniture, and architecture come and go. Some styles become outdated or may disappear. Others never really go away but reassert themselves, with some changes, over many years. A **fad** is a style of short duration. A **fashion** is a more lasting style. Both fads and fashions are engaged in by large groups of people. Fads of the past forty years include the hula hoop, hot pants, love beads, disco dancing, automobile "tail fins," and Klick-Klack Blocks. You may be*

thinking, "I've never heard of some of these fads" and for good reason: They have come and gone. Fashions stay with us. Miniskirts—once considered a fad—have enjoyed several revivals. Columns, a feature of ancient Greek architecture, have never gone out of style. You see them on public buildings and private homes— wherever a "classic" look is desired. Because fashions are more lasting than fads, they tend to be more socially acceptable. What is the difference between a fashionable person and a faddist? One is selective about which trends and behaviors to embrace, developing his or her own personal style. The other is swept along by each new fad that enjoys a brief popularity and seems to have no recognizable style.

According to this paragraph, both fads and fashions are forms of collective behavior, but they differ in duration. You can use this information to make inferences about other behaviors. For example, a few years ago, many drivers displayed this sign in their cars' rear windows. Now you rarely see the sign. Was it a fad or a fashion?

The "baby on board" sign was probably a fad because of its relatively short duration. Bumper stickers, which may have started as a fad, have become a trend of longer duration and are, therefore, fashionable. What about vanity plates— license plates with personal messages? Are they a fad or a fashion? What do you think?

EXERCISE **13.4**

APPLY WHAT YOU HAVE LEARNED about main idea, details, and implications by completing this exercise with group members. Follow the guidelines for successful collaboration that appear on the inside back cover. Read each paragraph. Then discuss the main idea, identify the details, and read the implications that are listed. If you think most readers would see these implications, check *yes*. If not, check *no*. In either case, explain your answer. When you reach consensus, record your conclusions on the lines provided. Then evaluate your work.

If you want to expand your vocabulary, there are two methods you might want to try. The first method involves making note cards and using them for recitation and review of words that you want to learn. Prepare each note card by writing the word on one side of the card and its definition on the other side. Recite to learn by pronouncing the word and saying its definition. Then turn the card over and check yourself. Do this with each card until you can recite all the definitions from memory. Review the words by repeating these steps once a week, or as often as needed, to keep the words in your memory. The second method for learning words involves keeping a word list as you read. As you are reading an assigned chapter in one of your textbooks, jot down in a notebook any unfamiliar words you encounter. Look at these words and write the definitions that fit the contexts in which the words appear. The next time you read a chapter from the same textbook, keep your word list handy. You can add to the list or use it to review definitions of your words when they appear in new contexts. These two methods have worked for many students.

Main Idea: If you want to expand your vocabulary, there are two methods you might want to try.

Details:

a. _____

_____

_____

b. _____

_____

_____

Implications:

	Yes	No
a. These vocabulary-building methods may work for you.	☐	☐

Explain your answer: _____

_____

_____

	Yes	No
b. Using one of these two methods is the only way to expand your vocabulary.	☐	☐

Explain your answer: _____

_____

_____

_____

Group Evaluation:

Evaluate your discussion. Did everyone contribute? Did you accomplish your task successfully? What additional questions do you have about the main idea, details, and their implications? How will you find answers to your questions?

_____

_____

_____

CONFIDENCE
Builder

Calculate Your Reading Rate

Does Speed Reading Really Work?

You may have read accounts of people who can "read" 1,700 words per minute, and you may have wished you could read that fast. Speed reading is a controversial issue. Although you may want to increase your reading rate in order to save time or improve your chances of answering all the items on a timed reading test, you may lose comprehension as you gain reading speed if you try to read *too* fast.

Let *efficient reading*, not speed reading, be your goal. To read efficiently, vary your reading rate with the *type of material* and your *purpose* for reading. For example, you can skim a news or magazine article that you read for personal interest, but when you read textbooks and other materials to gain and retain knowledge, you must read slowly and carefully for maximum comprehension.

Do you read everything at the same rate? If you do, then you are not reading as efficiently as you could. Use this formula to calculate your reading rate; then experiment with adjusting your rate to the type of material and your purpose for reading it.

$$\frac{\text{No. of words in passage}}{\text{Reading time}} = \text{Reading rate in words per minute (wpm)}$$

To estimate the number of words in a passage, find the average number of words per line and multiply that number by the number of lines in the whole passage (if the passage is less than one page) or by the number of lines on one page (if the passage is several pages). Then use a stopwatch, digital watch, or clock with a second hand to time yourself, in minutes and seconds, as you read. Finally, round off to the nearest minute to use the formula.

Knowing that your reading rate for difficult or unfamiliar material is naturally going to be slower than your rate for less complex kinds of information can help you plan your study time. Suppose you are taking a biology course and have been assigned a 60-page chapter to read for the next class meeting. First, time yourself to determine how many minutes it will take you to read one page. Then multiply your time by 60 (the number of pages in your assignment) to get your total time in minutes. Divide this total by 60 to determine how many hours and minutes you will need to schedule for reading the assigned chapter. If it will take you three hours to read 60 pages, then you may want to break up the time into three one-hour segments so that you stay focused. To read efficiently, adjust your reading rate and schedule your reading time to meet the demands of any reading task.

To pursue this topic further, do an online search using these key words as a starting point: *reading speed, reading rate, reading efficiency, reading retention.*

EXERCISE **13.5**

TO READ ACTIVELY, YOU MUST read critically, evaluating sources for authoritativeness, accuracy, objectivity, and bias. This is especially true when you are searching the Internet for information. Anyone can publish on the Internet; therefore, not everything you read on the Net is a credible source. How do you know whether to trust the information you have found on a web site? The following is a list of questions to ask. If the web site is a credible source, then it will provide answers to these questions.

Using the following questions, choose a site on a topic that interests you and evaluate it. Then share your findings with the rest of the class.

1. **Who says so?** Who publishes the web site, and what are the author's qualifications? Can you determine where the author lives and works? What degrees and awards does the author hold? What is the author's reputation in his or her field?

2. **Is the information objective?** Is the author or publisher self-interested? What does the author have to gain from publishing this information? For example, you can expect a company to endorse its own products. You can also expect information provided by special interest groups to reflect their biases.

3. **How current is the information?** One of the virtues of the Internet is that web sites have the potential for immediacy of data. However, some web sites are not kept current. Can you find a date on the web page that indicates when the information was last updated or revised?

4. **How extensive is the coverage of the information?** What is the purpose of the site? Is the site linked to other sites or pages, and if so, are the links of the same quality as that of the original page? Is the site organized in such a way that you can easily find the answers to your questions or the specific information related to the issue that you are researching?

For more information on evaluating Internet sources, see http://college.hmco.com/success for up-to-date URLs. Also check your college's web site for any information it may have on evaluating Internet sources.

Use a Textbook Marking System

MARKING YOUR TEXTBOOKS by *underlining* or *highlighting* and by *annotating* (making notes) improves your concentration for two reasons: It focuses your attention on the task of reading, and it provides a tactile pathway to the brain. You must think critically about what you read so that you can make decisions about what to underline, highlight, or annotate. When done well, marking your textbook saves time by providing you with specific information to review so that you do not have to re-read a whole chapter in order to study for a test. Whether you underline or highlight is a matter of personal preference. Highlighting pens come in a variety of colors, and the type of ink they contain may vary. Experiment with highlighters to find one that won't bleed through your pages. Underlining is best done with a fine-line ballpoint pen or felt-tip marker. Again, choose one that doesn't bleed through. A pencil may not be as good a choice for underlining. A sharp point may tear the paper; also, pencil smudges and fades and doesn't show up nearly as well as ink.

Marking your textbook is an essential part of any study system because it improves your reception and retention of information. In the next paragraph a student, Alex, describes the system he worked out for underlining and marking his textbook:

> I read one section at a time. After I read the section, I draw a bracket, [ ], around the main idea and put a star beside it in the margin. I underline the major details, and I put a number in a circle next to each detail. That way I can see how many details there are when I review the section for a test. If a word I don't know is defined in a section, I underline it and write "def." in the margin. If I have to look up a word that is not defined, I circle it and write my definition in the margin. Also, I don't underline everything in a sentence. I just underline key words. Before I did this, I used to underline too much; then I would end up having to re-read almost the whole chapter when I reviewed instead of studying just the important parts.

Alex makes a good point: Underlining too much is not useful (nor is underlining too little). The purpose of marking textbooks is to make the important ideas stand out and to provide memory cues. Then you can determine what you need to study in depth and what you can skip when you review. Here is what one of Alex's underlined passages looks like. Notice how he has annotated the passage in the margins.

(def.) grimace = expression of pain

Studies of infants show expressions are inborn.

People of all cultures react the same to same stimuli.

Similar facial responses: 4 examples

[Two types of evidence indicate that, as Darwin proposed, the basic facial expressions of emotions are innate.]

One source of evidence comes from infants. They do not need to be taught to (grimace) in pain or to smile in pleasure; they exhibit facial movements that are appropriately correlated with their well-being. Even blind infants, who cannot see adults in order to imitate them, show the same emotional expressions as do sighted infants (Goodenough, 1932).

A second line of evidence for innate facial expressions comes from research showing that, for the most basic emotions, people of all cultures show similar facial responses to similar emotional stimuli (Ekman, 1984, 1993; Ekman & Friesen, 1986). Studies that demonstrate the universality of emotional expressions ask people to look at photographs of faces and then pick what emotion the person in the photo is feeling. The pattern of facial movements we call a [1]smile, for example, is universally related to positive emotions. [2]Sadness is almost always accompanied by slackened muscle tone and a "long" face. Likewise, in almost all cultures, people [3]contort their faces in a similar way when presented with something disgusting. And a [4]furrowed brow is frequently associated with frustration or unpleasantness (Smith, 1989).

Douglas Bernstein et al., *Pyschology*, First Edition. Copyright © 1988 by Houghton Mifflin Company. Used with permission.

© Ron Sherman

Marking your textbooks focuses your attention on the task of reading and helps you think critically about what you read.

Try these guidelines for effective textbook marking. Then, like Alex, develop a system that works for you and use it consistently.

What to Mark in Textbooks

Deciding what to mark is the same as deciding what is important. *Definitions of terms* are important. Even if they are already italicized or printed in boldface, mark them anyway if you do not already know them. *Examples* used to illustrate theories are important; so are *experiments,* including who conducted them, what happened, and what they proved. *Names, dates,* and *historical events* are important. *Principles, rules,* and *characteristics* are additional examples of the kinds of information that may be important within the context of what you are reading.

How to Mark Your Textbooks

1. It is usually better to read before you underline and to read one section at a time. You may not be able to tell what is important until you have read a whole section to see how the ideas relate to each other.

2. In the margin, write key words or symbols that will serve as memory cues to call your attention to special terms, names, dates, and other important information.

3. Use your own words when you make notes in your textbook. Putting the author's ideas into your own words will help you test your understanding, and you will be more likely to retain them.

4. Decide on some symbols to indicate certain kinds of information and use your symbols consistently. Here are some common symbols students use. You probably already use some of them.

def. = definition

ex. = example

T = possible test item

* = an important point

1., 2., 3., etc. = used when sequence matters

5. Underline or highlight words and phrases only, not entire sentences.

Review for a test or prepare for class by reciting from what you have marked or annotated in the margin. Use your underlining and marking to identify processes or concepts you can illustrate, using charts or diagrams for easy review and recall.

EXERCISE **13.6**

APPLY THE GUIDELINES FOR UNDERLINING and marking textbooks to this excerpt from a textbook chapter. Read and mark the passage. Then answer the questions that follow to help you determine whether you correctly identified the most important ideas.

Guidelines for Wise Buying Over the Life Cycle
Examples of ways that people waste money could fill the pages of dozens of books. Fortunately, a few simple guidelines can yield savings of 10 to 20 percent during a year, equivalent to a sharp increase in income. Suggestions follow.

Control Buying on Impulse *Simple restraint will help avoid* **impulse buying,** *which is nothing more than buying without fully considering need and alternatives. Say, for example, you have shopped carefully by comparing various microwave ovens and have selected one at a discount store with the lowest price of $200. While at the store, you impulsively pick up some microwave cookware and a cookbook that you really don't need. The extra $45 spent on impulse ruined some of the benefits of the comparison shopping for the oven itself.*

Pay Cash *Paying cash whenever possible can help save money in two ways. First, it helps control impulse buying that is made easy by using credit cards to make purchases that one really can't afford. Second, use of credit can make financial planning more difficult by taking away financial flexibility and by adding to the cost of items. You may pay 12, 18, or even 24 percent more for your credit purchases, because you pay that much more in interest.*

Buy at the Right Time *Paying attention to sales and looking for the right time to buy will save money. As you probably know, 30 to 60 percent can be saved on telephone charges just by making calls in the evenings and on weekends. Many items, such as sporting goods and clothing, are marked down near certain holidays and at the* end of each climate season. Also, $5 or $10 weekly can be saved on food simply by stocking up on advertised specials. Make sure that what you buy on sale is something you will really use, however.

Don't Pay Extra for a "Name"   Some people have an "Excedrin headache" for 30 cents a dosage or an "Anacin headache" for 25 cents a dosage, and others have a plain aspirin headache for 2 cents a dosage. Scientific research (not the advertiser's research) consistently shows that the effectiveness of all over-the-counter pain relievers is about the same. This is why the ads say "none better" rather than "we're the best." Gasoline, vitamins, laundry and other soaps, and many grocery items are all products with minor quality differences. Buying generic products is a good way to save money. **Generic products** are sold under a general commodity name such as "whole kernel corn" rather than a brand name such as Del Monte. Savings can be especially significant for prescription drugs. Many states allow consumers to request that the pharmacist use a generic equivalent even if the physician writes the prescription under a brand name. In other states consumers can ask the physician to write the prescription generically. Also note that many less expensive, store-brand products (such as appliances sold at Sears and J. C. Penney) are actually made by the brand-name manufacturers....

The High Price of Convenience Shopping   A bottle of ketchup or jar of peanut butter bought at a supermarket probably costs 50 cents less than at a nearby convenience store, whereas bread and milk may be priced about the same. Buying a few items daily at a convenience store or neighborhood market rather than making a planned weekly visit to a grocery store can raise food bills 30 percent or more through higher prices and the more frequent temptation of impulse purchases. Also, although it may be convenient to shop for furniture and appliances in the local community, better prices on the same items may be found in larger, more competitive shopping areas, such as outlet shopping malls.

Life-Cycle Planning for Major Purchases   "You can't have everything," as the old saying goes, but many young Americans certainly try. This is one of the reasons why the average household headed by someone under age 25 spends 17 percent more than its disposable income. (How? By using credit, of course.) What is important to realize is that although one cannot have everything right now, planning will help keep things in perspective. Comparing what one has to [what] parents or older relatives and friends [have] is fine. But recognize that it takes a lot of time to build up the quantity and quality of possessions that they may have. Intelligently setting short- and long-term goals and recognizing budget limitations will enable you to reach goals for major purchases but not at the expense of financial security....

From Thomas E. Garman and Raymond E. Forgue, *Personal Finance,* Fourth Edition. Copyright © 1994 by Houghton Mifflin Company. Used with permission.

1. **What is the central idea of this passage?**

_____

2. **How many guidelines for buying are explained in the passage? Briefly list them on the following lines.**

_____

_____

_____

(Continued)

3. **How much can you save by stocking up on advertised specials at the grocery store?**

_____

4. **What is a good way to avoid impulse buying?**

_____

_____

_____

5. **Why is it not a good idea to shop at convenience stores?**

_____

_____

_____

6. **What is the advantage of paying cash for purchases?**

_____

_____

_____

7. **Define *disposable income* as it's used in the last paragraph, second sentence.**

_____

_____

_____

8. *Personal implication:* **Which of the suggested guidelines for buying do you use?**

_____

_____

_____

9. *Personal implication:* **What is one way you could save money that you haven't tried?**

_____

_____

_____

_____

10. *Inference:* **Why do you suppose so many young people try to have everything now, as the authors suggest?**

_____

_____

_____

CRITICAL THINKING

Examples A and B show the same passage as marked by two different students. Evaluate each student's markings for usefulness. Determine which student has successfully applied the suggestions for marking text-books that are explained in this chapter. Summarize your findings in writing.

Example A

Behavioral Stress Responses. Clues about people's physical and emotional stress reactions come from changes in how they look, act, or talk. Strained facial expressions, a shaky voice, tremors or spasms, and jumpiness are common behavioral stress responses. Posture can also convey information about stress, a fact observed by skilled interviewers.

Even more obvious behavioral stress responses appear as people attempt to escape or avoid stressors. Some people quit their jobs, drop out of school, turn to alcohol, or even attempt suicide. Unfortunately, as discussed in the chapter on learning, escape and avoidance tactics deprive people of the opportunity to learn more adaptive ways of coping with stressful environments, including college (Cooper et al., 1992).

Aggression is another common behavioral response to stressors. All too often...this aggressiveness is directed at members of one's own family (Hepworth & West, 1988; MacEwan & Barling, 1988). In the months after Hurricane Andrew hit south Florida in 1992, for example, the rate of domestic violence reports in the devastated area doubled....

Stress shows in your face, voice, actions, posture.

Cooper et al.: avoidance tactics keep you from dealing with stress

avoidance tactics

Aggression often directed at family

Example B

Behavioral Stress Responses. Clues about people's physical and emotional stress reactions come from changes in how they look, act, or talk. Strained facial expressions, a shaky voice, tremors or spasms, and jumpiness are common behavioral stress responses. Posture can also convey information about stress, a fact observed by skilled interviewers.

Even more obvious behavioral stress responses appear as people attempt to escape or avoid stressors. Some people quit their jobs, drop out of school, turn to alcohol, or even attempt suicide. Unfortunately, as discussed in the chapter on learning, escape and avoidance tactics deprive people of the opportunity to learn more adaptive ways of coping with stressful environments, including college (Cooper et al., 1992).

Aggression is another common behavioral response to stressors. All too often...this aggressiveness is directed at members of one's own family (Hepworth & West, 1988; MacEwan & Barling, 1988). In the months after Hurricane Andrew hit south Florida in 1992, for example, the rate of domestic violence reports in the devastated area doubled...

Avoidance tactics

Hepworth, West, MacEwan, Barling

Excerpts from Bernstein, Clarke-Stewart, Roy, Srull, and Wickens, *Psychology,* Third Edition. Copyright © 1994 by Houghton Mifflin Company. Reprinted by permission.

thinking *ahead* - - - - ->

What practical knowledge have you gained from this chapter that you can use to solve real-world problems? To find out, read the following scenario and complete the items after it.

After graduating from high school, Hector went to work as a delivery worker for a company that supplies gum, candy, tobacco products, and other assorted goods to stores and restaurants. He drives a company truck and has an excellent driving record. Although Hector enjoys driving a truck, making his rounds, and interacting with the customers on his route, he knows that his job offers no opportunities for advancement. Recently he applied for a job with a postal delivery company that would net him a salary increase, a benefits package better than the one he has now, and a chance for advancement to a management level.

Although his qualifications were good in every other aspect, Hector was denied the job because of his poor reading skills. "Reading is important," the personnel manager told Hector, "because our employees have to keep accurate records of deliveries, make sure packages get to the right addresses, and be able to use maps and directories. Moreover, employees on a management track must have superior communication skills and those include reading." Because she liked Hector and was impressed with his driving record and interpersonal skills, the personnel manager advised him to enroll at a community college to upgrade his reading skills. "Come back to see me," she said, "when you have your associate of arts degree." Hector has taken her advice and will soon be starting classes. Looking at the books he has just purchased for his courses, Hector is wondering how he will ever get through them. But he is determined to succeed because he really wants a better job.

1. What is Hector's problem?

_____

_____

2. What is Hector's goal?

_____

_____

3. In addition to taking a reading course, what else can Hector do to upgrade his communication skills?

_____

_____

_____

4. What plan can you suggest that will help Hector become an active reader?

_____

_____

_____

chapter **re**view

To review the chapter, reflect on the following confidence-building attitudes, complete **Concepts to Understand,** and practice your new skills at every opportunity.

ATTITUDES TO DEVELOP

- self-motivation
- commitment to learn
- desire to succeed
- persistence

CONCEPTS TO UNDERSTAND

Active reading is an essential part of any study system. To read actively, apply two strategies: (1) Read for _____, _____, and _____; (2) Mark your textbooks by underlining or highlighting and by _____.

To find a stated main idea, look for a _____ _____ in a paragraph. If the main idea is implied, you must infer it from the details, which consist of _____, _____, and _____.

Implications may be personal or inferential. _____ implications are those you discover when you relate the author's main idea and details to your own experience. _____ are implications based on an author's stated main idea and details.

Marking your text helps you concentrate and encourages you to think critically about what you read. The value of marking is that it makes important ideas stand out. To mark effectively, _____ or _____ key ideas and make notes in the margin to create memory cues to aid your review.

To access additional review exercises, see http://college.hmco.com/success.

SKILLS TO PRACTICE

- reading actively
- reading for ideas
- setting realistic goals
- making inferences
- using reading and marking systems

Your Reflections

Your Reflections

Reflect on what you have learned about active reading and how you can best apply that information. Use the following list of questions to stimulate your thinking; then write your reflections. Your response may include answers to one or more of the questions. Incorporate in your writing specific information from this chapter or from previous chapters as it's needed.

- Would you describe yourself as an active reader? Why, or why not?

- Of the strategies explained in this chapter, which ones are new to you? Which ones have you already used, and how?

- What kinds of reading activities do you perform well? What gives you trouble?

- Why is reading an important skill? How do you use reading in your daily life?

- Of the attitudes and skills listed in the Chapter Review, which do you think will be most useful at work or in your career?

Using Critical Thinking Strategies

WHAT ENABLES YOU to put two and

two together? How do you know what

you know? What is critical thinking, and what are

its lifelong benefits?

WHEN YOU ARE thinking critically, you are conscious, or aware, that you are thinking. At the same time, you are thinking with a purpose. For example, you may need to think through a personal or work-related problem to find a solution, or you may need to think about the ideas presented in a difficult reading assignment to achieve understanding.

What is *critical thinking*? Broadly defined, it is *the process of constructing and evaluating meaning*. More specifically, critical thinking is *logical, or analytical, reasoning* that helps you make sense of everything you read, see, and hear. Critical thinking is also the process of *self-reflection*, whereby you examine your actions and their consequences both to achieve self-understanding and to determine whether to make attitudinal or behavioral changes. Finally, critical thinking is both *conscious* and *purposeful*. You know that you are doing it, and you know why.

Making decisions, solving problems, finding and organizing information, and other important tasks all require critical thinking. This chapter explains four strategies that will help you think critically and confidently. Flow charts in each of the next four sections show how each strategy is linked to different skill areas. The first letter of each boldfaced word in the following list is part of the acronym *A PIE*, which you can use as a memory aid to recall these four strategies.

- Examine your **assumptions.**

- Make **predictions.**

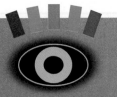

Awareness Check 20

ARE YOU A CRITICAL THINKER?

Yes	No	
☐	☐	*Check* yes or no *beside the following statements.*
☐	☐	1. I usually can predict what assignments will cover.
☐	☐	2. I always have a purpose for reading.
☐	☐	3. I relate what I learn in my courses to my experience.
☐	☐	4. I ask questions to guide my learning.
☐	☐	5. I read or listen for main ideas and details.
☐	☐	6. I can identify and follow organizational patterns.
☐	☐	7. I recognize an author's or speaker's purpose.
☐	☐	8. I look for implications in what I learn.
☐	☐	9. I evaluate what I learn from reading, observing, or listening.
☐	☐	10. I know how to evaluate Internet sources.

If you cannot honestly check yes *to every statement in the Awareness Check, then your thinking skills need improving. You* can *become a critical thinker and take control of your learning.*

- Sharpen your **interpretations.**
- **Evaluate** what you learn.

Examine Your Assumptions

AN *ASSUMPTION* IS an idea or belief taken for granted. Assumptions are based on what we know or have experienced. Everyone has certain assumptions about family, education, government—any aspect of one's life or world—and people's assumptions differ. For example, most people agree that some sort of health care reform is needed. Those who favor nationalized health care subsidized by government funding assume that under such a system costs for services would be lower, and more people would be able to afford health care as a result. Those opposed to nationalized health care assume that lower costs would mean lower payments for services, which would result in a decline in the quality of service. They may also assume that their taxes would be increased to pay for the program. What do those on either side of this issue stand to gain or lose? What evidence supports their assumptions? Are there other points of view?

These are the kinds of questions critical thinkers ask. To think critically, examine your assumptions—and others' assumptions—to determine what is known, believed, or taken for granted about the topic or issue at hand. Keep an open mind and be willing to change your assumptions based on new evidence or experiences. Before you read anything or listen to a lecture, examine your assumptions by asking yourself, "What do I already know about the topic?" and "What opinions have I already formed?"

Assumptions can be compelling. Your beliefs, the ideas you take for granted, shape your thoughts and actions. Figure 14.1 illustrates how examining your assumptions extends to several skill areas and activities.

Figure 14.1   Examine Your Assumptions: How You Can Use This Critical Thinking Strategy

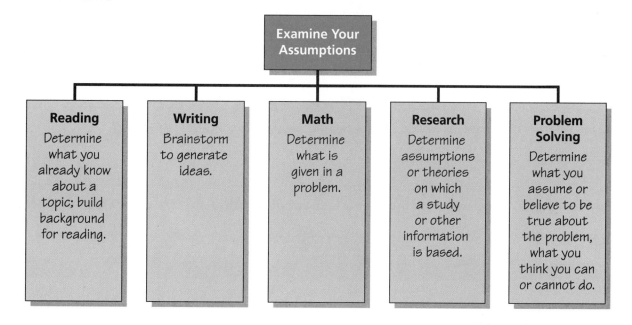

	Examine Your Assumptions			
Reading	**Writing**	**Math**	**Research**	**Problem Solving**
Determine what you already know about a topic; build background for reading.	Brainstorm to generate ideas.	Determine what is given in a problem.	Determine assumptions or theories on which a study or other information is based.	Determine what you assume or believe to be true about the problem, what you think you can or cannot do.

EXERCISE **14.1**

IT IS IMPORTANT TO RECOGNIZE and analyze the assumptions that you bring to everyday interactions with people as well as to the subjects you study.

To examine some of your assumptions about other people, look at the group in the following photograph, and then answer the questions.

© Bob Daemmrich/The Image Works

1. **Who are these people? What assumptions can you make based on their clothing or on other details in the photograph?**

_____

_____

2. **Where are they, and what do they seem to be doing? What details in the photograph help you make your assumptions?**

_____

_____

3. **Based on their expressions, what do these people seem to be thinking or feeling?**

_____

_____

4. **How do your assumptions about the people in the photograph relate to your own experiences?**

_____

_____

5. **Has your learning style either helped or interfered with your ability to complete this exercise? Explain your answer.**

_____

_____

Make Predictions

A *PREDICTION* IS a decision made beforehand about the outcome of an event. Predictions are based on assumptions. Because you believe that certain things are true, you expect or believe that certain things will happen. If you believe, for example, that you are good at math, then you can predict that you will do well in a math course. If you have a favorite author who has just published a new book, you can predict that you will probably like it. Your prediction is based on the assumption that the new book will be similar to others by this author that you have read and enjoyed.

Predictions are often the result of asking yourself questions and looking for answers. When you wake up in the morning, you may wonder, "What will the weather be like today? What should I wear?" You look out the window at a sunny, cloudless sky. You step outside, and it is breezy and cool enough for a sweater. You remember that yesterday's weather started out like this, but by noon the temperature had risen to eighty degrees. Predicting that today's weather will be the same, you dress in layers so that you can remove some of your clothing as the temperature warms. By lunchtime, however, clouds have begun to form. Friends tell you that rain has been forecast. You run out to your car to grab an umbrella from the trunk. In doing so, you have acted on the prediction that it will rain. Based on new information—the clouds and your friends' comments—you now think rain is a likely occurrence.

Before listening to a lecture, reading an assignment, or taking a test, make predictions by asking yourself questions such as these: "What will I learn from this lecture?" "How will this assignment help me?" and "What test questions can I anticipate?" Figure 14.2 illustrates how making predictions extends to several skill areas and activities.

Listen With a Purpose

When listening to lectures, make predictions that are *purposeful* and *flexible*. Suppose the speaker's topic is *five strategies for improving memory.* You can predict that the speaker will explain the five strategies and ways to use them. Your purpose is to listen for cues such as *identifying words* or *definitions* that will tell you what the strategies are, *numbers* that will indicate which strategy is being explained, and *examples* or *steps* that will tell you how to use each strategy. Suppose the speaker says, "Acronyms are another helpful memory aid" and writes *acronym* on the board. As you copy this term into your notes, you're thinking, "Is this a new strategy, or is it another example of the use of mnemonic devices, the third strategy mentioned so far?" You raise your hand to ask the question. Based on the speaker's answer that acronyms are indeed a mnemonic device, you predict that following the explanation of acronyms, the speaker will either provide an

Figure 14.2 **Make Predictions: How You Can Use This Critical Thinking Strategy**

Make Predictions

Reading
Turn headings into questions to guide your reading.

Writing
Have a purpose for writing. Have an organizational plan to follow.

Math
Determine the kind of answer you need: a fraction? a percent?

All Courses
Anticipate exam questions and make practice tests.

Decision Making
Look ahead to the outcome. What do you think will happen?

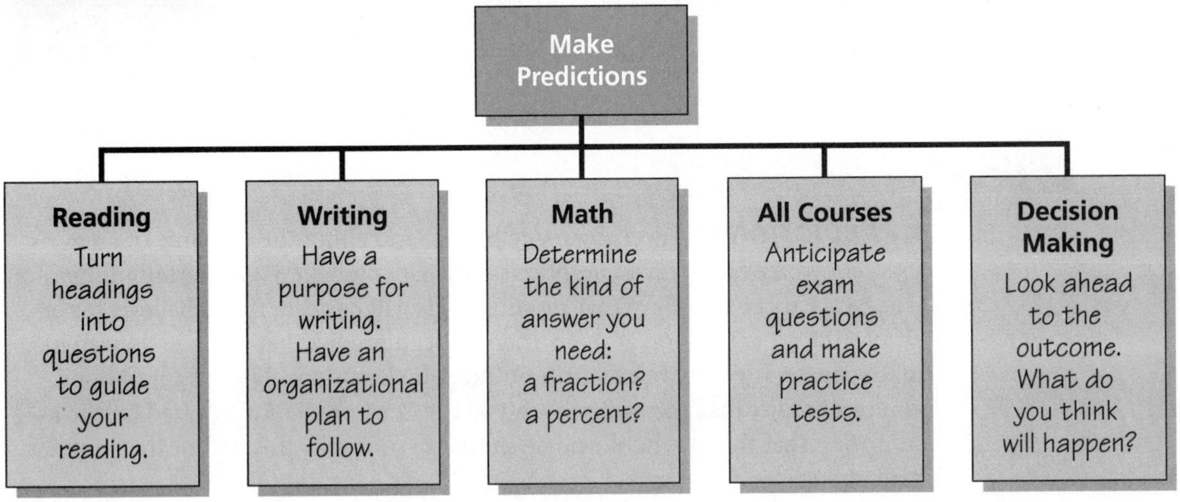

additional example of a mnemonic or will proceed to the fourth strategy. In either case, your question and predictions have helped you understand and follow the speaker's ideas.

Read with a Purpose

Predictions are useful for reading your textbooks as well as for understanding a lecture. To see how this critical thinking strategy applies to reading textbooks, look at the following chapter title and headings from *Personal Finance* by E. Thomas Garman and Raymond E. Forgue.

TITLE: THE IMPORTANCE OF PERSONAL FINANCE

HEADINGS: Reasons for Studying Personal Finance

Goals of Effective Personal Financial Management

Factors That Affect Personal Income

Steps in Personal Financial Management

What predictions can you make about the chapter's content? Notice how the writers of *Personal Finance* help you. They begin each heading with a key word that tells you exactly what to look for in each part of the chapter: *reasons, goals, factors,* and *steps.* Here are some guide questions you could ask to start thinking about personal finance in general—and your own attempts to manage money:

• What do these authors think is important about personal finance?

• Why should I study personal finance?

- What are the goals of financial management?

- Which factors affect personal income, and what are their effects?

- How many factors are there?

Asking guide questions like these and making predictions about content enable you to read with a *purpose*. There are three main purposes for reading informational material (such as that found in most textbooks) and three strategies best suited to each purpose. Figure 14.3 shows these relationships among the different purposes and strategies.

When you read a chapter for the first time, you should use the first strategy. Read every word so that you will understand ideas and comprehend the author's meaning. Read actively, turning headings into questions and anticipating the answers.

After reading a chapter, you may need to search for a fact or for the answer to a question you missed on a test. To do this, use the second strategy. Decide what kind of fact you're looking for: a number, name, or place, for example. Then scan the chapter section that is likely to contain the fact. If you're looking for a date, ignore everything else and read only the dates until you find the right one.

If a passage is difficult, use the third strategy. Read it again slowly and carefully. If you still don't understand the passage, read one sentence at a time. If sentences are long, break them down into parts and restate them in your own words. Read aloud. Sometimes hearing yourself read a difficult passage helps you make sense of it, especially if your preferred learning style is auditory.

Figure 14.3   Purposes and Strategies for Informational Reading

PURPOSE	STRATEGY	WHEN TO USE
Reading to understand ideas and construct meaning	Read carefully at normal speed; slow down for difficult parts; try to relate ideas; ask guide questions.	The first time you read a chapter
Reading to find facts	Scan-read for dates, names, places, lists of steps, or other factual matter. (*Scan* means to glance rapidly over a page, looking for specific information or the answer to a question.)	To look for an answer to a question missed on a test; to look for information you know will be on a test; to look for answers to questions covering a chapter; to verify information in your notes; to survey and review chapters
Reading to analyze difficult or complex passages	Read slowly; pay attention to every word; break sentences into parts and express the parts in your own words; summarize difficult passages.	To read a sentence or passage that you don't understand; to analyze a complex or difficult section that you want to understand more fully; to read literature, especially poetry

The first purpose and strategy will help you understand how the author constructed the arguments or discussions in the text. Reading with the second purpose in mind will help you make predictions and discover the author's intent. The third purpose and strategy will help when you read complex or technical material as well as literature.

EXERCISE **14.2**

BEFORE READING THE FOLLOWING PASSAGE, test your assumptions about homosexuals on campus by answering questions 1 and 2. Then read the passage and answer the questions that come after it.

1. **Do you think that most students support equal rights for homosexuals? On what do you base this assumption?**

   _____

   _____

2. **Do you think most students' attitudes toward homosexuals on campus are positive or negative? On what do you base this assumption?**

   _____

   _____

> Several years ago, a group of gay students at a large state university picked a date and announced, "If you are gay, wear blue jeans today." Nobody sought to quantify the result, but can you guess what may have happened? (Fewer students than usual wore blue jeans.) Studies show that although most Americans support equal rights, attitudes toward gay men and lesbians are generally negative (Herek, 1988). Based on a recent poll, Time magazine found that 53 percent of American adults believe that homosexual relationships between consenting adults are morally wrong, and 64 percent believe that marriage between homosexuals should not be recognized by law (Henry, 1994).
>
> Not everyone harbors anti-gay prejudice, of course, and there is a wide range of individual differences of opinion. The problem is that people with negative attitudes toward homosexuals may also discriminate in important matters. In one study, Geoffrey Haddock and his colleagues (1993) told student subjects that their university's student government had to cut funding to campus-wide organizations by 20 percent—and that they wanted to hear student opinions on where to make these cuts (two weeks earlier, each subject's attitude toward homosexuals had been assessed). Subjects were then given a list of ten campus organizations, including one for gays and lesbians. As you might expect, negative attitudes were linked to discriminatory decisions. Those with the most anti-gay sentiment proposed an average budget cut of 45 percent, compared to 26 percent among subjects with the least negative attitudes. Discrimination can take on many forms. In a recent survey of 800 American adults, 75 percent said they would vote for a homosexual political candidate and only 39 percent said they would see a homosexual doctor (Henry, 1994).
>
> Saul Kassin, _Psychology_. Copyright © 1995 by Houghton Mifflin Company. Reprinted by permission.

3. What is the author's topic?

_____

_____

4. What evidence from paragraph 1 does the author provide to support the opinion that Americans' attitudes toward homosexuals are generally negative?

_____

_____

5. What seems to be the relationship between attitudes toward homosexuals and discrimination? Use evidence from paragraph 2 to support your answer.

_____

_____

6. If an announcement were to appear in your college newspaper saying, "If you are not gay, wear red next Friday," how do you think students would respond, and why?

_____

_____

7. Define the words _sought_ (paragraph 1, sentence 2) and _harbors_ (paragraph 2, sentence 1).

_____

_____

Now look at your answers to Exercise 14.2. Did you write them in your own words, or did you copy directly from the passage? Often the wording of a test question will be different from the wording that appears in your textbook. When information in your textbook is complex or unfamiliar, be sure you understand it first; then summarize it in your own words so that you can remember it more easily and can recognize it on a test, no matter how it is worded.

Predict Test Questions

Predicting test questions is another way you can use critical thinking. When you study for a test, try to anticipate the questions your instructor will ask. This is a good activity for a study group. Each member of the group may have different assumptions about what is important. By pooling your information gathered from lecture notes and other sources, you may be able to determine the essential concepts or skills your instructor expects you to have learned. Based on those assumptions, you should be able to predict the questions he or she might ask. Then make up your own questions and answer them. First, find out what kinds of questions will be on the test—essay or multiple-choice, for example—so you can construct questions of the same type.

Sharpen Your Interpretations

READING OR LISTENING occurs on two levels. The *literal level* is the stated meaning, the author's or speaker's main idea and details. The *implied level* is the suggested meaning—what you can infer, conclude, or guess from what is said or deliberately left unsaid. An *inference* is an informed guess based on experience and stated information. Figure 14.4 shows how sharpening your interpretations can extend to other skill areas and activities. Now read the following poem.

On Reading a
Favorite Poem
Carol Kanar

Deep in the Maine woods,
On a starless September night,
Lights flicker, then go out.
Miles from any incandescence,
I sit in the middle of fear,
Black, thorough,
And mourn the sudden loss of sight
As if it were not temporary.
The mind adjusts, takes its measure
Of eternity.
My book lies open in the dark;
I read by lights I cannot see.

On a literal level, you know that the events described in this poem take place in September in the woods of Maine on a dark night. You also know that the lights go out. Specific words in the poem tell you these facts.

On an implied level, what more can you infer from these lines? Because the night is starless, you could infer that it is cloudy, maybe even stormy. Perhaps a utility line is down—that would explain why the lights went out. Also, you could infer that the person in the poem is isolated in the deep woods, far from neighbors or a town. Your experience can help you make more inferences. If you have ever been in the woods at night, you know how dark it gets, especially if you can't see the moon and stars. If you have ever lived in Maine, you know that by September the weather is starting to get cold, and it is not unusual for a frontal storm to pass through at night, causing a power outage. Your interpretation of a poem—anything you read—is affected by the experience you bring to it.

Your experience also affects how you read textbooks. If you have some prior knowledge about a subject, understanding may come easier. New material and unfamiliar concepts make greater demands on you as a reader. Reading on two levels of meaning will help you think critically about your assignments and sharpen your interpretations. At the literal level, pay attention to what an author *says:* the main idea and supporting details. At the implied level, determine what an author *means* by reading between the lines and making *inferences* about the significance of the information or ways to apply it. For example, when you read a chapter in an algebra textbook, determine what rules or steps are involved in solv-

Figure 14.4   **Sharpen Your Interpretations: How You Can Use This Critical Thinking Strategy**

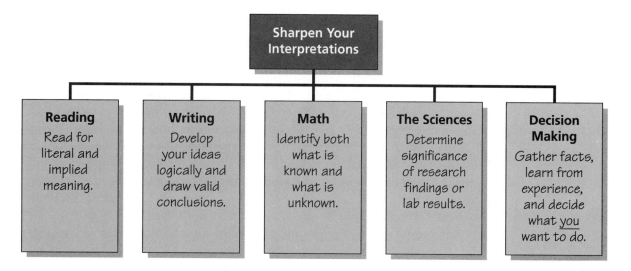

ing a certain kind of problem. Then practice applying the rules and steps to similar kinds of problems in the chapter. When you read a chapter in a psychology textbook, read about experiments on two levels. At the literal level, determine who conducted the experiment, why, what data were collected, and what happened. At the critical level, determine the experiment's significance. What did it prove, and why is it an important piece of research?

Sharpening your interpretations also means making useful inferences outside of your studies. If you have children, you have had to learn to tell whether your child has a harmless cold, has a bad case of the flu, or is pretending to be sick to get attention or get out of doing an unpleasant task. Cold and flu symptoms are similar, but with the flu they are more pronounced and last longer. A child may have a fever with either a cold or the flu, but if the child is faking, there is no fever. Mothers and fathers are good at making inferences about the severity and meaning of their children's symptoms based on their experiences. No matter what the situation, the more facts you have and the more experience you have had in similar situations, the better your inferences will be.

Here is a six-step approach to sharpening your ability to interpret information on two levels:

- Understand the author's or speaker's purpose.

- Read or listen for a main idea and supporting details.

- Read or listen for an organizational pattern.

- Find implications in what you learn.

- Define new or unfamiliar terms.

- Read and understand graphics.

Understand an Author's or Speaker's Purpose

The textbook author's purpose is to inform, provide information, and impart knowledge. Textbook authors use various devices to make information accessible to students. For example, the author of an introductory biology text uses formal language but defines technical terms in context as they occur within chapters and also may include a glossary of terms at the end of the book. The textbook preface provides clues to the author's structure and emphasis, and may explain the book's features and how to use them.

Because textbook authors know that much of their information will be new to you, each chapter contains illustrations, charts, tables, and other graphics that help condense and clarify complex ideas. Textbook authors use a standard format and structure in every chapter so that you can predict and follow the development of ideas. Once you become familiar with an author's format, you will be able to predict a great deal about each chapter. Survey the textbook to get a feel for important topics and examine your assumptions about each topic before you begin your careful reading.

Instructors who lecture also use various methods to make information accessible. They may use visual aids such as overhead transparencies and illustrations on a chalkboard. They may give verbal cues, numbering their examples or singling out a point for emphasis, saying, "This is important" or using other emphatic expressions. Their language may be formal or informal, depending on their personalities and teaching styles. Determine a purpose for listening by asking yourself questions like "Why is this important?" or "What concept or skill am I supposed to learn?" Listen carefully for clues to the instructor's purpose.

Read or Listen for the Main Idea and Details

Whether you are reading a textbook chapter or listening to a lecture, determine the author's or speaker's main idea. Then read or listen for the details that support or elaborate upon it.

As explained in Chapter 13, look for the *central idea* of a textbook chapter in the introductory paragraphs. Look for a sentence that tells you what the whole chapter is about and what you should gain from reading it. The chapter's title may provide a strong clue. Because the central idea of a textbook chapter is often a general statement of a complex idea, section headings will tell you how this idea is broken down. Read one section at a time. Determine its *main idea* by using the heading as a clue. Then identify the important *details* that explain the main idea. Before going on to the next section, determine how the main idea and details of the section you have just read relate to the chapter's central idea. Reading for main ideas and details keeps your attention focused on what is important in a chapter and improves your comprehension.

Reading for main ideas and supporting details is a skill you can apply to any type of material. For newspaper and magazine articles, look for the central idea near the beginning and use the headline or title as a clue. Read each paragraph for a main idea and for details that support or expand upon the central idea. Although newspaper and magazine articles are usually not broken down into sections with subheadings to guide your reading, you may find a topic sentence at the beginning of some paragraphs that will state the main idea.

Just as you read for main ideas and details, also listen for them during lectures. Don't miss the beginning of a lecture because the speaker's opening

EXERCISE **14.3**

APPLY WHAT YOU HAVE LEARNED so far about making inferences by completing this exercise with group members. Follow the guidelines for successful collaboration that appear on the inside back cover. Read the following paragraph and determine whether you can make the inferences that follow it. Discuss each inference, arrive at consensus, and then check *yes* or *no* for each statement. Finally, evaluate your work.

Susan is not doing well in her composition course. She missed the first two days of class because she was dropping and adding other courses. She missed the introduction to the course and the instructor's description of the course requirements. Her instructor gave her a syllabus, but she didn't read it. As a result, she was not prepared for the first grammar test, and she earned a D on it. She decided that the advisor was too demanding, and she tried to get into another section. Unfortunately, the drop-add period was over. Susan's advisor convinced her to stay in the course and suggested that she make an appointment with the instructor to see what she can do to catch up. The advisor believes that if Susan begins right now to take a serious interest in the course, do the assignments, and keep up with the syllabus, she can still do well in the course because it is early in the semester.

Yes No

☐ ☐   1. **Susan will fail the course.**

☐ ☐   2. **The instructor is too demanding.**

☐ ☐   3. **If Susan had read the syllabus, she might have known that a test was scheduled.**

☐ ☐   4. **The instructor may be willing to let Susan make up what she missed on the first two days of class.**

☐ ☐   5. **It is important to attend the first few days of class.**

Group Evaluation:

Evaluate your discussion. Did everyone contribute? Did you accomplish your task successfully? What additional questions do you have about making inferences from facts? How will you find answers to your questions?

_____

_____

_____

_____

_____

_____

_____

_____

_____

_____

remarks usually contain a statement of the lecture topic and the main idea. If you arrive late, you may miss the main idea and never catch up. If you know what the main idea is, then listen for key words or numbered steps or stages that will identify important details. One advantage that listening to lectures has over reading is that when you're in doubt, you can always ask the speaker a question.

A speaker's concluding remarks are just as important as the opening remarks. Some students begin packing up their books and getting ready to leave before a lecture ends, missing important details or a summary that may be the key to understanding the whole lecture. Maintain your concentration from beginning to end and listen for the main ideas and details, and you won't miss anything.

EXERCISE **14.4**

EACH GROUP OF SENTENCES CONTAINS one sentence that expresses the main idea and three sentences that present supporting details. Working with a partner or on your own, underline each main idea.

1. a.   Many parents support sex education courses and programs in the public schools.

   b.   Students should have access to accurate information about sexually transmitted diseases.

   c.   Some birth control methods are more effective than others, and students should know what their options are.

   d.   It is easier for students to talk about sex with peers and teachers than with parents.

2. a.   Take your car to a commercial car wash instead of washing it at home.

   b.   Don't leave the water running while brushing and flossing your teeth.

   c.   A few simple guidelines can help you save money while conserving water.

   d.   Take baths or limit your showers to no more than two minutes.

3. a.   Chat rooms and newsgroups provide opportunities for students to share their information and opinions with others.

   b.   Many students enjoy the convenience of shopping on the Net.

   c.   Students can research topics for papers and reports on the Internet.

   d.   The Internet has a number of practical uses that make it attractive to students.

4. a.   The sticker price may be only a fraction of the real price you pay to own a car.

   b.   The costs of maintenance and repairs vary with the make and model of the car you buy.

   c.   Gas mileage and insurance premiums are additional factors that may increase your cost of operating a car.

   d.   If you finance your car, interest rates may make it cost twice as much by the time you pay off the loan.

Read or Listen for an Organizational Pattern

Common organizational patterns link main ideas and details. If you can spot the pattern early in a chapter or lecture, you can use it as a guide to predict what will follow. Key words may suggest how ideas are organized. For example, if the author's or speaker's main idea is that memory is a three-stage process, then the key words *three-stage process* should alert you to the **process** pattern of organization. Read or listen for the explanation of each stage and how it works.

You can learn to recognize six other common organizational patterns that help you follow an author's or speaker's ideas:

1. If two things are being compared, the pattern is **comparison and contrast.** Read or listen for similarities and differences.

2. If an author or speaker explains *why* something happens, the pattern is **cause and effect.** Read or listen for reasons and results.

3. If an author or speaker groups items into categories, the pattern is **classification.** Determine the number of categories and identify the characteristics of each category.

4. If an author or speaker supports a main idea by giving examples, the pattern is **example.** Read or listen for key introductory phrases such as *for example* and *for instance.*

5. If an author's or speaker's details follow a certain order, the pattern is **sequence.** Read or listen for numbers in a sequence or for events that are explained according to time periods. A sequence is often part of a process, especially when the stages of a process occur in a certain order or at specific times. Processes explain *how* things happen. Sequences explain *when* things happen.

6. If an author or speaker provides an extended meaning of a word or a concept, the pattern is **definition.** Read or listen for words and phrases such as *the meaning is, can be defined as,* and *to define.*

An author or speaker who brings together more than one organizational pattern in a single explanation is using **mixed patterns.** For example, someone might use classification to describe the kinds of students who attend a certain college and then use comparison and contrast to describe the similarities and differences among them. Identifying organizational patterns requires slow and careful reading. Similarly, careful listening may help you identify key words that can serve as clues to a speaker's pattern.

Find Implications in What You Learn

To find the implications or understand the significance of what you are learning, try to see the big picture. If you are taking a writing course, you know that one of the course objectives is to help you develop good writing skills. As you learn each new skill, determine its significance by asking questions such as "How will this skill improve my writing?" and "What should I be able to do when I have mastered this skill?"

Once you have the big picture, find the details. Read your instructors' comments on your returned papers and determine why you missed certain items on tests. What do the comments tell you about your writing—the way in which you have expressed yourself or your level of skill mastery? What can you learn from your mistakes so that you will be less likely to repeat them?

Finally, relate what you are learning in college to other areas of your life. Your psychology course may give you a better understanding of your own motives and

EXERCISE **14.5**

THE FOLLOWING STATEMENTS MIGHT BEGIN sections of a textbook chapter or an article. Read each statement to predict the author's organizational pattern. Write the letter of your answer in the space provided.

A. cause and effect   **C. sequence**   **E. classification**   **G. process**

B. example   **D. comparison and contrast**   **F. definition**

1. _____ A computer is an information-processing system that, in some ways, works much like your brain.

2. _____ Numbering consecutive pages in a document is easy if you follow these steps.

3. _____ A computer has five major units: input, control, storage, retrieval, and output.

4. _____ Computer-managed inventory control systems have proven beneficial to small businesses for a number of reasons.

5. _____ In the following section, we will examine two data-processing programs and their advantages and disadvantages.

6. _____ The ability to move sentences and paragraphs around is but one example of the features of a word processor that make writing easier.

7. _____ People who have never used computers can be grouped into three general categories: those who are afraid learning will be time consuming and difficult, those who resist learning for personal or other reasons, and those who want to learn but have neither the means nor the opportunity to do so.

8. _____ What does it mean to be *computer literate?*

9. _____ The next section traces the development of the computer from a crude piece of equipment that was little more than a calculator to the complex information processor it has become.

10. _____ Learning how to use a word-processing program can be easy if you follow these steps.

behavior. What you learn about art, music, and literature in a humanities course may lead you to new interests in these areas. Examine the ways in which you are changing as the information you are absorbing tests your assumptions and challenges your beliefs.

Define New or Unfamiliar Terms

Most academic disciplines use special terminology to describe theories, concepts, and principles. You may have encountered the terms *id, ego,* and *superego* in a psychology course; *photosynthesis* in a biology course; and *integer, binomial,* and *polynomial* in a math course. In order to understand the information presented in each course, you must know the meaning of the special terms related to each discipline. Make a habit of using a dictionary and textbook glossaries. An excellent way to develop your vocabulary is by reading. The more you read, the more you are exposed to new words and ideas that will increase your store of knowledge.

Read and Understand Graphics

Textbooks and other printed sources of information are filled with graphics that are essential to your understanding of what you read. Graphics condense and summarize a great deal of information. Graphics illustrate relationships among ideas, and they provide a visual supplement to the text they accompany. Make reading graphics an important part of your study system. Figure 14.5 shows five common types of graphics you can learn to recognize.

Circle or "Pie" Charts. Pie charts illustrate part-to-whole relationships. Slices of the pie represent amounts and percentages. The size of each slice in relation to the other slices and to the whole pie indicates its significance. For example, where a student's monthly income goes could be illustrated on a pie chart, with each slice representing a different expenditure.

Bar Graphs. Bar graphs illustrate relationships between *variables*, or quantities, such as time and amount. They also show trends such as an increase or decrease in amount over a period of time. One variable is measured on a vertical axis; the other variable is measured on a horizontal axis.

Line Graphs. Like bar graphs, line graphs illustrate relationships among variables. Trends are represented by lines instead of bars or columns. Voter turnout among different age groups over several presidential elections could be illustrated by either a line graph or a bar graph.

Diagrams. Diagrams are drawings that illustrate functions or processes. A *process diagram* may illustrate the steps and stages of a process or trace a sequence of events. The stages of pregnancy and the events that occur during cell division are two examples. *Function diagrams* illustrate parts of a whole, such as the separate bones of a skeleton.

Tables. Tables are organized lists or rows of numbers or text. They classify and compare large amounts of information or statistical data. A table that lists contraceptive methods and their rates of effectiveness is one example.

To read a graphic with understanding, determine its *purpose*, discover what *relationship* it illustrates, and read the *text* that accompanies it. To help you recall these steps, remember the acronym **PRT**:

1. To determine the **purpose**, read the title of the graphic and its caption for any clues they may provide.

2. To help you discover the **relationship**, determine the graphic's type. For example, if you have identified a graphic as a process diagram, then determine what process is illustrated, trace the steps, and understand what happens at each stage.

3. For an explanation of the graphic, read the **text** that accompanies it. For each part of the explanation in the text, find its counterpart in the graphic. To test yourself, recite the explanation in your own words while looking at the graphic. Then close your eyes and visualize the graphic.

Figure 14.5   Textbook Graphics: Some Common Types

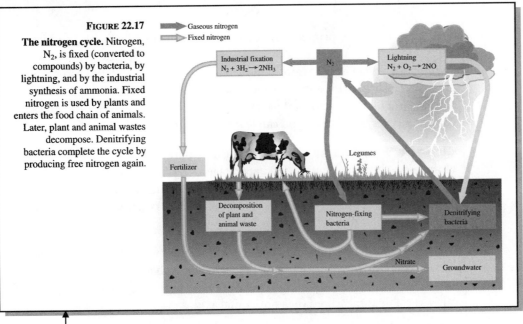

FIGURE 22.17

The nitrogen cycle. Nitrogen, N₂, is fixed (converted to compounds) by bacteria, by lightning, and by the industrial synthesis of ammonia. Fixed nitrogen is used by plants and enters the food chain of animals. Later, plant and animal wastes decompose. Denitrifying bacteria complete the cycle by producing free nitrogen again.

diagrams

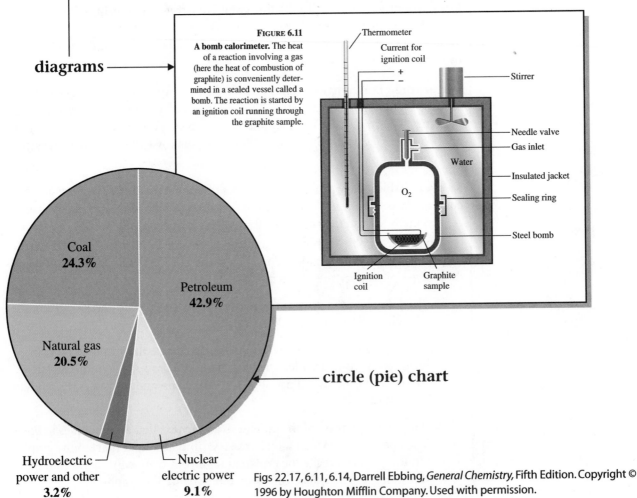

FIGURE 6.11

A bomb calorimeter. The heat of a reaction involving a gas (here the heat of combustion of graphite) is conveniently determined in a sealed vessel called a bomb. The reaction is started by an ignition coil running through the graphite sample.

circle (pie) chart

Figs 22.17, 6.11, 6.14, Darrell Ebbing, *General Chemistry*, Fifth Edition. Copyright © 1996 by Houghton Mifflin Company. Used with permission.

Figure 14.5   **Textbook Graphics: Some Common Types (continued)**

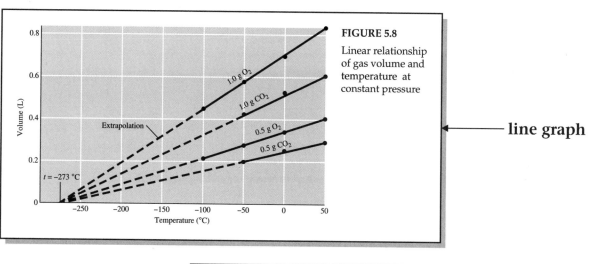

FIGURE 5.8

Linear relationship of gas volume and temperature at constant pressure

line graph

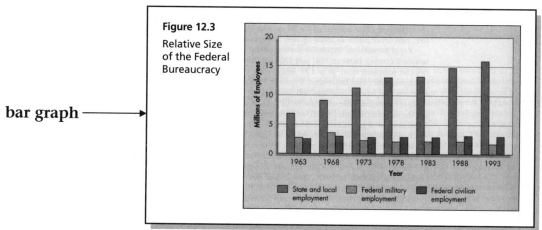

Figure 12.3

Relative Size of the Federal Bureaucracy

bar graph

tables

Fig. 5.8 and Table 5.1 from Darrell Ebbing, *General Chemistry,* Fifth Edition. Copyright © 1996 by Houghton Mifflin Company. Used with permission. Fig. 12.3 from Alan R. Gitelson et al., *American Government,* Fourth Edition. Copyright © 1996 by Houghton Mifflin Company. Reprinted by permission. Table 3.3 from Thomas E. Garman and Raymond E. Forgue, *Personal Finance,* Fourth Edition. Copyright © 1994 by Houghton Mifflin Company. Used with permission.

EXERCISE **14.6**

CHOOSE A GRAPHIC FROM ONE of your textbooks. Using *PRT*, read the graphic and interpret it by answering the following questions.

1. What is the graphic's title?

_____

2. Is there a caption? If so, summarize what it says.

_____

3. Based on your answers to questions 1 and 2, what is the graphic's purpose?

_____

4. What type of graphic is it?

_____

5. Based on your answer to question 4, what relationship does the graphic illustrate?

_____

_____

6. What is the connection between your graphic and the text that accompanies it?

_____

_____

_____

Evaluate What You Learn

To *evaluate* means to determine worth or value. To evaluate also means *to judge*, that is, to make decisions about whether something is right or wrong, good or bad, fair or unfair. If you decide to withdraw from a course, you must evaluate that decision on the basis of whether doing so will be good or bad for you. On the one hand, withdrawing from a course may have a negative effect on your grade point average. But a positive effect might be that it would leave you more time to devote to your remaining courses. Evaluating your progress in a course means checking yourself for improvement. What skills have you mastered since the beginning of the term, and what effect has the application of these skills had on your grades?

Making evaluations is a critical thinking strategy you use in other areas of your life besides college. Deciding whether to take a job, quit a job, marry, divorce, or buy a home all depend on making judgments about these important decisions. At work, you may be asked to judge which machines, tools, or procedures produce the desired outcomes.

An evaluation is a *measurement* of worth. "How much will this help or hurt me?" and "How important is this to me?" are questions you can ask when making evaluations. To make evaluations, you need a standard to go by. To evaluate the worth of continuing a relationship that has proved unsatisfying, your standards might be the expectations you have for a good relationship. To evaluate the purchase of a car, your standards might include the car's safety, dependability, and affordability. There are many criteria, or standards, by which you can make sound evaluations. As a college student, you can evaluate what you learn by applying three basic standards: *reliability, objectivity,* and *usefulness.* Figure 14.6 shows how making evaluations extends to several skill areas and activities.

Reliability

A good way to check for reliability is to ask yourself three questions:

- Who says so?

- What are his or her credentials?

- How does he or she know?

As you read, research, and listen to lectures, remember that primary sources are more reliable than secondary sources. A *primary source* is a first-hand or direct source of information. A *secondary source* is an interpretation of a primary source. For example, if the President of the United States addresses the nation on television, the text of his speech is a primary source. If a newscaster summarizes what the President said, the summary is a secondary source. A newspaper account of the President's speech is also a secondary source unless the newspaper reprints the entire text of the speech. Have you ever listened to a newscaster's summary of a speech you just heard and wondered whether the newscaster heard the same

| **Figure 14.6** | **Evaluate What You Are Learning: How You Can Use This Critical Thinking Strategy** |

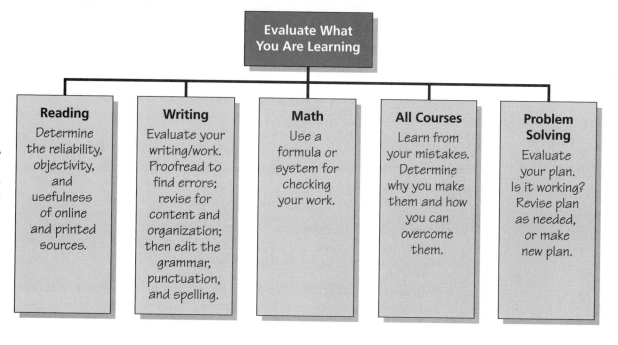

speech you heard? A secondary source is only as reliable as the person who interprets the primary source to create it.

When you are researching a topic, you may have difficulty determining whether a source is primary or secondary. Look at the bibliographies at the ends of books and articles. If the same titles and authors appear over and over again, chances are good that they represent either primary sources or reliable secondary sources of information. If you are just beginning to do research, your instructor or a librarian can help you select sources and evaluate their reliability.

Another way to evaluate reliability is to look at an author's background or credentials. If you are doing research on a scientific topic such as the greenhouse effect, a research scientist with a Ph.D. who is on the faculty at a major university will be a more reliable source than a concerned political activist who writes letters on the subject to the local newspaper. Instructors try to select textbooks that are reliable sources of information, written by experts who may be instructors themselves. The title page of a textbook usually includes a college affiliation underneath the author's name.

Objectivity

To determine whether an author's or speaker's presentation is objective, ask yourself three questions as you read or listen:

- What is the author's or speaker's purpose?

- Are all sides of the issue being presented or acknowledged?

- Is the language free of slanted or manipulative words and phrases?

If an author's or speaker's purpose is to inform, then you should expect factual details and reasoned opinions. You should also expect fair treatment of differing viewpoints and language that is free of words and phrases designed to provoke emotional reactions that could cloud your judgment. Although most authors and commentators—including textbook authors and college lecturers—would probably say that they are objective, some may have a motive or viewpoint that influences their choice of words or examples.

An author or speaker who has something to gain by a change in readers' beliefs or behaviors will not be as objective as one who has nothing to gain. Those whose purpose is to persuade may write forcefully in favor of one viewpoint. If they try to persuade fairly, they will acknowledge other viewpoints. Those who attempt to persuade unfairly are likely to distort facts, leave out facts, state opinions as if they were facts, and use manipulative language. Usually they have something to gain by appealing to your emotions or changing your beliefs or behavior. Advertisers want your money. The proponents of various interest groups want your support. Politicians want your vote. Where self-interest is high, objectivity is low.

Can you spot the manipulative language in these two examples?

- An animal rights activist says, "We must stop the needless torture of animals in medical experiments that serve only to provide researchers on college campuses with lucrative grants."

- A medical researcher says, "No one in our profession sets out to torture animals in painful experiments, but some pain and even death may be necessary if, through these experiments, we can effect cures that will prevent the loss of human life."

In the first example, the activist tries to manipulate your feelings by suggesting that research is an excuse to get grant money, that animals in experiments are always tortured, and that the experiments are needless. In the second example, the researcher denies that anyone in his or her profession would deliberately cause an animal pain. At the same time, the researcher suggests that some animal pain or death is acceptable if it will save human lives. In this example, the researcher manipulates your thinking so that you must make a choice: your life or an animal's life.

Manipulative language is characterized by simple arguments that seek to explain complex issues. Read the next two examples.

Passage A

It is becoming impossible to find good candidates willing to run for public office. A politician's life is an open book. The would-be candidate for office must dodge photographers and news reporters lurking in the bushes around his house, eavesdropping on his conversations in restaurants, and spying on him through binoculars when he thinks he has escaped from their prying eyes. If a person has ever taken a drink, smoked a marijuana cigarette, had a meaningless affair, or cheated on an exam, his chances of winning an election are compromised. The press has gone too far. Everyone, even a political candidate, is entitled to a private life.

Passage B

As soon as someone runs for election, it is understood that she gives up her right to privacy. Indeed, the U.S. Constitution guarantees no one a right to privacy. We the public have a right to know what to expect from those who seek office. Cheating on one's husband or on an exam is not the issue. The real issue is whether we can trust a person who has a history of dishonesty or poor judgment. We want our elected officials to be responsible people. Therefore, the press performs a valuable public service by exposing candidates' indiscretions.

Both passages oversimplify the issues their proponents raise. Both authors manipulate your thinking by appealing to your emotions instead of to your reasoning. The author of the first passage blames the press for making people afraid to run for office. The author of the second passage praises the press for exposing the weaknesses of potential candidates. The first author wants you to identify with the candidate whose privacy has been violated. The second author appeals to your right as a citizen to know as much as you can about a candidate. Are members of the press scandalmongers or public servants? Neither passage offers convincing evidence.

Usefulness

To evaluate the usefulness of what you are learning, consider what you have already gained from it. Has it improved your understanding of the subject? Have you gained a skill or knowledge you can use now or in the future? Can you relate the knowledge or skill to your course objectives? Has the information made you more interested in the topic it covers? If you answered *no* to all of these questions, then try to figure out what is missing and what you might need to learn next. Figure 14.7 lists the questions you can ask to evaluate information.

EXERCISE **14.7**

IDENTIFY WORDS OR PHRASES IN each of the previous passages that appeal to readers' emotions and manipulate their feelings.

Passage A: _____

_____

_____

_____

_____

_____

Passage B: _____

_____

_____

_____

_____

_____

Figure 14.7	**Standards of Evaluation: Questions to Ask**
Reliability	• Who says so?
	• What are his or her qualifications?
	• How does he or she know?
Objectivity	• What is the purpose?
	• Are all sides of the issue presented?
	• Is the language free of slanted or manipulative words and phrases?
Usefulness	• What have I learned?
	• Will I use what I have learned either now or in the future?
	• Does the new knowledge relate to my courses?
	• Having learned the material, am I now more interested in the topic?

CRITICAL THINKING

Many large companies spend millions of dollars a year on magazine advertising. They must believe that people respond to magazine ads, or they wouldn't pay large sums for full-page ads in widely read magazines such as *Time, Newsweek,* and *People.* Advertisers profit by researching and appealing to the market for their products and services. Thinking critically about ads will make you a more informed consumer.

I am not finicky.
But I'm simply not accustomed
to that unsavory copy paper.

Don't blame your printer (or other machines) when the problem is actually your paper. Georgia-Pacific Papers are guaranteed to print trouble-free. And they come in a complete menu of reasonably priced choices, from higher brightness for sharper blacks and richer colors to beefier weights to minimize see-through. Plus, our resealable polywrap package keeps your paper clean and uncrumpled. Visit our web site at www.gp.com or call 1-800-635-6672, and watch your printer become a different animal.

The right paper makes all the difference.℠

©1999 Georgia-Pacific Corporation.

GP *Georgia-Pacific Papers*®

Courtesy of Georgia-Pacific Corporation

(continued)

Working on your own or with a partner or group, examine the Georgia-Pacific Papers ad on the previous page. Then answer the following questions.

1. To whom does the ad appeal?

2. To what consumer need does the ad appeal?

3. What is Georgia-Pacific Papers' guarantee to consumers?

4. According to the ad, what are the advantages of using Georgia-Pacific Papers instead of other brands?

5. Who are some of Georgia-Pacific Papers' competitors?

6. What relationships do you see among the image of the ape, the message printed across the image, and the words *menu, beefier,* and a *different animal* in the ad copy?

7. What is your reaction to the ad, and what, specifically, in the ad copy or image chosen provokes this reaction?

8. What inferences can you make from the slogan "The right paper makes all the difference."

9. Evaluate the ad for usefulness: What is its purpose? Does it accomplish this purpose? How?

10. If you need to buy copy paper, would you be tempted to try Georgia-Pacific's brand? Why or why not?

EXERCISE **14.8**

Looking back through all the chapters of *The Confident Student* that you have already read, choose one topic that you would like to pursue further such as time management, concentration, memory, critical thinking—anything that interests you. Research your topic on the Internet. Find two different web sites that deal with this topic and evaluate them for reliability, objectivity, and usefulness. Be prepared to discuss in class the topic you chose, a brief summary of the information found on the websites you selected, and your evaluation of the websites.

CONFIDENCE
Builder

Thinking Creatively

Creative thinking is a skill you can develop.

How does creative thinking differ from critical thinking? The tool of the critical thinker is *analysis*. The tool of the creative thinker is *invention*. Analysis is the process of logical reasoning. When you think through the steps of a process or consider all sides of an issue or argument, you are using analysis. When you come up with a solution to a problem, or when you use what you know to discover what you don't know, you are using invention.

Critical thinking and creative thinking work together. The COPE problem-solving method provides a good example. The COPE method defines a problem as a *challenge*, which is a positive way of looking at a difficult situation. Your first step is an analytical one: to clearly identify your challenge. Suppose you have gained 10 pounds. Your challenge is "I need to find a weight-loss program I can live with." To add a creative thinking step, ask yourself, "What is in conflict with the result I want? You might say, "My conflicts are that I hate diets, and I don't have time for exercise." Now you have a clue that will help you work through COPE's second step, considering your *options*. Since any effective weight-loss program involves a combination of diet and exercise, you must choose from among the possible options one that will help you overcome your conflicts. Analysis helps you determine what the options are. Invention helps you arrive at a *plan*, the third step of COPE. Your plan will be one that you create that combines a diet you can live with and an exercise program you can follow in the time you have available.

The last step of COPE, *evaluate*, works by both analysis and invention. Suppose that after five weeks, you have lost only two pounds. Now you must analyze what has happened. Did you stick to your diet? Did you make time for exercise? What has gone wrong? More importantly, what can you do about it? Again, thinking creatively about your challenge will help you discover ways to modify your weight-loss plan and to get back on track.

No matter what your challenge, a valuable question to ask that starts the creative thinking process is "What if?" This question takes you beyond what you know to imagine what could be. For example, what if you could avoid procrastination? What if you could fight your distractions and control your concentration? What if you took charge of your learning by designing your own study system that incorporated strategies known to increase comprehension and improve retention? Imagine what you could achieve.

By using a combination of critical and creative thinking, you can meet any challenge. Invention and analysis are your tools.

To pursue this topic further, do an online search using these key words as a starting point: *creativity, thinking creatively, creative thinking.*

thinking *ahead* ┅┅➤

What practical knowledge have you gained from this chapter that you can use to solve real-world problems? To find out, read the following scenario and complete the items after it.

The members of a work team in a large company were having trouble using the company's new software. Scott had re-sisted learning the program because he thought it was too difficult. Tasha and Trina were angry because they had liked the old program better. The team leader agreed that the inability to get help conveniently was the program's greatest problem. Jonas and Joy wondered, "What if help were more readily available? Wouldn't we be more willing to work with the new program?" They approached the team leader, who involved everyone in thinking of a solution. After discussing various options, someone suggested bringing in a technical writer to produce an in-house manual that would simplify the operations procedures of the program. Another suggested holding an in-service training session conducted by someone who is an expert in using the program. Everyone on the team agreed that these solutions might work.

1. Why were team members having trouble with the new software?

_____

_____

_____

_____

2. What options did they explore?

_____

_____

_____

_____

3. Which team members showed inflexible attitudes?

_____

_____

_____

_____

4. Which team members displayed creative thinking?

_____

_____

_____

_____

chapter **re**view

To review the chapter, reflect on the following confidence-building attitudes, complete Concepts to Understand, and practice your new skills at every opportunity.

ATTITUDES TO DEVELOP

- self-reflection
- openness to new ideas
- flexibility

CONCEPTS TO UNDERSTAND

Critical thinking is the process of constructing and evaluating meaning. Critical thinking is logical, analytical, self-reflective, conscious, and purposeful. Four strategies can help you think critically: Examine your _____, make _____, sharpen your _____, and _____ what you learn.

Your _____ are your beliefs, what you take for granted. Determine what your beliefs are. Relate new information to prior knowledge and experience. Be willing to change your opinions in light of new information.

Your _____ are your expectations or anticipations based on the information you have. To make _____, have a _____ for reading and listening. Anticipate what will follow in your reading or in a lecture. Ask questions to guide your thinking.

Your _____ are the meanings you get from what you read or hear on two levels: the _____ level and the _____ level. Reading or listening for the purpose, main idea, details, organizational patterns, and implications will improve your understanding of meaning on both levels.

To _____ what you learn, determine its worth or significance by using three standards of evaluation: _____, _____, and _____.

To access additional review exercises, see http://college.hmco.com/success.

SKILLS TO PRACTICE

- reading and listening actively
- thinking critically and creatively
- using standards of evaluation

Your Reflections

Your Reflections

Reflect on what you have learned about critical thinking and how you can best apply that information. Use the following list of questions to stimulate your thinking; then write your reflections. Your response may include answers to one or more of the questions. Incorporate in your writing specific information from this chapter or from previous chapters as it's needed.

- Would you describe yourself as a critical thinker? Why, or why not?

- Of the strategies explained in this chapter, which ones are new to you? Which ones have you already used, and how?

- Why is critical thinking an important skill? Explain how you use critical thinking.

- What have you learned from this chapter that you can apply to the way you think and learn?

- Of the attitudes and skills listed in the Chapter Review, which do you think will be most useful at work or in your career?

Index